In SEARCH of the HEBREW PEOPLE

GERMAN JEWISH CULTURES

Editorial Board:

Matthew Handelman, *Michigan State University*
Iris Idelson-Shein, *Goethe Universität Frankfurt am Main*
Samuel Spinner, *Johns Hopkins University*
Joshua Teplitsky, *Stony Brook University*
Kerry Wallach, *Gettysburg College*

Sponsored by the Leo Baeck Institute London

IN SEARCH OF THE HEBREW PEOPLE

Bible and Nation in the German Enlightenment

Ofri Ilany

Indiana University Press

This book is a publication of

Indiana University Press
Office of Scholarly Publishing
Herman B Wells Library 350
1320 East 10th Street
Bloomington, Indiana 47405 USA

iupress.indiana.edu

First published in Hebrew by the Leo Baeck Institute
and Zalman Shazar © 2014 by Ofri Ilany.
English language rights licensed from the Hebrew-language publisher.
English translation © 2018 by Ishai Mishory
All rights reserved

No part of this book may be reproduced or utilized in any form or by any means, electronic or mechanical, including photocopying and recording, or by any information storage and retrieval system, without permission in writing from the publisher. The paper used in this publication meets the minimum requirements of the American National Standard for Information Sciences—Permanence of Paper for Printed Library Materials, ANSI Z39.48-1992.

Manufactured in the United States of America

Library of Congress Cataloging-in-Publication Data

Names: Ilany, Ofri, author. | Mishory, Ishai, translator.
Title: In search of the Hebrew people : Bible and nation in the German Enlightenment / Ofri Ilany ; English translation by Ishai Mishory.
Other titles: ?Hipu?s a?har ha-?am ha-?Ivri. English
Description: First edition. | Bloomington, Indiana : Indiana University Press, [2018] | Series: German jewish cultures | Includes bibliographical references and index.
Identifiers: LCCN 2018000957 (print) | LCCN 2018000289 (ebook) | ISBN 9780253033857 (e-book) | ISBN 9780253033512 (hardback : alk. paper)
Subjects: LCSH: Bible. Old Testament—Criticism, interpretation, etc., Jewish—History—18th century. | Enlightenment—Germany. | Politics in the Bible. | Jews—History—To 70 A.D. | Michaelis, Johann David, 1717–1791. | Jewish law—Biblical teaching.
Classification: LCC BS1186 (print) | LCC BS1186 .I5313 2018 (ebook) | DDC 221.60943/09033—dc23
LC record available at https://lccn.loc.gov/2018000957

1 2 3 4 5   23 22 21 20 19 18

For Iair

Contents

	Acknowledgments	ix
	Introduction	1
1	Troglodytes, Hottentots, and Hebrews: The Bible and the Sources of German Anthropology	17
2	The Law and the People: Mosaic Law and the German Enlightenment	43
3	The Eighteenth-Century Polemic on the Extermination of the Canaanites	66
4	"Is Judah Indeed the Teutonic Fatherland?" The Hebrew Model and the Birth of German National Culture	86
5	"Lovers of Hebrew Poetry": The Battle over the Bible's Relevance at the Turn of the Nineteenth Century	113
	Conclusion	145
	Bibliography	151
	Index	175

Acknowledgments

As someone who grew up in the State of Israel and experienced firsthand its ideologically laden educational system, I absorbed the imagery of a place where the Bible and its characters have a palpable, at times almost inescapable, presence. In this place, covenants, calamities, and wars recorded thousands of years ago still, sometimes tragically, seem to decide people's fates. Deeds of the deepest past are reflected in and reverberate through the most contemporary of developments. A chilling example is Israel's first prime minister, David Ben-Gurion, who claimed that the 1948 Arab-Israeli war was the ultimate acting out of the Book of Joshua, providing an ultimate exegesis next to which all other interpretation pales.

The Bible-centered ideology marks the boundaries of the Israeli worldview, so that those born and raised there sometimes have to journey as far as the universities of eighteenth-century Germany to understand the way the biblical past appears to their eyes. Being the son of a Bible-loving zoologist, biblical natural history played a formative role in my upbringing: everywhere my father went, he carried a copy of the Hebrew Bible in which he marked verses relating to gazelles, leopards, hyraxes, acacia trees, and the like. I remember him troubled by a mysterious verse in Genesis 36 about a man called Anah: "that found the mules in the wilderness, as he fed the asses of Zibeon his father." As opposed to the English and German translators, who deftly deduced that the original animals mentioned in Hebrew were "mules," the word for the animal in the Hebrew original, "yemim," is unclear. So which exactly were the animals Anah had found? My father tried to find them his entire life. Biblical natural history was his way of interpreting hard-to-decipher biblical verses. Only during my university studies did I come to realize that this form of interpretation—wrestling with hard biblical verses by observing the "orient's" natural and human phenomena—was developed by Protestant, and particularly German Bible scholars of the early modern period.

I would like to thank my parents who fostered my curiosity for ancient texts and myths as well as other cultures and forgotten periods.

I thank my teacher Shulamit Volkov for supporting me and my work from the beginning, when my thesis was only a sketch.

The writing of the dissertation on which this book is based was made possible by an Israeli Council for Higher Education Nathan Rotenstreich Scholarship for PhD Students in the Humanities, which allowed me to devote my time to research. I am also grateful for Lichtenberg-Kolleg, Georg-August-Universität x | Acknowledgments

Göttingen, for inviting me as a visiting scholar and allowing me to use both its extensive university library and the Michaelis archive.

Turning my dissertation into a book was made possible by a Hebrew University Franz Rosenzweig Minerva Research Center Postdoctoral Fellowship, a Minerva Stiftung Postdoctoral Fellowship, and a Ben Gurion University Center for the Study of Conversion and Inter-Religious Encounters Postdoctoral Fellowship.

An earlier version of chapter 3 of this book has been published in the *Journal of the History of Ideas*, volume 73, 2012, and an earlier version of chapter 4 has been published in *Naharaim*, volume 8, 2014. Both are reprinted with permission.

I am grateful to the staff of the Leo Baeck Institute, who made publication of the Hebrew edition of the book possible and worked on it from beginning to end, as well as the staff of the Zalman Shazar Center, Jerusalem.

I thank Haifa University School of History for awarding my dissertation the Gilad Margalit Prize for outstanding doctoral work on European history and the Historical Society of Israel for awarding the Hebrew edition of the book the Bella and Solomon Bartal Am and Olam Prize.

I owe my teachers at Tel Aviv University's history department and other departments, from whom I learned the craft of history writing, a debt of gratitude. Joseph Mali, Billie Melman, Amnon Raz-Krakotzkin, Shmuel Feiner, Jonathan Sheehan, Moshe Sluhovsky, Avi Lifshitz, Avihu Zakai, Jan Eike Dunkhase, Yehonatan Alsheh, Kathrin Wittler, Yotam Feldman, Yitzhak Laor, Shai Lavi, Avner Ben Amos, Sharon Gordon, Hannan Harif, Dominik Huenniger, Yosefa Raz, and Shai Zamir read parts of the book at different stages and gave me invaluable advice.

I thank Markus Witte, who hosted me at Humboldt University Faculty of Theology, as well as Jan Assmann of University of Konstanz and Christoph Bultmann of University of Erfurt, who helped me and gave advice on many ideas.

A special thanks goes to Iris Idelson-Shein, coeditor of the German Jewish Cultures series at Indiana University Press, who accompanied the book's editing and publication from its inception.

Thanks to the translator, Ishai Mishory, for his concise and inspiring translation. My gratitude goes also to Avner Greenberg for the language editing.

And finally I thank my partner, Iair Or, who dove with me into the world of Michaelisiana.

IN SEARCH OF THE HEBREW PEOPLE

Introduction

"THE ONLY WAY for us to become great, and indeed—if this is possible—inimitable, is by imitating the ancients," argued the German antiquarian Johann Joachim Winckelmann.[1] But which ancients should be imitated? For Winckelmann, as well as other German scholars of the eighteenth and nineteenth centuries, the answer was clear: the Greeks.[2] While the influence of Greek legacy on German culture is undisputable, this book delineates a no less important path to understanding the evolution of this culture, presenting the Hebrews as "alternative ancients" who likewise played a central role in German intellectual and cultural discourse. From the middle of the eighteenth century, "Hebrew lovers" competed with "Greek lovers" for the nascent national-cultural hegemony in their bid to formulate an aesthetic and political blueprint for German culture.

In fact, over two centuries, German theologians and philosophers mulled German nationalism's relation to the Old Testament. As far back as 1798, Georg Friedrich Hegel described the Bible as a foreign myth that prevented Germans from developing "a national fantasy" of their own.[3] This trend gathered strength with the advent of the German national movement of the nineteenth century. Writers and national leaders in Germany sought to purify German national culture of influences perceived as foreign, thereby to create a German Christianity free of Jewish influence—namely, purged of the religious ritual of the Old Testament. In *Aryan Jesus*, Suzanna Heschel addresses attempts by antisemitic theologians to fashion an Aryan Christianity by detaching Jesus from the Jews.[4] German national Christianity, however, was beset by tension between two opposing trends: that which sought to purify Christian German culture of the Bible and another that chose to *return* to the Old Testament to draw legitimacy precisely from the biblical notion of *chosenness*. The latter trend can be traced back to the dawn of national thought in Germany during the second half of the eighteenth century.

In striving to establish their national identity, eighteenth-century German thinkers sought historical models that could serve as an alternative to those formulated by the thinkers of the French Enlightenment.[5] The extensive literature written in German on the ancient Hebrews constituted an attempt to propose the Hebrew people as an alternative to classical antiquity. Endeavoring to distinguish themselves from Enlightenment thinkers such as Voltaire and the Deists, who defamed the Hebrews by describing them as barbarous and bloodthirsty, some

German thinkers were motivated by a desire to rehabilitate the Hebrew historical myth as a source of inspiration.

German Bible scholars took the lead in the construction of a modern image of the biblical past. The church played a dominant role in eighteenth-century German intellectual life, and many prominent writers were theologians.[6] Following Luther's instructions, they studied Hebrew alongside Greek to gain an understanding of the Psalms and the Prophets. During the second half of the eighteenth century, German universities became the center of scientific biblical scholarship in Europe.[7] German scholars published dozens of works about the Old Testament, examining the process of the Bible's compilation as well as the historical events it describes. As part of this effort, they sketched the portrait of ancient Israel by employing new disciplines such as ethnography and comparative linguistics. Their work marks the genesis of the modern historiography of ancient Israel, which formulates it as a historical entity and a scientific object of research.

Contemporary images of the Israelites often portray them as Bedouins or as Arab peasants decked out in *jalabahs*, dresses, or sheepskins. Yet up until the modern age, they were represented differently. In Medieval and Renaissance paintings, for instance, Abraham, Moses, and David are dressed in the painters' contemporary garb. Prior to the seventeenth century, artists did not, in fact, try to recreate the Israelites' ancient way of life, attaching little significance to the difference between the biblical period and their own.[8]

In the ecclesiastic tradition, the events of the Old Testament were generally interpreted as signs prefiguring the events of the New Testament. Biblical narrative was subjugated to ecclesiastical redemption history—the fulfillment of the divine plan leading from creation through the advent of Jesus Christ and into the End of Days. God revealed himself in historical events through a series of significantly recurring "types." Episodes of the life of the patriarchs were considered to be transhistorical archetypes of the life of Jesus; thus, Noah's ark symbolizes the church, and the Binding of Isaac, the Crucifixion.

In his classic essay *Figura*, Erich Auerbach demonstrates how, since Augustine, an interpretive tradition viewing the Old Testament as a prefiguration of the Gospels took root in the church based on Paul's reference to the Israelites: "Now all these things happened unto them for examples" (1 Corinthians 10:11).[9] In fact, according to Auerbach, "The figural interpretation changed the Old Testament from a book of laws and a history of the people of Israel into a series of figures of Christ and the Redemption."[10] A striking example of this figural reading is the Book of Joshua. The contemporary reader would tend to understand this book as a chronicle of military maneuvers, battles, and conquests. But ecclesiastical interpretation, since the time of the church fathers, has addressed the text quite differently. In fact, it did not regard

Joshua as a military personage at all but rather perceived him to be a figure that anticipated Jesus—a "Jesus of the Old Testament," subject in all things to Christ.[11] The people of Israel themselves, as described in the Bible, act, in Christian interpretation, as a Figure of the church.

In traditional ecclesiastical interpretation, there is thus no room for a political understanding of this people's history. Literal understanding of the text was condemned as a "Jewish" reading, and Christian exegetes were enjoined to eschew reading "the letter," "for the letter killeth, but the spirit giveth life" (2 Corinthians 3:7). Allegorical reading was directed at an eternal, spiritual sphere elevated above the plane of transient historical events. This approach toward reading the Old Testament endured after the Reformation. In his early interpretations of the Old Testament, Luther still employed the *Quadriga* (or "fourfold sense") interpretive method, in which the text is read allegorically rather than literally.

For Luther, the Old Testament has no meaning when detached from the Gospel. He regarded the Psalms as the most important part of the Old Testament, albeit claiming that they deal exclusively with Jesus. In this respect, the great reformer did not stray far from the path of the ancient church fathers.[12] Thus, for instance, does he interpret the verse "yet have I set my king upon my holy hill of Zion" (Psalms 2:6):

> But in this Zion there is a figure. For, by Zion, we are not to understand the wood and stones of Zion, but those who inhabit Zion. And even this is only the corporal Zion; and it teaches us that we should expect that King, who is called King of Zion. For if you understand by Zion the material Zion, it is all over with us gentiles, because we do not possess this mountain now, it is in the hands of the wicked Hagarenes. But now, all our salvation and consolation lies in this—that we have the King of Zion, and confess him, and embrace him ... And as God the Father himself gave this promise to David, Christ is rightly said to be set by God himself as King on Mount Zion, where David reigned.[13]

Even geographical terms such as *Zion*, which appear in the Psalms and Prophets, require, according to Luther, an allegorical reading in relation to the Christian gospel. According to Luther's method, the kingdom of the Jews was supplanted by Jesus's universal celestial reign, so that even the Prophets' words concerning a return to Zion have no more earthly validity.

Only in his later writings did Luther shift toward the literal sense and reject allegorical interpretation, calling allegory "a beautiful harlot."[14] However, the conception whereby the narratives of the Bible took place in a foreign, ancient world emerged fully only in the seventeenth and eighteenth centuries. It was during this period that an understanding began to take shape, which today seems intuitive to us: that the lifestyle of the Israelites differed markedly from that of the Europeans. From the end of the seventeenth century and up to the beginning of the nineteenth, the way the Bible was read changed fundamentally. Allegorical interpretation was supplanted by a view of the Bible as a historical document describing a distant and exotic existence. The Hebrews were subsequently depicted as an ordinary people subject to the laws of nature and history, and in many instances, in fact, as a particularly wild and coarse lot.

One of the most resounding attacks on the traditional concept of the Israelites' chosenness was formulated in Benedict Spinoza's contentious treatise, *Tractatus Theologico-Politicus*. Spinoza portrayed the Hebrews as a childish, uncultured people, who "had no understanding of the excellence of virtue."[15] He rejected the assertion that God had chosen the Hebrews above all nations and claimed that this kind of election would run counter to God's nature.[16] Following Spinoza, deist philosophers and pamphleteers went out of their way to undermine the Bible's authority and present it as pernicious fiction. In the context of their attacks on organized religion, English deists Matthew Tindal, Thomas Morgan, and Lord Bolingbroke, and French philosophers such as Voltaire undermined the biblical narrative sanctified by the church. These attacks reverberated powerfully through the period's "republic of letters"; most eighteenth-century scholars, however, chose a different route: that of reasserting the Bible's authority.

Responding to the deist challenge, Bible scholars of the period reconstructed the Bible using historical tools. The Hebrews' history was now described as the transformation of a migratory people into a sedentary one. Simultaneously, the Bible itself was now read as a national history: the history of the Hebrew people. This book deals with the shaping of this historical image.

The scholars discussed in this book endeavored to characterize the Hebrews' emergence as a natural development within the larger historical and scientific context of the birth of nations. For instance, the chapter on the Hebrews in philosopher Johann Gottfried Herder's *Ideas of the Philosophy of Human History* [*Ideen zur Philosophie der Geschichte der Menschheit*] constitutes a stage in his description of the emergence of human civilization and cosmic development writ large. Herder places the Hebrews' emergence on a chronological axis beginning with cosmic phenomena and moving on to the civilizations of the ancient Near East. The Hebrews are positioned somewhere between the Babylonians and the Phoenicians.

The historicization of Bible scholarship is linked to a wider intellectual and social trend commonly referred to as the *Enlightenment*, a term which has been diversely defined in philosophical, cultural, and social terms. In fact, its precise definition troubled the thinkers of the period itself and remains controversial to this day.[17] However, it is generally agreed that at the core of the Enlightenment project lies the belief in the "education of mankind" (the title of Gotthold Ephraim Lessing's influential tract) and the organization of the world according to universal rationalist principles. The thinkers of the Enlightenment sought to examine social institutions and natural phenomena critically and without prejudice. Criticism—*Kritik*—therefore lay at the very heart of this movement.

Until several decades ago, historians tended to depict the Enlightenment as an intellectual movement characterized by a rift with Christian tradition and religion. In this context, historians stressed its critical view of scripture.[18] They focused on the Enlightenment's radical avant-garde, which vehemently rejected the validity of the tradition and the authority of religious institutions. And indeed, treatment of scripture in the eighteenth century was characterized by virulent attacks by anticlerical writers. However, contemporary research has established that these antireligious critics constituted a small and even marginal group within the Enlightenment movement. In recent decades, scholars have stressed that the Enlightenment did not simply oppose religion but was tightly bound up with it.[19] They point to the fact that many of the reformers did not regard their work as an act of apostasy but on the contrary, one of re-Christianization, of purification of belief of its superstitious elements, elements that hindered realization of its uncorrupted goals.

Indeed, addressing Protestant biblical scholarship as part of the secularization process overlooks the fact that the German Enlightenment's historical criticism was not directed against the biblical tradition. In many cases, it was rather intended *to inaugurate* precisely such a tradition. With few exceptions, German biblical scholarship never fully severed itself from theology. Even when formulated in response to anticlerical writers such as the deists and the *Philosophes* historical criticism sought to strengthen and entrench religion in an ever-changing world.

Description of ancient Israel in the eighteenth century combines modern anthropological concepts and traditional Christian images. Most German Bible scholars were educated in theology and their vocation was built on the protestant tradition of biblical exegesis that had evolved in the German-speaking regions from the time of the Reformation. However, unlike that of previous generations, the historicist methodology of eighteenth- and nineteenth-century exegetes, developed mainly at the University of Göttingen, was based on a novel historical perspective; biblical events were now no longer interpreted symbolically as prefigurations of the life of Jesus. Instead, they were situated in the concrete context of the history of an "archaic" and "oriental" people.

The two founders of modern German study of the Old Testament were the orientalist Johann David Michaelis (1717–1791) and the philosopher Johann Gottfried Herder (1744–1803). The publication of Michaelis's first books in the 1750s in Göttingen may be considered the starting point of critical-historical Bible research in the German principalities. These works—and in particular the voluminous *Mosaic Law* (*Mosaishces Recht*, 1771)—heralded the beginning of a

German-Hebraistic Renaissance.[20] Several dozen monographs on the Hebrews appeared around the turn of the century, most bearing titles such as *Archaeology of the Hebrews* or *Antiquities of the Hebrews*.[21] This extensive literature forms the basis of Herder's *On the Spirit of Hebrew Poetry* (*Vom Geist der ebräischen Poesie*, 1782–1783), which is recognized by many as the most influential eighteenth-century work on the Hebrews.[22]

These German scholars sought to explain biblical events while avoiding supernatural explanations. The theological narrative of the divine revelation of Mosaic Law on Mount Sinai was given a new meaning. No longer was it the story of the emergence of a religious tradition, it was now the history of a nomadic clan's [*Stamm*] transformation into a nation.

The new and significant component that emerged within the discourse of the German Enlightenment is the positing of the Hebrew *people* as an object of scientific inquiry. Whereas the authors of previous generations had engaged in religious polemic with the Mosaic tradition, the orientalists and biblical scholars at the German universities now sought to reconstruct the ancient Hebrew people, who they viewed as the originators of the biblical text. Using allegedly objective and impartial ethnographic and demographic tools, these scholars proceeded to characterize, measure, define, and quantify the Hebrew nation. Going beyond an interpretation of the biblical text, this new literature on the ancient Hebrews constituted an attempt to restore the "body" of the people.

The various meanings that German scholars attributed to the history of ancient Israel reflected their political outlooks. Their depiction of events, such as the emergence of Israel, the enslavement in Egypt, the granting of the law, and the establishment of the kingdom served as a laboratory for discussing concepts of ethnicity, civil society, social reform, government, and patriotism.

These modern political concepts—some of which were still in embryonic form at this stage—not only shaped the description of biblical history but were, in turn, themselves shaped by it. As Anthony Smith argues, the transition from religious to modern national self-perception was fragmented but continuous, with biblical images resonating in the way that modern nationalist movements perceived themselves.[23] It is in this context that I seek to establish to what extent the Israelites served as a model for German nationalism, and to identify Hebraistic elements in the early German national movement.

*

Eighteenth-century German writing on the Bible and Hebrew tradition spanned several disciplines. The principal field in which this topic had been discussed up until then was the historiography of Bible interpretation and biblical criticism during the Enlightenment.[24] But the subject was also addressed in writing about the Jews, in the ethnographic description of ancient or "savage" peoples, and in German philosophy during the Enlightenment. The past decade has seen a growth of interest in Christian Hebraism, namely Christian scholars' research into Hebrew and Jewish sources, especially during the sixteenth and seventeenth centuries.[25] Once perceived as a marginal phenomenon, Christian Hebraism is now widely recognized as an important intellectual movement, encompassing hundreds and even thousands of writers following the Reformation.

It should be noted, however, that these scholars did not call themselves Hebraists—this term emerged in its current configuration only during the second half of the nineteenth century. Furthermore, no commonly accepted definition of the academic term *Christian Hebraism* exists since it relates to diverse phenomena in different works.[26] Several scholars define it as the study of the Hebrew language by Christians, while others conceive it to be the use of rabbinic and kabbalistic sources for exegetic and theological purposes.[27] An alternative definition refers to philosophical or political writing that addresses and draws inspiration from the Hebrew constitution or the Hebrew state—a practice sometimes referred to as "political Hebraism."[28] In the context of this book, *Hebraism* refers to systematic research into the Hebrew nation and Hebrew history as well as imitation and adulation of the ancient Hebrews. In this sense, Hebraism is both a field of knowledge and a cultural-political ideal, similar to the way that the term *classicism* describes both the investigation of Greco-Roman creation and its perception as a cultural ideal.

While Dutch, English, and American Hebraism have recently been the objects of considerable scholarly interest, many studies treating the phenomenon of Hebraist nationalism disregard or marginalize its existence in Germany. Although several scholars have studied Herder's and Michaelis's major works dealing with the Hebrews, existing research has focused primarily on the history of biblical criticism rather than on the history of political thought.[29] The most comprehensive study of this subject is Jonathan Sheehan's *The Enlightenment Bible*, which surveys philological research and the translation projects of the Old and New Testaments in England and Germany.[30] Taking issue with the prevailing conception, according to which the Enlightenment's move toward secularization resulted in a "dwindling" of biblical scholarship, Sheehan claims that interest in the Bible actually *grew* throughout the eighteenth century. The effort to "reinvent" scripture, he explains, was powered by a religious desire to conserve the Bible's status as an active agent in modern life. Yet within the German context, Sheehan's study focuses mainly on academic biblical criticism and theology, and fails to address one of the most important aspects of German Bible reading, namely the use of the Old Testament as a political model.

Michaelis's biblical interpretation was recently treated by Michael Legaspi, who focused on the author's contribution to the academization of biblical study and the transformation of scripture into a subject of philological scientific research.[31] Michaelis's writing on Mosaic Law is discussed further in Jonathan Hess's book *Germans, Jews and the Claims of Modernity*.[32] Hess convincingly analyzes the Bible's transformation into an exotic text and the positioning of the Hebrews as objects of an orientalist discourse. However, his analysis focuses almost exclusively on Michaelis's stated intentions, as set out at the beginning of *Mosaisches Recht*, and thus does not address the multifaceted content of the text itself. In my view, Hess disregards several important aspects of Michaelis's work, overemphasizing German biblical scholarship's anti-Jewish tendencies and failing to pay sufficient attention to the central role that the Bible played in the life of Christian German society itself.

The aforementioned studies focus on the secularization process and highlight the prevalence and transformation of the biblical tradition in the German Enlightenment. However, historians have rarely analyzed the actual content of those treatises dealing with the ancient Hebrews, and the image they reflect of biblical history and its protagonists. Perception of the Enlightenment as a secular project shifted scholarly focus away from a history of Bible reading toward a history of Bible negation and to an emphasis on the undermining of the biblical narrative rather than on the inauguration of the modern image of the biblical past. The very categorization of eighteenth-century biblical scholarship as "biblical criticism" excludes from the discussion numerous works that sought to describe and recreate the biblical period and the biblical world—a literary genre that flowered during the eighteenth century, especially in Germany.

The following investigation highlights a different aspect of German Bible culture, namely the introduction of political and national concepts to textual interpretation. Rather than simply replacing religious with national concepts, the political reading of the Bible played a key role in the creation of religious nationality.

Many of the historians and philosophers who have addressed nationalism and the conditions that encouraged its formation have cited the ancient Israelites as a case of modern nationalism *avant la lettre*. One of the first writers to pursue this subject was Hans Kohn. In *The Idea of Nationalism*, Kohn described the biblical Israelites as an ancient historical iteration of a people imbued with a national consciousness, millennia before the modern age.[33] Even contemporary scholars, such as Steven Grosby, have identified genuine national elements among the ancient Hebrew people from the seventh century BCE onward.[34] Other writers, however, point to a fundamental difference between modern nationalism and the ancient form of ethnicity portrayed in the Bible, arguing that to equate a modern ideology with texts written in the depths of antiquity renders the concept of nationalism devoid of all meaning as a theoretical category.[35]

Far wider agreement exists, however, on the profound influence exerted by the biblical narrative of the Israelites' history on the formation of national consciousness among various European groupings. Many forms of collective identity that evolved during the early modern period drew inspiration from the Hebrew model—a phenomenon that Kohn has termed *Hebraic nationalism*.[36] According to Kohn, three constituent elements of modern national ideology grew out of the reading of the Bible: the idea of a chosen people, the national-messianic vision, and what he characterizes as a shared pool of past memories and future hopes.[37]

The notion of Hebraist nationalism has gained renewed attention over the past two decades. In his book, *Chosen Peoples*, Anthony Smith—the leader of this trend—endeavors to uncover nationalism's "sacred foundations." Nationalism, he claims, is distinct from other modern ideologies, such as socialism and liberalism, in that it is not totally secular but is rather a belief system centered on the nation. Furthermore, he attributes what he calls the rise of the "ethnic election" political model to biblical influence.[38] Smith's main, if not only, examples of this form of nationalism are the Dutch and English national identities as they evolved in the seventeenth century.

A similar approach is elaborated by Adrian Hastings in *The Construction of Nationhood*.[39] He traces the roots of the European nations back to the Middle Ages, claiming that the Bible, which was viewed as "a mirror for national self-imagining," provided an early, influential model of divine choice of a particular nation.[40] Within the context of scripture, it is the Old Testament that is relevant to the formation of national ideology, since the New Testament does not offer the element of chosenness necessary to the Christian nations. Hastings claims further that a biblical model of national chosenness appears as early as the eighth century with Bede (672–735), but became especially popular in the Netherlands and England in the seventeenth century. Likewise, Liah Greenfeld has shown how during the early modern era, it was the Old Testament that provided the language through which to express a national consciousness.[41]

Referring mainly to the Netherlands, historical sociologist Philip Gorski has gone so far as to posit a "Mosaic moment" during the formation of nationalism;[42] Pasi Ihalainen has conducted a wide-ranging historical survey of the use of the biblical chosenness idea in English, Dutch, and Swedish sermons of the seventeenth and eighteenth centuries, stressing the clear preference accorded to the Old rather than the New Testament in protestant political language.[43] These theories all demonstrate that nationalism's Hebraist phase was linked to protestant political movements in the early modern period. Other historians have discerned similar traces of a protestant Hebraism in the works of the American founding fathers, for instance, Thomas Jefferson.[44]

The first to take note of the Hebraist aspect of German nationalism was Salo Baron, who, together with Kohn, was among the first scholars to address the connection between the Bible and the emergence of European nationalism.[45]

Regarding Germany, Baron stresses the link between Phillip Jacob Spener's (1635–1705) Pietist Hebraism and the rise of German nationalism and notes that during this period, the wider German public was better acquainted with the Bible than with German literature. Yet he maintains that the Old Testament "influenced cultural, though not political, nationalism."[46] The distinction he makes between the two phenomena remains unexplained.

Several other scholars have addressed Herder's Hebraist nationalism. In his essay, "The Hebraic Roots of Herder's Nationalism," politologist and Herder scholar Frederick M. Barnard offers a systematic investigation of the German writer's Hebraist nationalism.[47] In his opinion, in fact, Herder's idea of nationhood was not grounded in the German political reality of his time but rather grew out of his interpretation of Hebrew history.[48] According to Barnard, even though Herder's primary academic motivation was religious, his interest in politics grew over time. According to this reading, the model of the Hebrew state offered Herder an alternative to the Natural Law tradition with its emphasis on private rights.

Another scholar who investigated Herder's biblical model is Bernd Fischer, who traced the formation of a national identity in the German literature of the eighteenth century. Fischer presents the Old Testament as "the state's mythological-poetic paradigm" underlying Herder's political thought. According to this reading, Herder regarded the Hebrew state as an example of a theocracy with a nomocratic constitution based on patriarchal custom rather than on abstract principles.[49] Liliane Weissberg argues that Herder's praise of the Hebrews served to stress the difference between this ancient people and the Jews of his time.[50] Mary Ann Perkins and George Williamson have also written about the impact of the Hebrew idea of chosenness on German nationalism.[51]

In summary, while the major works dealing with the Hebrews—mainly Herder's, but also some of Michaelis's writings—have been well researched, writing about the ancient Hebrews as a whole has not been sufficiently investigated, and German Hebraism has yet to be researched as an independent phenomenon. Moreover, the many lesser texts that formed part of the discourse on the Hebrew people and state have not been addressed academically at all. The history of the quest for the Hebrew people in the German Enlightenment reveals an interesting path in the annals of German culture, one that touches on many figures and phenomena in that nation's history.

*

The first section of the book deals with the diverse body of research on the historical character of the Hebrew people during the period under discussion. It focuses on the work of Michaelis, the founder of the historical-critical school of Bible scholarship, as well as the writing of his disciples. The second section observes how German writers of the second half of the eighteenth century used the Old Testament as a cultural and political model. Political Hebraism is shown to constitute one of the means they employed to integrate and fashion a cultural identity in the German-speaking space.

Chapter 1 deals with ethnographic descriptions of the Israelites. German Bible scholars attempted to pinpoint the Hebrews' emergence within the general historical and scientific context of nation formation. Reading the patriarch narratives in Genesis, they sought to characterize the stage of development that humanity had reached at the time. The principle that guided them in gauging a people's historical evolution was their advance toward higher levels of development, from a community of nomadic shepherds [*Hirtenvolk*] to a sedentary civil society [*bürgerliche Gesellschaft*].

Chapter 2 reviews the debate concerning the role of biblical law in German jurisprudence. It revolves around Michaelis's *Mosaisches Recht*, the most influential German work on biblical law written during this period. His inquiry into the history of Mosaic Law signified a novel research methodology with his use of modern ethnographic and philological tools. Like Martin Luther and other Protestant exegetes, Michaelis distinguished between universal legislative principles and particular elements of customary Hebrew law. In doing so, he revealed a new cultural and ethnic layer in the Old Testament. Having lost its universal validity, Mosaic Law was imbued with new significance as a paragon of particular legislation suited to its people's national conceptions [*Nationalbegriffe*].

The ways in which eighteenth-century German writers treated the biblical account of the conquest of Canaan by the Israelites and the extermination of its inhabitants is the subject of chapter 3. It surveys the attacks by anticlerical philosophers on the morality of Moses's extermination decree and focuses on attempts made by advocates of the Bible to affirm its legitimacy. Defending the legitimacy of the Canaan campaign and the extermination of the land's residents became a hallmark of German Bible scholars. Nevertheless, the historical methodology they used fundamentally altered the image of the biblical past, signifying a break from traditional readings of scripture. The focal point of the debate in this context shifted from the issue of a religious war's legitimacy to the question of historical rights to a territory and the link between a people and a land.

Chapter 4 surveys the discussion of Hebrew poetry during the second half of the eighteenth century, the manifestations of German Hebraism in literature, and the ideology that underlay them. The exemplar of Hebrew poetry played a pivotal role in the work of a group of influential writers, in particular, members of the *Sturm und Drang* movement. The most prominent of these was Friedrich Gottlieb Klopstock (1724–1803), widely regarded as the harbinger of modern German poetry. In his work, Klopstock created a poetic-theological synthesis of

German identity, Protestant belief, and fierce fidelity to the Old Testament and the Hebrew model. Thus, German literary Hebraism was linked to two contemporaneous cultural conceptual developments. The first was a notion of Hebrew as an authentic, primordial, and sublime language. Imitation of the Hebrews and their poetry became an important element in the sentimental style of *Sturm und Drang*, inextricably linked to Pietist Protestant ideology. A second, no less important, development was the conception of the Hebrews as an alternative to the dominant Greek-Roman model, with a view to establishing an authentic German culture. The Hebrew model served as one of the cultural elements through which the German literature of that period could distinguish itself from French-associated neoclassical literature and develop its own stylistic and thematic avenues.

The chapter furthermore surveys attempts to read the Old Testament as a German political myth. It focuses on the way Herder interpreted the Bible, turning it into a political prototype suited to the German people and its needs. Herder's writing on Hebrew nationality was part of a new discourse that evolved in German literary circles following the Seven Years' War, moving away from the Enlightenment's universalist political conceptions and engaging with the new concept of "national literature" [*Nationalliteratur*]. His book, *Vom Geist der Ebräischen Poesie*, offers a novel appraisal of the Hebrew people; rather than stressing their role as disseminators of the universal religion, Herder acclaims the Hebrews for having evolved their own national religion and culture. Hebrew particularism, so reviled by Enlightenment writers, was now lauded as the element that imbued Hebrew poetry with its power and entitled it to become a role model for the Germans.

Chapter 5 addresses the persistent political discourse on the Hebrews in the generation after Herder. It surveys the growing tendency to write the Hebrew tradition out of German culture, first by describing it as sensual and irrational and later by asserting that it was foreign to German culture. Attempts by poets and theologians to reassert the Bible's validity in the face of these attacks and to reintegrate it into German culture are evident, inter alia, in their political use of the Hebrew model. One of the major avenues through which writers of this period endeavored to "save" the Bible was by transforming it into mythology. By so doing, they sought to integrate "Hebrew myth," alongside the Greek classics, into the *Bildung* of the German educated classes.

This Christian discussion of the Hebrew Bible impacted the emerging Jewish Haskalah movement. Specifically, its transformation of "ancient oriental poetry" into a cultural artifact triggered a new set of aesthetic and cultural values within Jewish intellectual circles. Herder, for instance, expressed hope that the "Hebrew epic" would be revived by "a poet of the Hebrew nation," and his call was taken up by Jewish authors who created poetic adaptations of biblical themes, among them Naftali Herz Wessely's *Shirei Tif'eret* ("*Poems of Glory*") or *Moseide*, considered one of the pioneering works of modern Hebrew literature.

Notes

1. Johann Joachim Winckelmann, "Thoughts on the Imitation of Greek Works in Painting and the Art of Sculpture (1755–1756)," in *Johann Joachim Winckelmann on Art, Architecture, and Archaeology*, trans. David Carter (Rochester, NY: Camden House, 2013), 3.
2. Winckelmann, "Thoughts on the Imitation of Greek Works," 3.
3. Georg Wilhelm Friedrich Hegel, "The Positivity of Christian Religion," in *Early Theological Writing*, trans. T. M. Knox (Chicago: University of Chicago Press, 1948), 146–147.
4. Susannah Heschel, *The Aryan Jesus: Christian Theologians and the Bible in Nazi Germany* (Princeton, NJ: Princeton University Press, 2008).
5. See, for example: Hans-Martin Herrmann, *Machtphantasie Deutschland: Nationalismus, Männlichkeit und Fremdenhaß im Vaterlandsdiskurs des 18. Jahrhunderts* (Frankfurt am Main: Suhrkamp, 1996); George S. Williamson, *The Longing for Myth in Germany: Religion and Aesthetic Culture from Romanticism to Nietzsche* (Chicago: University of Chicago Press, 2004), 19–72.
6. See, for example: Thomas Albert Howard, *Protestant Theology and the Making of the Modern German University* (Oxford: Oxford University Press, 2006); and Jonathan Sheehan, *The Enlightenment Bible: Translation, Scholarship, Culture* (Princeton, NJ: Princeton University Press, 2005), 148.
7. See, for example: Jonathan Sheehan, *The Enlightenment Bible*; Rudolf Smend, *From Astruc to Zimmerli: Old Testament Scholarship in Three Centuries* (Tübingen: Mohr Siebeck, 2007), 35–40; Rudolf Smend, *Bibel und Wissenschaft: historische Aufsätze* (Tübingen: Mohr Siebeck, 2004); Rudolf Smend, *Deutsche Alttestamentler in drei Jahrhunderten* (Gottingen: Vandenhoeck & Ruprecht, 1989); Emil G. Kraeling, *The Old Testament since the Reformation* (London: Lutterworth, 1955); Hans-Joachim Kraus, *Geschichte der historisch kritischen Erforschung des Alten Testaments von der Reformation bis zur Gegenwart* (Neukirchen-Vluyn: Neukirchener, 1969); Hans W. Frei, *The Eclipse of Biblical Narrative: A Study in Eighteenth and Nineteenth Century Hermeneutics* (New Haven, CT: Yale University Press, 1974); Henning Graf Revenlow, Walter Sparn, and John Woodbridge eds., *Historische Kritik und biblischer Kanon in der deutschen Aufklärung* (Wiesbaden: Otto Harrassowitz, 1988), Elinor S. Shaffer, *"Kubla Khan" and the Fall of Jerusalem: The Mythological School in Biblical Criticism and Secular Literature* (Cambridge, UK: Cambridge University Press, 1980).
8. See, for example, Michael Zell, *Reframing Rembrandt: Jews and the Christian Image in Seventeenth-Century Amsterdam* (Berkeley: University of California Press, 2002), 33–58.
9. Erich Auerbach, "Figura," in *Scenes from the Drama of European Literature*, trans. Ralph Manheim (Gloucester: Peter Smith, 1985), 44.
10. Auerbach, "Figura," 49.
11. Thomas R. Elssner, *Josua und seine Kriege in jüdischer und christlicher Rezeptionsgeschichte* (Stuttgart: W. Kohlhammer, 2008), 301–305.
12. Emil G. Kraeling, *The Old Testament since the Reformation*, 9.
13. Martin Luther, "Commentary on the First Twenty-Two Psalms," in *Selected Works*, trans. Henry Cole (London: Bensley, 1826), 493.

14. Martin Luther, *Werke: kritische Gesamtausgabe* (Weimar: Böhlau, 1883), WA 42.667. See Jon Whitman, "Introduction," in *Interpretation and Allegory: Antiquity to the Modern Period* (Leiden: Brill, 2000), 3.

15. Benedict Spinoza, *Tractatus Theologico-Politicus*, trans. S. Shirley (Leiden: Brill, 1989), 84.

16. Spinoza, *Tractatus Theologico-Politicus*, 89.

17. Dan Edelstein, *The Enlightenment: A Genealogy* (Chicago: University of Chicago Press, 2010).

18. Such a stance is taken, for example, in: Paul Hazard, *La Pensée européenne au XVIIIème siècle, de Montesquieu à Lessing* (Paris: Fayard, 1963); Peter Gay, *The Enlightenment: An Interpretation: The Rise of Modern Paganism* (London: Weidenfeld and Nicolson, 1966). For a debate on Enlightenment-era historiography, see, for example: Dorinda Outram, *The Enlightenment* (Cambridge, UK: Cambridge University Press, 2005); Daniel Brewer, *The Enlightenment Past* (Cambridge, UK: Cambridge University Press, 2008).

19. See, for example: Sheehan, *The Enlightenment Bible*; David Sorkin, *The Religious Enlightenment: Protestants, Jews, and Catholics from London to Vienna* (Princeton, NJ: Princeton University Press, 2008); Wolfgang Altgeld, *Katholizismus, Protestantismus, Judentum: Über religiös begründete Gegensätze und nationalreligiöse Ideen in der Geschichte des deutschen Nationalismus* (Mainz: Matthias-Grünewald, 1992); S. J. Barnett, *The Enlightenment and Religion: The Myths of Modernity* (Oxford: Oxford University Press, 2004); James Van Horn Melton, "Pietism, Politics, and the Public Sphere in Germany," in *Religion and Politics in Enlightenment Europe*, ed. James E. Bradley and Dale K. Van Kley (Notre Dame, IN: University of Notre Dame Press, 2001); Horst Carl, "Die Aufklärung unsres Jahrhunderts ist ein bloßes Nordlicht ... Konfession und deutsche Nation im Zeitalter der Aufklärung," in *Nation und Religion in der deutschen Geschichte*, ed. Heinz-Gerhard Haupt and Dieter Langewische (Frankfurt am Main: Campus, 2001), 105–141.

20. Johann David Michaelis, *Mosaisches Recht* (Frankfurt am Main.: J. Gottlieb Garbe, 1775).

21. For example: Johann Ernst Faber, *Archäologie der Hebräer* (Halle: Curt, 1773); Wilhelm Nicolaus Freudentheil, *Ossian und die Hebräischen Dichter / Über die Siegslieder der Hebräer* (Leipzig, 1774); Johann Jakob Hess, *Geschichte der Patriarchen* (Zürich: Orell, Gessner, Füssli, 1776); Heinrich Ehrenfried Warnekros, *Entwurf der hebräischen Alterthümer* (Weimar: Hofman, 1782); Theodor Jakob Ditmar, *Geschichte der Israeliten bis auf den Cyrus* (Berlin: Maurer, 1788); Babor, Johann, *Alterthümer der Hebräer* (Vienna: V. Kurzbeck, 1794); Karl Wilhelm Justi, *Nationalgesänge der Hebräer* (Marburg: Neue Akadem, 1803); Friedrich August Carus, *Psychologie der Hebräer* (Leipzig: Barth & Kummer, 1809).

22. Johann Gottfried Herder, *Vom Geist der Ebräischen Poesie*. Dessau: Buchhandlung der Gelehrten, 1782–1783.

23. Anthony D. Smith, *Chosen Peoples: Sacred Sources of National Identity* (Oxford: Oxford University Press, 2003), 9–19.

24. For an extensive and up-to-date survey of modern-era Biblical interpretation, see: Magne Saebo ed., *Hebrew Bible / Old Testament: The History of Its Interpretation* (Göttingen: Vandenhoeck & Ruprecht, 2008). On the pioneers of Biblical criticism in England and France, see, for example: Richard Popkin, "Bible Criticism and Social Science," in *Methodological and Historical Essays in the Natural and Social Sciences*, ed. Robert Cohen and Marx Wartofsky (Dordrecht: Reidel, 1973).

25. See especially: Stephen G. Burnett, *Christian Hebraism in the Reformation Era (1500–1660): Authors, Books, and the Transmission of Jewish Learning* (Leiden: Brill, 2012); Yaacov Deutsch, *Judaism in Christian Eyes: Ethnographic Description of Jews and Judaism in Early Modern Europe* (Oxford: Oxford University Press, 2012); Allison Coudert and Jeffrey S. Shoulson, eds., *Hebraica Veritas? Christian Hebraists and the Study of Judaism in Early Modern Europe* (Philadelphia: University of Pennsylvania Press, 2004); Christoph Bultmann and Lutz Danneberg, eds., *Hebraistik—Hermeneutik—Homiletik: Die "Philologia Sacra" im frühneuzeitlichen Bibelstudium* (Berlin: Walter de Gruyter, 2011).

26. Deutsch, *Judaism in Christian Eyes*, 21–22. On the concept of Hebraism, see also: Michael A. Signer, "Polemic and Exegesis: The Varieties of Twelfth-Century Hebraism," in *Hebraica Veritas?*, 21–23.

27. See, for instance: Jerome Friedman, *The Most Ancient Testimony: Sixteenth-Century Christian-Hebraica in the Age of Renaissance Nostalgia* (Athens, OH: Ohio University Press, 1983), 1–2.

28. See especially: Gordon Schochet, Fania Oz-Salzberger, and Meirav Jones, eds., *Political Hebraism: Judaic Sources in Early Modern Political Thought* (Jerusalem: Shalem Press, 2008). And see also: Eric Nelson, *The Hebrew Republic: Jewish Sources and the Transformation of European Political Thought* (Cambridge, MA: Harvard University Press, 2010); Phillip S. Gorski, "The Mosaic Moment: An Early Modernist Critique of Modernist Theories of Nationalism," *American Journal of Sociology* 105, no. 5 (2000): 1428–1468; Pasi Ihalainen, *Protestant Nations Redefined: Changing Perceptions of National Identity in the Rhetoric of the English, Dutch and Swedish Public Churches, 1685–1772* (Leiden: Brill, 2005); Eran Shalev, *American Zion: The Old Testament as a Political Text from the Revolution to the Civil War* (New Haven, CT: Yale University Press, 2012).

29. Saebo, *Hebrew Bible / Old Testament*; on the pioneers of biblical criticism in England and France, see, for example, Richard Popkin, "Bible Criticism and Social Science."

30. Sheehan, *The Enlightenment Bible*.

31. Michael Legaspi, *The Death of Scripture and the Rise of Biblical Studies* (Oxford: Oxford University Press, 2010). Another scholar who has lately taken up Michaelis's and Herder's biblical exegesis is Daniel Weidner, who focuses on the conceptual and semiotic shifts that the reading of the Bible underwent during the eighteenth century. See: Daniel Weidner, *Bibel und Literatur um 1800* (Munich: Wilhelm Fink, 2011).

32. Jonathan M. Hess, *Germans, Jews and the Claims of Modernity* (New Haven, CT: Yale University Press, 2002).

33. Hans Kohn, *The Idea of Nationalism: A Study in Its Origins and Background* (New York: Macmillan, 1944), 41–47, 633.

34. Steven Elliott Grosby, *Biblical Ideas of Nationality: Ancient and Modern* (Winona Lake, IN: Eisenbrauns, 2002).

35. For a detailed discussion of this subject, see: Anthony D. Smith, *The Nation in History: Historiographical Debates about Ethnicity and Nationalism* (Hanover, NH: University Press of New England, 2000), 48–51.

36. Kohn, *The Idea of Nationalism*, 633.

37. Kohn, *The Idea of Nationalism*, 36.

38. Anthony Smith, *Chosen Peoples: Sacred Sources of National Identity* (Oxford: Oxford University Press, 2003), 66–77.

39. Adrian Hastings, *The Construction of Nationhood: Ethnicity, Religion, and Nationalism* (Cambridge, UK: Cambridge University Press, 1997).
40. Hastings, *Construction of Nationhood*, 18.
41. Liah Greenfeld, *Nationalism: Five Roads to Modernity* (Cambridge, MA: Harvard University Press, 1992), 51–54.
42. Philip S. Gorski, "The Mosaic Moment: An Early Modernist Critique of Modernist Theories of Nationalism," *The American Journal of Sociology* 105, no. 5 (March 2000): 1428–1468; and see also: Theodor Dunkelgrün, "'Neerlands Israel'—Political Theology, Christian Hebraism, Biblical Antiquarianism, and Historical Myth," in *Myth in History, History in Myth*, ed. Laura Cruz and Willem Frijhoff (Leiden: Brill, 2009), 201–236.
43. Pasi Ihalainen, *Protestant Nations Redefined*, 109.
44. See, for example: Adam Sutcliffe and Jonathan Karp, "A Brief History of Philosemitism" in *Philosemitism in History*, ed. Jonathan Karp and Adam Sutcliffe (Cambridge, UK: Cambridge University Press, 2011), 86–87; Eran Shalev, *American Zion: The Old Testament as a Political Text from the Revolution to the Civil War* (New Haven, CT: Yale University Press, 2012).
45. Salo Wittmayer Baron, *Modern Nationalism and Religion* (New York: Harper, 1947), 214.
46. Baron, *Modern Nationalism*, 135.
47. Frederick M. Barnard, *Herder on Nationality, Humanity, and History* (Montreal: McGill-Queen's Press, 2003), 17–38.
48. Barnard, *Herder on Nationality*, 17–18.
49. Bernd Fischer, *Das Eigene und das Eigentliche: Klopstock, Herder, Fichte, Kleist* (Berlin: Schmidt, 1995), 191–195.
50. Liliane Weissberg, "Juden oder Hebräer? Religiöse und politische Bekehrung bei Herder," in *Johann Gottfried Herder: Geschichte und Kultur*, ed. Martin Bollacher (Würzburg: Königshausen & Neumann, 1994), 191–211; for further references, see also: Wolf-Daniel Hartwich, *Romantischer Antisemitismus: von Klopstock bis Richard Wagner* (Göttingen: Vandenhoeck & Ruprecht, 2005); Anders Gerdmar, *Roots of Theological Anti-Semitism: German Biblical Interpretation and the Jews, from Herder and Semler to Kittel and Bultmann* (Leiden: Brill, 2009).
51. Mary Anne Perkins, *Nation and Word, 1770–1850: Religious and Metaphysical Language in European National Consciousness* (Aldershot: Ashgate, 1999), 155–157; George S. Williamson, *The Longing for Myth in Germany: Religion and Aesthetic Culture from Romanticism to Nietzsche* (Chicago: University of Chicago Press, 2004), 34.

1 Troglodytes, Hottentots, and Hebrews: The Bible and the Sources of German Anthropology

IN 1773, ORIENTALIST Johann Ernst Faber (1745–1774) published the first volume of what was to be his final work, *Archäologie der Hebräer*, in Halle—he died a year later at the age of twenty-eight, with the book uncompleted. The published text, entitled *Haüslisches Alterthum*, begins with a clarification: with so many previous publications about "the antiquity of the Hebrews" [*Altherthümer des Hebräer*], yet another essay might seem superfluous. The writer offers this justification for its publication: his work does not purport to deal with the Hebrews' religious or legal history but rather to address their "private lives." "Since no essay has been dedicated to that antiquity dealing with the Hebrews' daily lives, lodgings, nutrition, arts, and sciences.... I allow myself to dedicate this archeology to this mission ... to describe the private life of this nation."[1]

With this work, Faber inaugurated a tradition of monographs on Hebrew history that included numerous essays over the following decades. A native of Limmerhausen (Saxony), Faber underwent standard training in the burgeoning field of biblical orientalism, studying under Michaelis at Göttingen and rounding off his education with ethnography and natural history.[2] In 1770, he took up the post of lecturer in oriental languages at Kiel, where he founded the Oriental Society. He published two books on Arabic grammar and established close ties with Herder, who planned to study Hebrew and Arabic under him. The plan fell through when Kiel became part of Danish territory, and in 1772, Faber relocated to Jena, where he completed two years of study before his death. Besides his essays on grammar, he also penned some works on biblical topics, such as animals in the book of Zephaniah and the manna the Israelites consumed in the desert.[3] He furthermore edited an anthology of travelers' accounts of biblical lands translated from English.[4] During these years, he was embroiled in a fierce academic dispute with Michaelis. His untimely death, attributed by some of his colleagues to overzealous academic preoccupation, left the three planned volumes of *Archaologie der Hebräer* uncompleted.[5]

The novelty of Faber's book is evident from its very first chapter. Unlike previous scholars who had engaged with the subject, Faber does not begin the text with Moses (or, in fact, with Abraham). Rather, the book's first section deals with the troglodytes—the cave-dwellers he claimed lived in and around Canaan prior to Abraham's arrival there. Mentioned by Herodotus and other Greek writers, the troglodytes were a favorite object of eighteenth-century scholarship. Anthropological writing of the period describes them as semihuman dwarves who lived in faraway lands, and Carl von Linné (1707–1778), in his influential biological system of classification, went as far as to dedicate an entire species to these mysterious beings. Linné divided the genus Homo into two species—*sapiens* and *troglodyte*, identifying the latter with the ape we now refer to as the orangutan.[6]

As cave-dwellers play no role in the Bible, Faber had to muster an interpretive effort to incorporate them into the narrative of Hebrew history. He relied principally on Josephus, who mentions "a land of Troglodytes" as the place in which Abraham's sons from his wife Keturah settled on their father's command.[7] Faber developed Josephus's casual remark into a comprehensive theory of humanity's ancient history in its wild state [*wilder Zustand*], adding that caves were humankind's earliest dwelling places, where shelter from rain and thunder was found.[8]

Faber finds proof of cave-dwelling in several biblical stories as well as in various accounts of travelers to the Orient, from which he deduces that "there are entire settlements and peoples dwelling in caves."[9] This form of existence, he argues, had proliferated since the time of Cain, who was the original troglodyte. Faber further claims that the majority of the peoples dwelling in the land of Canaan were, in fact, made up of troglodytes, in particular the Chorites, the Hivites, and the Raphaites. All of these flourished in the land until their downfall, which was brought about by the invasion of the Israelites: "The many caves that can be seen to this day in Palestine give credence to the conjecture that Palestine—including the other side of the Jordan—in the past housed many Troglodytes, who were, however, banished with the invasion of the Israelites."[10]

In contrast to the cave-dwellers, the Israelites brought a different, more advanced form of life to Canaan, namely shepherding and tent dwelling. A prevalent contemporary Enlightenment social theory defined shepherding as the second of four stages of human development—occupying the rung between hunting-gathering and agriculture. According to Faber, the shepherds' way of life began to evolve just before the Flood, initiated by Cain's son Jabal. After the Flood, humanity was divided into troglodytes and shepherds. He claimed further that permanent homes were rare—even though Noah was taught the art of architecture directly by God. Abraham and his offspring lived as nomads and tent dwellers [*Sceniten*]—the most prevalent way of life in Mesopotamia, Abraham's homeland, which he brought westward with him to the land of Canaan.[11]

Faber's version of "the archaeology of the Hebrews" presents the biblical account of the Israelites' origins as a progression of civilization. Their early history is tied to the ancient state of humanity as a whole, with the patriarchs' entrance into Canaan signifying the end of a base form of existence, that of the troglodytes. As I show later, in describing the battle between Hebrew shepherds and troglodytes in Palestine, Faber was developing a theory hatched before him by, among others, his master and nemesis, Michaelis. The question revolving around the origin of the Israelites occupied many German writers of the period and gave rise to many a scholarly essay.

In what follows, I discuss theories developed by thinkers of the German Enlightenment regarding the Israelites' origin and their emergence as a distinct group. While traditional Christian interpretation treated Abraham's story as a moment of religious revelation—and as humanity's first step on the way to salvation—German scholars of the mid-eighteenth century began reading it as a description of the emergence of a people or a clan. This view accorded new meanings to Hebrew history, a view that was incorporated into universal history.

As Reinhart Koselleck has argued, the foremost characteristic of the modern concept of history as fashioned in the eighteenth century was the move to a homogenous, linear time frame.[12] Other scholars have maintained that the fundamental innovation associated with the new historical writing that evolved at Göttingen University during this time was the move toward natural circumstantial rationalization, which focused on singular events and their placement in contextual webs alongside other events.[13] Indeed, scholars of the Enlightenment—especially German Bible scholars of the historical-critical school—sought to place the appearance of the Hebrews within the wider historical and scientific context of the emergence of peoples at the dawn of mankind. Reading the stories of the patriarchs in Genesis, they grappled with questions such as: Where had this people come from? What stage in its development had humanity reached during the period in which they lived? What parallels may be drawn between them and other peoples? And what enduring imprints did its formative stage leave on the Israeli nation—until its exile and even thereafter? The question of this people's origin is a highly charged one, as it holds the key to the Hebrew people's "fundamental" characteristics.

Through readings of various texts that describe the ancient Israelites, I trace the link between the emergence of the Hebrews' historical image and the anthropological discourse of the time—both in its historical guise (descriptions of ancient peoples) and its ethnographic aspects (descriptions of "wild" peoples penned by travelers to the Orient and the New World). I thus seek to ascertain the place the Hebrews were allotted within Enlightenment-era scholars' *Weltanschauung*. In the context of this debate, I introduce and discuss several key figures in German research into the antiquity of the Hebrews: central figures such as Michaelis and Herder as well as less prominent scholars, who nonetheless capture the sentiments and conceptions of the time.

The First Nation of Believers: The Israelites in Salvation History

Investigation into the origins of humanity and the emergence of peoples and cultures during the eighteenth century was frequently conducted as part of scholarly engagement with "universal history." This genre was well developed in German universities as far back as the sixteenth century under the influence of the Protestant humanism of Philip Melanchthon (1497–1560).[14] It produced lengthy essays following mankind's history that were typically divided into different chapters that constituted the different stages of salvation.[15] Within this genre, the history of biblical times and ensuing eras was conceived as a single comprehensive system leading from the world's creation to the present day.

According to the traditional Christian conception of salvation history, the Israelites played a prescribed and meaningful role as God's chosen people and as the first "nation of believers."[16] This description highlighted Abraham's role as "the father of believers" [*Vater der Gläubigen*]. God's covenant with Abraham was perceived as having inaugurated the third chapter in his dealings with humanity, following the previous covenants with Adam and with Noah.[17]

This conception was likewise prevalent among many orthodox theologians of the eighteenth century. Thus, in the chronicle *Introduction to Universal History* [*Einleitung zu der Universal-Historie*] published in 1740 by Pietist scholar Johann Friedrich Hochstetter (1698–?), Abraham's appearance on the stage of history is explained solely in the context of the history of faith: "From the moment people began to disperse across the earth; they gradually forgot God and became more and more immersed in contemptuous idolatry; and that is what led God to take Abraham, son of Terah, out of Chaldea, where his kin had dwelt, and reestablish in his home the rite of the True God."[18]

According to this narrative—a mainstay of holy history biblical chronicles—the origin of the Israelites was of major significance: they were the first people to shed idolatry and ignorance, a process which was to culminate in the arrival of Christ. Abraham's appearance on the historical scene signifies the transition from an age of idolatry to an age of belief in the true God [*Verherung des wahren Gottes*]. Therefore, many of these texts contain a lengthy description of the prevalence of idolatry in the era preceding the Israelites' history.

As Frank Manuel has shown in *The Eighteenth Century Confronts God*, the received wisdom among most early modern scholars was that idolatry first appeared at some point following the Flood, when the sons of Noah were dispersed in different lands.[19] In fact, belief in the one true God originated with Adam, and this belief was passed on through the generations to Noah and his sons; but life's hardships in the era following the Flood, humankind's ongoing estrangement from its ancient sources, and the accumulation of a string of misdemeanors that emanated from the feeble human mind brought about a gradual weakening and degeneration of belief.

One of the proponents of this theory was the Dutch humanist scholar Gerhard Vossius (1577–1649). According to Vossius, Noah still preserved the major religious traditions concerning the immortality of the soul, the Trinity, and the Last Judgement. As Noah's offspring spread over the earth, they lost touch with the antediluvian tradition. Idolatry emerged alongside the gradual corruption of tradition.[20]

According to a particular outlook prevalent among church scholars, idolatry was spread by the sons of Ham—especially the Egyptians and the Canaanites. Belief in the one true God endured only among the sons of Shem, even while idolatry spread among the rest of humanity. Luther went so far as to adopt a stance previously elaborated in the Talmudic tractate *Nedarim*, according to which Shem himself was the figure referred to in Genesis as Melchizedek—and that it was he who passed the belief in the true God on to Abraham.[21]

This narrative recounting the transmission of tradition, religion, faith, or ancient divine knowledge accords Abraham and his offspring a special place at the center of world history by virtue of their sole function as bearers of the faith. Abraham is seen as a link in a chain beginning with Adam and Noah and continuing through David and Jesus. Whether narrating seamless knowledge transmission from Noah to Abraham or describing the renewal of the True faith following God's revelation to Abraham, this traditional description of the patriarch is constructed as an answer to the question of the roots of faith.

Transformations in the understanding of human history in the early modern era undermined the Israelites' status as a nation of believers elected by God. The causal description of history obliged writers to adhere to natural explanations, feeding into a rationalist theology that undermined the legitimacy of particular election. Tracts rejecting the Jewish people's singular status in history appeared in the Netherlands, France, and England as early as the first half of the seventeenth century. The most resounding attack on the traditional concept of the Jews' election was formulated in Spinoza's *Tractatus Theologico-Politicus*, which rejected the assertion that God chose the Hebrews above all nations and claimed that this kind of choice would run counter to His nature. Spinoza went on to portray the Hebrews as a childish, vulgar people, maintaining that Moses had actually chosen them in order to bind them to his rules and persuade them to uphold the covenant.[22]

Spinoza's ideas left a lasting impression on radical Enlightenment circles and were adopted by several German anticlerical philosophers, including Johann Christian Edelmann (1698–1767) and Hermann Samuel Reimarus (1694–1768). However, as Ernst Cassirer has shown, the German Enlightenment traced its origins not to Spinoza but to the intellectual tradition of the Reformation, and thinkers of the *Aufklärung* sought not to deconstruct the biblical text, or to undermine its authority and supremacy, but rather to distill its original meaning, dismantling the hermeneutic intermediaries that rendered it inaccessible.[23]

Well into the 1770s, scholars in German universities took care not to topple the edifice of salvation history altogether but to preserve the Israelites' role in it. In major essays of the period, the Israelites are accorded a new role—this time as harbingers of the Enlightenment. This idea was manifested in various ways, some closer to traditional Christian historical schemes and others based on a "philosophical" system, that is, a rationally oriented conceptual system. The roots of these theories are to be found in the writings of Renaissance and Baroque-era Christian Kabbalists and Hebraists who sought to narrate the transmission of ancient knowledge or religion, of *prisca theologia* or *philosophia perennis* from Adam to Abraham and Moses.[24]

One of the most prominent figures of early German Enlightenment and classicism, Johann Christof Gottsched (1700–1766), claimed in 1733 that Hebrew philosophy was the most ancient in existence—apart from that of the Chaldeans. According to Gottsched, Abraham's family preserved much of the knowledge accumulated by humankind prior to the Flood (and which was subsequently lost), passing this "somewhat faulty" wisdom from father to son and conveying it to Palestine. His family then developed further ideas to ease human life, especially in the realms of morals and the economy.[25]

The chosen people's religious calling is exchanged in Gottsched's work for *Weltweisheit*, a term denoting a moral—but not religious—philosophy.[26] In 1750, Friedrich Andreas Walther (1727–1769), head of the Göttingen philosophy faculty, published an entire essay devoted to the wisdom of the Hebrews, *The History of the Ancient Hebrews' Wisdom [Geschichte der Weltweisheit der alten Hebräer]*. He describes Abraham as the first philosopher of the epoch following the Flood: "If we opt not to reduce the meaning of the word philosopher . . . it could include Abraham, as well. Scripture describes him as a man endowed with exceptional wisdom and intelligence. . . . In ancient times just as in new, it could not have escaped people's attention that Abraham must be regarded as one of the great philosophers, as well as the man responsible for bringing all wisdoms to the Orient at large."[27]

In the same spirit, the Israelites as a whole are described as a nation of philosophers—the bearers of reason in the ignorant post-Flood world.

This version of the holy history, however, was challenged by growing criticism of the idea of the chosen people. The mid-eighteenth century witnessed a proliferation of iconoclastic attacks on the Bible, which appeared in different European countries; Voltaire's critique, published in 1765 in his *La philosophie de l'histoire* under the title "De Bram, Abram, Abraham,"[28] could be considered the most provocative. Voltaire claimed that Abraham was, in fact, an ancient Indian sage whose name was connected to Brahma or the Brahmins.[29] He proceeded to assert that the Hebrews appropriated the figure of the oriental sage to enhance their people's stature. In his entry for "Jews" in his historical dictionary, Voltaire ignored the era of the patriarchs altogether, placing the beginning of Jewish history in Egypt.[30]

German Bible scholars were, on the whole, hesitant to join these attacks. In their research, they strove toward a historical description of the Bible, and favored the rational incorporation of biblical events into contemporary anthropological models and theories on the natural progression of civilizations. While they employed methods similar to those used by the iconoclasts and were influenced by those essays that attacked the Old Testament's authenticity, these scholars sought to achieve something very different. Rather than undermine biblical description, they endeavored to establish the stories of the patriarchs as an empirical historical past. As Michael Carhart has discerned, if one is to understand fully the scholarly motivations of many of the German scholars of the eighteenth century, one must differentiate between criticism and religious skepticism.[31] In many cases, their aim was actually to safeguard traditional historic conceptions in light of the new skeptical stances that eschewed biblical narrative's credibility and authenticity.[32] The new orientalist image of the Bible forced leading scholars of the German Enlightenment to formulate new apologies of Revelation, the Bible and the Hebrew people at its center.

Abraham: From Faith Father to Clan Father

In 1756, the Royal Society of Science in Göttingen held its fifth annual conference. Michaelis, the editor of the society's periodical (*Göttingische gelehrte Anzeigen*), delivered the keynote address.[33] His talk was devoted to the subject "The Wandering Shepherds of Ancient Palestine" and was based on fresh research.[34] The scholar, who would publish his major works only some twenty years later, was at this stage still a young professor engaged in crystallizing his method of historical-critical Bible interpretation.

Michaelis was born in Halle and received his basic philological training from his father, orientalist Hans Benedict Michaelis (1680–1764), head of that city's Pietist Collegium Orientale. Both the study of Hebrew and rote memorization of the Bible as a moral guide and communal ethical code played a central role in this educational institution, a stronghold of the Pietist movement. To that end, Pietist text scholarship was combined with systematic philological investigation of oriental (Coptic, Ethiopian, Arab, and other) manuscripts.[35] The young Michaelis also attended lectures on German history, medicine, and the natural sciences, choosing at first to follow in his predecessors' footsteps. Between 1733 and 1740, for instance, he wrote a distinctly conservative dissertation about the divine inspiration of biblical cantillation.

On completing his dissertation, the young Michaelis traveled to Leiden, where he studied with Albert Schultens (1686–1750), a Dutch scholar who wrote an essay on the use of Arabic for biblical interpretation. Schultens's principal claim, which was novel in his time, was that Hebrew was not a divine language given to Adam but rather an offshoot of the Semitic family of languages. After his Dutch sojourn, Michaelis proceeded to England, where he attended lectures by Bishop Robert Lowth (1710–1787) and other scholars.

After returning from England, Michaelis's lectures attracted a growing following, and in 1745, he was invited to Göttingen University. Leaving his familiar surroundings and setting down roots in Göttingen was a turning point in his career: Göttingen was a new university, founded in 1737 as one of the first academic institutions in which the theology faculty did not reign supreme. Influenced by the philosophical ideas of Scottish liberalism, the university dedicated itself to the experimental sciences, natural history, and critical historical research.[36] Thus, historiography was not perceived as a mere didactic aid but was placed in two quite novel contexts; it was used as a legal interpretive instrument (for the investigation of the context in which laws were formulated) and recognized as an "art" unto itself.

The social circle to which Michaelis belonged in Göttingen comprised historians, ethnographers, natural scientists, and critics. During these years, he accumulated a considerable body of knowledge on the history of religions, philology, and the natural sciences, as well as—by 1750—a mastery of the Hebrew language; he also studied Aramaic, Arabic, and Syriac. He corresponded with scholars throughout Europe in an attempt to assimilate any philological or scientific developments that might promote his project of investigating the scriptures.

Michaelis was especially impressed with the work of English Hebraist Benjamin Kennicott (1718–1783), who in the 1750s, published a codex of 615 biblical manuscripts copied before the invention of print. By means of comparison, Kennicott attempted to arrive at a version "free of the many mistakes and deceptions inserted into the Bible by the Jews," which stemmed partly from the cantillation marks added by the Masorites.[37] Michaelis, however, concluded that version comparison was insufficient to safeguard the text's authenticity, since, in his opinion, even the version preserved by the Jews had been corrupted long ago. Michaelis posits the Jewish interpretation of the Bible as a paradigm of the text's obfuscation: the modern Protestant interpreter must free himself from the Jewish interpretation and its influences if he is to arrive at an authentic understanding of the text.

Conversely, the only way to understand fully the text's original meanings would be "to become acquainted with the circumstances of that world," namely, the time and place of its writing. Already, in his first works in Göttingen, Michaelis stresses the idea that the Bible is first and foremost an oriental creation, and that the skills required for its understanding are primarily "knowledge of Oriental languages, a close acquaintanceship with the customs of ancient times and a good grasp of natural sciences."[38] Philology, therefore, had evolved into a comprehensive scientific investigation that far exceeded the mere comparison of versions and texts. Michaelis marshaled all the contemporary scientific disciplines to outline an anthropological, archaeological, and natural portrayal of the biblical world.

His discussion of the "Palestinian shepherds" is typical of the nascent discipline of biblical orientalism. Rather than revolving around a problem in biblical interpretation, the entire lecture—delivered to scholars of a wide array of disciplines—took the form of a debate on a scientific-historical question. The Hebrews themselves are contained within the more general category of "Oriental shepherd peoples"—a category that includes Arabs as well.

Michaelis began his lecture with a general overview of a "way of life" [*Lebensart*], which he claimed had been prevalent in Mesopotamia, Palestine, and Arabia after the destruction of the Tower of Babel. He then proceeded to delineate the fundamental characteristics of shepherd society. The principal concern he addresses is the question of the existence of property among the herders—one of the most controversial issues among scholars of the time. According to Michaelis, Hebrew shepherds recognized the concept of private property and upheld "the shepherds' law" [*Recht der Hirten*], which allowed them joint rights to pasture and movement within their grazing areas—including those inhabited by other peoples.[39] Michaelis is tacitly offering a daring argument here, that Abraham, in fact, did not migrate to Canaan in obedience to a divine command—his wandering to Canaan was nothing but a routine passage on the part of wandering shepherds to their familiar pastures in the west: "In Abraham's time this land still belonged to Mesopotamian tent-dwellers [*Sceniten*], and whoever wanted to adopt that way of life moved there. According to the Hebrew text, Abraham at first received no divine command to leave the land of his forefathers as long as his father was alive. . . . And so, even before having been commanded to do so, and unconnected to [that command], he moved with his father and a whole shepherd clan to Palestine, the homeland of tent-dwellers."[40]

This argument is emblematic of the fundamental transformation that Michaelis inaugurated in the manner in which early Hebrew history was described and explained—especially when understood against the backdrop of Christian tradition, in which God's revelation to Abraham signifies the point of departure of holy history. In his various writings on ancient Hebrew history, Michaelis contributed more than any other scholar to the crystallization of a new narrative regarding the Israelites' origin.

Several years later, a strikingly similar description of the Hebrew people's origin appeared in the short essay "Hebrews" [*Hebräer*] in Johann Gottfried

Herder's *Ideas on the Philosophy of Mankind's History* [*Ideen zur Philosophie der Geschichte der Menschheit*]: "The Hebrews' national traditions recount that their clan father, who was a caravanserai Sheikh, crossed the Euphrates and finally settled in Palestine. He liked the place because he could carry on his shepherd fathers' way of life as well as worship his forbears' gods, according to clan custom."[41]

The way Herder describes Abraham—as the Sheikh of a nomadic shepherding group who made his way to Palestine from the eastern bank of the Euphrates closely follows Michaelis's theory of east-to-west migration. Herder goes even further in underscoring the continuity that marks Abraham's story, who, according to Herder, strove to maintain his forebears' religious way of life. Herder's book, which begins with the words "Our earth is a star among stars," narrates the history of the human race and of the world in general; yet Abraham does not appear at the beginning of the book nor indeed in any chapter of it.[42] The creation of the Hebrew clan [*Stamm*] is posited as just another stage within an all-encompassing narrative of the evolution of human civilization and of the cosmic progression in its entirety. Herder places the appearance of the Hebrews somewhere between the Babylonians and the Phoenicians on a chronological axis that begins with cosmic phenomena and passes through the ancient civilizations of the Orient.

In *The German Enlightenment and the Rise of Historicism*, Peter Hanns Reill traces the transformations in the way German historians characterized historical figures and actions during the first third of the eighteenth century.[43] Reill locates the turning point in the 1740s, when German scholars abandoned Christian Wolff's (1679–1754) deductive-speculative method in favor of an empiricist-legal approach, spearheaded by Christian Thomasius (1655–1728). According to Reill, until this turn, scholars had based themselves on transhistorical generalizations—be they abstract political ideas or theological categories—in which the historical figure was reduced to an ideal type and events were described as examples, symbols or test cases. The German *Aufklärer*, by contrast, attempted to characterize concrete historical events and to situate them within a temporal progression and causal development.

This transformation is indeed manifested in Abraham's changing characterization during the eighteenth century. In the transhistorical narrative of the advancement of the true faith, Adam, Noah, Abraham, and Moses functioned as markers along a route leading to salvation, each of them no more than a reflection of the other and a harbinger of the arrival of Christ. The primary—and sometimes only—characterization pinned to Abraham was "Faith." The project of historicizing the biblical past, however, sought to situate Abraham within his surroundings (the Orient) and in his time (the era of the shepherds). Therefore, if until then Abraham was described first and foremost as a "believer," he was now characterized above all as a wandering herder, an Emir, or a Bedouin.

The germination of the Hebrew clan in the geographical and ethnic seedbed of the ancient Orient; the exact circumstances of its formation and the environmental influences that contributed to shaping his ethnic characteristics—all these issues became central to the debate on the Israelites that commenced in the 1760s. Orientalists, biblical scholars, and theologians searched the scriptures for clues and traces that would allow them to outline exhaustively the people's origin, all the while employing the innovations of natural sciences. Michaelis, for example, claims that Sarah's pigment was lighter than that of Canaanite women, since Abraham's family had come from a geographical area located at least ten degrees further to the north.[44]

However, swapping symbolic interpretation for naturalistic readings of genealogical tables posed several problems. For instance, should Abraham's description as "a father of many nations" (Genesis 17:5) be read literally? And indeed, should the Israelites be regarded as his genetic offspring? Several scholars voiced doubts regarding the claim that the Israelites were indeed the offspring of Abraham.

This was the stance taken, for example, by Theodor Jacob Ditmar (1734–1791), professor of history and geography at Berlin's Köllnisches Gymnasium, who published his *Geschichte der Israeliten bis auf den Cyrus* in 1788.[45] The author maintains that this text is intended to guard the scriptures' authenticity against the attacks of its enemies, although it includes several unorthodox speculations regarding the formation of the Hebrew people. Ditmar claims, for instance, that Abraham was nothing other than the leader of a shepherd people—the Hebrews—which had already come into being in Chaldea. The title "father of the Hebrew people," he maintains, should be understood politically rather than physically. According to this reading, the names of the father of nations represented in the Bible as Abraham's sons are nothing other than the names of the colonies [*Stammcolonie*] he founded.[46]

Ditmar's text should be noted as an exceptional case in eighteenth-century German Bible scholarship. It is a theory that employs ethnographic and orientalist knowledge drawn from other sources to undermine the literal sense of the biblical narrative of the Israelites' origin, and by which he seeks to reconstruct a different historical reality that supposedly underlies the text. It should come as no surprise, then, that Wilhelm Martin Leberecht de Wette (1780–1849), the first German Bible critic to unequivocally rule out the Bible's validity as a description of actual historical reality, cited Ditmar's theory on several occasions.[47]

The Hebrews and the "Savage Peoples"

In his different works, Michaelis fashioned biblical scholarship as an intellectual project bound up with ethnographic research. The periodical he edited from 1771 until his death, *Orientalische und Exegetische Bibliothek*, offered European travelers' accounts, philological and grammatical essays on oriental languages (especially Hebrew, Arabic, Syriac, Aramaic, and Greek), reviews of Bible translations, and critiques of theological essays.

The German biblical exegete's "long arm" extended, in fact, to the deserts of the Arabian Peninsula. In 1756, he convinced Frederick V of Denmark to sponsor a mission to Yemen to investigate the languages and customs of the Near East and thereby further the understanding of the Israelites. Although he himself stayed behind in Göttingen, Michaelis was the effective manager of the Arabia Felix mission (1761–1767), advising the travelers and coaching them in Arabic. He even composed "a series of questions" arising out of the biblical text which the travelers were instructed to address. Unfortunately, all the mission's members perished in the desert—save Carsten Niebuhr (1733–1815), who published an account of the journey.[48]

According to Frank Manuel "the obsession with ethnography" was what set Michaelis and other Enlightenment Bible scholars apart from the Protestant Hebraists of the seventeenth century, who frequently based their works on Hebrew rabbinic texts, and seldom relied on ethnographic observations.[49] During the eighteenth century, ethnographic reconstruction of the Hebrews' ancient way of life came to supplant the philological textual interpretation of the previous century; oriental desert accounts supplanted rabbinic literature as the main aide for understanding the text.

To fully appreciate this "ethnographic turn" in biblical interpretation, Michaelis's method must be situated within the history of ethnographic discourse on the Bible and in particular, within the history of comparisons between Hebrews and "savages." One of the most common impressions found in the earliest travelers' accounts from the fifteenth century onward, was the similarity they discerned between the customs and beliefs of non-European peoples and certain events described in the scriptures. The European "discovery" of the Americas unleashed a wave of essays that claimed to have uncovered a link between the Native Americans and the Jews. An example is *Jewes in America*, by English missionary Thomas Thorowgood (1600–1669), published in 1650.[50] Thorowgood bases his claims on several beliefs and customs he found to be prevalent among the natives in some parts of the Americas, such as the washing of feet and the separation between men and women inside their wigwam tents. Among the sources on which he relied was the book *Miqveh Yisrael*, written by Menasseh Ben Israel (1604–1657), in which he claimed that the descendants of the ten lost tribes of Israel were to be found in America. It bears mentioning that Thorowgood does not differentiate between the ancient Hebrews and the Jews of his day. Furthermore, the essay's main thrust is missionary, as Thorowgood advocates the conversion of American Jews to Christianity to hasten the end of days. This and similar essays are linked to the millenarian groups that sprang up in England in the seventeenth century.[51]

Indeed, several travelers throughout the seventeenth and early eighteenth centuries made comparisons between the Jews and the Native Americans. William Penn (1644-1718) went as far as to claim that whoever met the natives might feel he was actually walking along Berry Street in London, on which the city's central synagogue was located.[52] Similar claims were made by authors such as Marc Lescarbot (1570-1641) and Antoine Le Mothe-Cadillac (1658-1730).[53]

The most renowned comparison between the Hebrews and the peoples of America was penned in 1724 by Jesuit priest Joseph-François Lafitau (1681-1746), a missionary among the Canadian Iroquois. Lafitau discerned many similarities between the customs of the Iroquois and those described in the Bible (especially those of the patriarchs). He concluded that the people, who, so he asserted, had arrived in America in the period after the Flood, were the sons of an ancient "joint religion" close to that of the Israelites.[54] More pertinent to our current debate, however, is the use made by Lafitau of several indigenous customs to illuminate biblical passages dealing with the Israelites. Thus, he refutes the claim that Sarah was Abraham's sister (a contention that featured prominently in deist criticism of the Israelites). Referring to Iroquois kinship structures, Lafitau, in fact, deduces that Sarah was actually the patriarch's niece. Lafitau's discourse offers an early attempt at ethnographic interpretation of the Bible.

According to Howard Eilberg-Schwartz, the identification of Jews with Native Americans stemmed from the similar position the two groups occupied in the early modern European concept of the "chain of being." Both these peoples were regarded as anti-Christian, and both were viewed as only partly human. However, when we place these early ethnographic comparisons between Jews and "savages" within the wider context of conceptions of human history that remained prevalent well into the mid-1700s, a common thread running through the works of Thorowgood, Lafitau, and the others emerges: in all of their texts, the perceived similarity between Hebrews and Native Americans is attributed to actual kinship, rather than merely a comparable degree of human development. The Native Americans are presented as Hebrews (or as relatives of the Hebrews) who have descended into savagery. The principal issue at stake here, which the comparison is intended to resolve, is that of the Native Americans' origin—one of the major intellectual challenges that occupied Europeans following the discovery of the New World.

Claims pertaining to similarities in belief and customs led also to the identification of African peoples with the Hebrews. In 1719, astronomer and adventurer Peter Kolbe (1675-1726) wrote an account of his travels in southern Africa, entitled *The Cape of Good Hope Today* [*Caput Bonae Spei Hodiernum*]. Born in a village near Bayreuth, the young Kolbe traveled to Halle to study Hebrew, mathematics, and astronomy. On completing his doctoral dissertation, he was appointed secretary to Prussian Baron Friedrich von Krosigk, in whose service he was sent to conduct astronomical readings at the Cape of Good Hope, where he lived between 1704 and 1713.[55] The major section of his book, which gained a wide readership and was soon translated into several other languages, comprised an ethnographic description of the so-called Hottentots—the colonial term employed to refer primarily to the Khoi people that lived in that area.

After describing some of the Hottentots' customs—among them hospitality and lion worship—Kolbe concludes that they have "much in common with the Jews and the Troglodytes."[56] In fact, he claims that these were the troglodyte descendants of Abraham mentioned by Jospehus. A reading of the text in its entirety reveals that Hebraist-educated Kolbe identified other phenomena he encountered in Africa by referring to the scriptures. Thus, he identifies a banana-like tree as the mandrake mentioned in Genesis and believes that a certain species of shark was that which the "great fish" that swallowed Jonah belonged to. As was common among early modern scholars, the book of nature is interpreted here according to the book of Revelation.[57]

For Kolbe, as well as for the other ethnographic essayists enumerated here, the Bible and classical literature still constituted the only corpus available for understanding the order of being; rather than employing ethnographic data to aid understanding of the Bible, they viewed scripture itself as the primary guide to the interpretation of new observations. The conceptual framework within which the comparisons of Africans and Native Americans to Hebrews were made served to generate a historical narrative of degeneration and loss of faith. Rather than regarding them as "savages" frozen in time, Americans and Africans are both described as groups that strayed from tradition, veering off the route of Judeo-Christian history and forgetting or distorting true belief. Lacking a temporal development scheme, these writers are untroubled by questions of the progress of civilizations; for the same reason, they fail to make a clear distinction between the ancient Hebrews and the Jews of their time. Lafitau's text, in a way, is an embryonic ethnographic Bible interpretation; yet it cannot be considered an ethnography in the modern sense, as it does not revolve around that exalted object of ethnography—primitive man.[58]

In light of this, we may conclude that until the early eighteenth century, even when the Hebrews were compared to Native Americans or Africans, this was not to designate them as a "primitive people" in the modern sense of the term. However, the ability to compare the Hebrews with peoples described by travelers to the four corners of the earth laid the groundwork for delineation of an entirely new set of relations between ethnographic objects. This new configuration was facilitated by a major transformation in the conception of history associated with the rise of the anthropological theory of the four stages of development—hunting, herding, agriculture, and commerce.[59]

It is against this backdrop that we witness the rise of the "savage Hebrews" genre of descriptions by French and English deist philosophers, who, by denigrating the Jews, sought to undermine scripture. If, during the seventeenth century, scholars exploited the supposed similarity between Hebrews and Native Americans to buttress the scriptures' authority and relevance, in the early eighteenth century, similar comparisons were employed to besmirch biblical protagonists and through them, Judaism and Christianity as such. The fiercest of the Hebrews' critics was, as already mentioned, Voltaire, who consistently mocked the Hebrews in his many works. He described them as a stubborn, provincial people that had zealously guarded their pathetic and cruel customs while living between the two great civilizations of the Orient—the Egyptians and the Chaldeans—refusing to adopt any of their wisdom. In 1756—the same year that Michaelis presented his Arab nomads theory—Voltaire likewise employed a comparison with the Arabs, designed to underscore the Israelites' cruelty during their occupation of Canaan. He remarks that "it seems they behaved according to the customs prevalent to this day in arid, desolate Arabia."[60] In fact, he goes so far as to conclude that the Israelites practiced bestiality and human sacrifice, precisely because these are banned by Mosaic law. This method—the "negative reconstruction" of the Hebrews' customs according to the prohibitions contained in their laws—was also adopted by the German Bible scholars, although it led them to totally different conclusions.

The characterization of Judaism as a materialist, sensual religion—as opposed to the spiritual characterization of Christianity—is an ancient theological concept harkening back to Paul's writings, and it infiltrated both the deists' and Voltaire's anti-Jewish criticism. However, it is important to differentiate between earlier presentations of the Hebrews as "coarse," "stubborn," or "materialist" and later descriptions as a "primitive" or "undeveloped" people. The traditional Christian criticism of the Jews makes no claim regarding the degree of their civilization's progress or development. And, although later descriptions of the Hebrews as a primitive people build on this ancient characterization, it is important to differentiate between the two. The modern view of the Hebrews is closely connected to the transformation of orientalism into a distinct academic field of expertise in the eighteenth century, which marks the establishment of the modern orientalist worldview. The state of the "orientals" became inextricably associated with sensuality, coarseness, and fanaticism. Once established, "oriental wisdom" [*Orientalische Weisheit*] was now ironically invoked to represent excess and fantasy.[61]

However, we should note that at the time that Voltaire and the deists were painting a portrait of the Hebrews as cruel oriental savages, a different tradition of biblical ethnography was taking shape in England. Bishop and orientalist Lowth pioneered the interpretation of the Bible as a literary work that should be understood from the perspective of the life of an oriental people living amid nature. In his *De sacra poesi Hebraeorum*, Lowth describes biblical poetry as the expressive outpouring of sublime forces through the tumultuous expressive means of the primordial soul.[62] The biblical hymns, he claims, were initially created as chants that served to transmit the people's history and laws from generation to generation. He stresses that the orientals were "the farthest removed of our customs and manners," and that among all the orientals, the Hebrews were the most removed. To understand the Hebrew original, the exegete needs to make a special effort to "see everything through the eyes" of the Hebrews.

Lowth's method of historical interpretation was adopted by a whole generation of German theologians and Bible scholars.[63] Two men in particular were responsible for introducing the new interpretive method into the German scholarly milieu: Moses Mendelssohn (1729–1786), who wrote the first German review of Lowth's book, praising the English bishop's innovativeness; and Michaelis, who published an edition of the book in Göttingen.[64] Exposure to Lowth's ideas led Michaelis to undergo a theological transformation: he began to recognize the scriptures' human-historical, time-and-geography contingent element, as well its authors' national character.[65]

These two images—the deists' "Hebrew savages" and Lowth's "natural Hebrews"—constituted the source of Michaelis's (and subsequently other German scholars') description of the people. Another no less important source, however, bears mentioning, namely the philological-orientalist tradition that developed in Michaelis's hometown of Halle. As Maike Oergel has shown, German ethnographic discourse is closely linked to this philological tradition, which has exerted considerable influence over German culture since the seventeenth century.[66] Michaelis's research into oriental languages did not appear ex nihilo; he acquired his aptitude for languages from his father, Christian Benedikt Michaelis, who studied Syriac, ancient Ethiopian (Ge'ez), and other oriental languages for purposes of biblical interpretation long before Michaelis junior published his findings. In 1708, the father published several essays on Islamic law and subsequently wrote about the patriarchs' way of life.[67] Interestingly, Michaelis junior almost totally ignored these texts, while it was ironically his nemesis, Faber, who cited them.[68]

The academic milieu within which Michaelis grew up shaped the orientalist context of his description of the Hebrews. He tended to compare them to Arabs rather than to Native Americans or Africans; he was, however, well aware of the existence of these other comparisons. In his *Mosaisches Recht*, he frequently interprets Hebrew customs in light of ethnographic descriptions of other peoples throughout the world. Thus he compares, for instance, different Pentateuch commandments to the customs of natives of West Africa as recorded by Jena University Pietist missionary Christian Georg Oldendorp (1721–1787), following his conversations with Caribbean Island slaves.[69] Michaelis also compares the biblical customs surrounding the blood feud to the customs of Caribbean peoples as described by French missionary Jean-Baptiste Labat (1663–1738).[70] In *Orientalische und Exgetische Bibliothek*, too, he reviews ethnographic records of American and African peoples, records which, so he claims, contributed to the understanding of the Bible.

A reevaluation of Michaelis's writing against the backdrop of the comparisons made by Thorowgood, Kolbe, and Lafitau would highlight the novelty of his understanding. Michaelis is skeptical of—and indeed sometimes rejects outright—the attempts to show that various peoples around the world were descendants of the Hebrews. These theories originated in the humanist traditions of the Renaissance and the Baroque, which assigned the Hebrew language a special status as the mother of all languages.

As part of his move to "normalize" the ancient Hebrews, Michaelis fundamentally eschews the special status accorded to their tongue. He articulates this stance in his criticism of Irish traveler James Adair's book of 1775, which offers twenty-three mostly etymological proofs that Native Americans were descended from the ten lost tribes of Israel. He sarcastically ridicules Adair's claim that *Ishtohooloo*—supposedly the savages' name for their God—is close to the Hebrew word for God, *Elohim*, while at the same time decrying the "epidemic" of essays describing Hebrew as the source of all other languages.

To a large extent, Michaelis's work can be seen as the concluding chapter of the "dynastic tradition" that sought to explain the customs, beliefs, and vocabulary of "savage" peoples according to their ancient connections with the Hebrews, as well as to place them in the genealogical tables listed in Genesis. It should be noted, however, that traces of this tradition crop up in his new ethnographic conception as well. Thus, he explains the method of reconstructing Hebrew customs through observation of Arab customs, for instance, by asserting that the residents of Arabia are "descendents of Abraham."[71]

Nevertheless, the interest that Michaelis showed in the customs of "nature peoples" [*Naturvölker*] was of a different order than that of earlier travelers. They concerned him only insofar as they reinforced his conceptions of the Hebrews. This was primarily a move toward the Israelites' naturalization and relativization, an attempt to prove that their laws and customs were *not* unique, but rather "natural." Michaelis was especially fond of reports—contained in the earlier accounts mentioned above—of "savage" peoples' propensity to circumcision as proof of their Hebrew origin. Michaelis transformed the comparison into a form of attack on Jewish circumcision—a custom that was the target of repeated Christian attacks ever since Paul and the distinct symbol of the revoked "covenant of the flesh." We find a further example of this in a comprehensive review he wrote of the Tahiti accounts of Prussian-Scottish traveler Johann Reinhold

Forster (1729–1798). Referring to Forster's accounts of Tahitian circumcision, Michaelis writes: "This fact is interesting, in that it supplies new evidence that the circumcision command handed down from God to Abraham was, in fact, not a totally new invention. It may be something that nature itself induces in hot climates, and which existed among other peoples."[72]

Michaelis thus enlists ethnographic observation in the service of Christian criticism of circumcision. He presents the Abraham covenant as nothing more than a custom that was prevalent in warm climates, be they those of Tahiti or Canaan. The condition in which Abraham and his descendants lived is thus represented as a primordial "state of nature" by bundling ethnography and theology into a single system of meaning.

Historian Rolf Engelsing argues that a revolution in the reading culture of the German educated classes occurred in the mid-eighteenth century. Until around 1750, he claims, the reading culture of those classes was "intensive"— recurrent reading of a limited number of books, especially scripture and Latin religious texts. Scholars took pride in having read the Old Testament dozens of times throughout their lives. After this point, however, their reading became "extensive"—encompassing a larger array of books, many in German, covering a wide range of topics. Engelsing notes especially the growing popularity of periodicals, which gained a wide readership.[73]

And indeed, Michaelis' *Orientalische und Exegetische Bibliothek* can be seen as a clear manifestation of this new, extensive, reading culture. While its main purview was exegesis, Michaelis included in it reviews of books on a wide range of topics to highlight his broad knowledge and familiarity with the different sciences as well as with travelers' accounts. This shift in practice had a profound effect on the way the Bible was read. Earlier generations of scholars "read" the world through the lens of the Bible, which, as far as they were concerned, was the only matrix for the organization of reality. In this vein, Kolbe, a graduate of the Pietist University of Halle, describes African trees as biblical flora and the residents of the Cape of Good Hope as the Hebrews' black kin. Michaelis, another Halle alumnus, turns the tables in expanding the interpretive corpus to contain the most exotic ethnographic observations. The people of the Bible are subsequently described as a "nature people."

Summary: The Hebrews and the Origin of History

By 1800, the year that Georg Lorenz Bauer (1755–1806) published *Handbuch der Geschichte der hebräischen Nation*, Abraham's image as a migrant Bedouin was already well-entrenched in the scholarly milieu. And this Bible scholar of Altdorf indeed employs the entire arsenal of orientalist expressions to describe the patriarch. "He was an Upper Asian man, an Emir or head of a wandering clan, who first meandered from Chaldea to Mesopotamia, and from there moved with his herds to Palestine, where he sought pasture. He was no different than any other inconsequential Bedouin or Arab Sheikh of his time, but was to become, if we look at the peoples that originated from him and the revolutions they brought about in both spirit and matter, a very important man in history."[74] This brief description epitomizes the ambivalent manner in which the German Enlightenment fashioned the figure of Abraham—and the ancient Hebrews in general. It contains, as in a nutshell, the dialectical tension between the two images those Bible scholars of Michaelis's school foisted onto Abraham's character—the wandering Bedouin as well as the man who played such a decisive, and revolutionary, role in the history of humanity.

Enlightenment exegesis was woven into a changing set of contexts characterized by repeated modifications of contemporary conceptual frameworks. Holy history's enduring signposts were gradually exchanged for a developmental continuity and a measured coming-into-being dictated by a natural, immanent logic. The Bible came to be described as a "document" [*Urkunde*], a kind of time capsule that preserved ancient man's authentic way of life.

These scholars' reading of the Bible was reoriented within newly formed bodies of knowledge such as natural history, ancient history, and ethnography. The assimilation of the Israelites into the natural history of early humanity put them on a par with other ancient peoples, as well as with the Arabs and other oriental peoples. In this way, these scholars fashioned a new portrait of the patriarchs in particular and of the ancient Hebrews in general. The Israelites' theological role as "the People of God" [*Volk Gottes*] was transformed into an ethnographic characterization of the Hebrews as a "natural people" and as a group of oriental herders.

Enhanced exposure to ethnographic accounts of oriental and New World peoples influenced the discipline of Bible exegesis. Exegetic scholars found parallels between Abraham's and the Israelites' way of life and those portrayed in the accounts of travelers. As we have seen, this similarity was explained in different ways. The necessary condition for the fashioning of the image of the Hebrews as savages or a nature people was a change in the conception of historical directionality. Conceived as being the most ancient of peoples, with which all historical chronicles began, the Hebrews' status was contingent on how the very sources of history were viewed.

A dominant paradigm in early modern historical thought viewed history as a process of decline and decay.[75] According to this paradigm, mankind had originally held divine knowledge, which was then lost after the Flood. The Hebrews, accordingly, gained the aura of an ancient people, the bearers of the ancient traditions of the first generations of humankind. This conception was gradually superseded, during the eighteenth century, by a notion of general and constant progress. The establishment of political institutions and the accumulation of knowledge were now regarded as outcomes of a gradual process of *Bildung*. The origin of history was more widely conceived as a savage time when men were coarse and ignorant. At the same time, the image of the biblical past itself was gradually transformed, and the Hebrews were, at times, assigned a character similar to that of Native Americans in the New World.[76]

Indeed, one of the two interlocutors in Herder's *Of the Spirit of Hebrew Poetry* [*Vom Geist der Ebräischen Poesie*] refers to the Hebrews as "those Hurons of the Orient" [*morgenländische Huronen*].[77] Most Bible scholars, however, neither thought of the Hebrews as Native Americans, nor regarded them as total savages. The more the rules governing the ethnographic discourse on the Hebrews became set, the more scholars tended to distinguish them from savage peoples. The essays that address the era of the patriarchs stress that from the very outset of their history, the Hebrews had reached the second stage of development of civilizations—the herding life. No wonder, then, that as early as his 1756 lecture on the nomads, Michaelis devotes a good part of his debate to proving that Abraham owned property. This is a fundamental assertion, as in all versions of the "four stages" theory, it is property ownership that differentiates the shepherd from the savage. The notion is further developed in later texts, in which the Israelites' status is highlighted through their comparison to a wilder, baser people—the Canaanite troglodytes. Thus, Heinrich Ehrenfried Warnekros (1752–1807)—another Göttingen alumnus—contrasts cave dwelling and herding in his 1782 *Entwurf der hebräischen Alterthümer*, claiming that "as lofty and august as is the life of the shepherd, so is the life of the cave dweller deplorable. These people were called 'Chorites' by the Hebrews and 'troglodytes' by the Greeks. The Greeks in fact painted a horrific portrait of their actions, describing them as the greatest of robbers. The Hebrews were at first very afraid of this human type."[78]

In this context, the occupation of Canaan and the annihilation of its residents are presented as a step in overcoming barbarism, a progression of humankind from ignorance toward rationality. Several scholars, such as Ditmar, even go so far as to describe Abraham's peregrination as a voyage undertaken with the intention to establish colonies in wild, unsettled lands—with Abraham himself as colony leader [*Colonieführer*]. Although mere herders, the Hebrews were the representatives of progress in the dark world of the beginning of history.

The idea of progress is expressed not only in the appearance of the Hebrews, but in descriptions of all biblical events, with the Hebrews' history construed as a developmental progression. The guiding principle of historical development here is a motion between forms of existence in the people's *Bildung* process: from a nomadic herding people [*Hirtenvolk*] to a settled civil society [*Bürgerliche Gesellschaft*]. These texts subsequently propose a division of Hebrew history into several periods—a scheme that varies from one author to the next, but which generally comprises three stages paralleling the levels of progress achieved by humanity at large. The first period is the era of the patriarchs (from Abraham to Moses), characterized by patriarchal rule and the way of life of nomadic herdsmen; the second period extends from Moses to the coronation of either Saul or David, during which a gradual move to agriculture took place and a loose political structure evolved; the third phase is the monarchical period leading up to the Babylonian exile, when the Hebrews reached the peak of their developmental. While signifying an earlier stage of human evolution, Hebrew history as a whole embodies the entirety of that development.

Despite the use of secular terminology, the echoes of traditional salvation history still reverberate in this story. The tripartite division into levels of social development unsurprisingly parallels the traditional theological periodization that goes back to Augustine: Abraham to Noah ("childhood"); Noah to David ("adolescence"); and finally, David to the exile ("adulthood").[79]

This developmental scheme of the Hebrew people's history is laid out in Gotthold Ephraim Lessing's (1729–1781) "Education of the Human Race" (*Die Erziehung des Menschengeschlechts*), which was to become the canonical manifesto of German Protestant rationalism. Here Lessing reinterprets the idea of revelation, describing it as a gradual evolution of the human mind from savagery to rationality and refinement. "What education [*Erziehung*] is to the individual—revelation is to all humankind," he states in the essay's opening sentence. This idea is tangibly formulated in the form of a new, philosophical version of salvation history, which still revolves around the Israelites. It was this people that God chose to be educators of mankind: "Why however, one might ask, educate such a savage people, a people with which God had to start from the absolute beginning? I answer: so that, in the fullness of time, some of its individuals could be used safely as educators of the rest of the peoples. He educated in it the future educators of humankind. This is what Jews turned into: this thing only Jews could be, only a people educated in this way."[80]

As Jonathan Israel has noted, although he was opposed to Lutheran orthodoxy, Lessing was also at odds with the deists in his desire to avoid direct confrontation with theology. His aim was to bridge the gap between the rationalist worldview and religious tradition,[81] and to this end he merges the revelation narrative of "God's people" with its modern description as a crass people who gradually became refined. He defends the role allocated to "The Israelite people" [*das Israelitische Volk*] in the process of revelation, but stops short of defending the Hebrew people themselves. In this version, God had chosen a people "still so fully in its infancy" to disseminate rationality among humanity and initiate the process of universal education. "But when He neither could nor would reveal Himself any more to each individual man, He selected an individual People for His special education; and that exactly the most rude and the most unruly, in order to begin with it from the very commencement. This was the Hebrew People."[82]

It was because the Israelites were "so crass and unfit for abstract thought," that is, still at the very earliest stage of Enlightenment, that they were to become the chosen people.[83] This notion of the Hebrews as humanity's first educators was embraced by other commentators as well. In 1790, Friedrich Schiller (1759–1805) penned an essay entitled "Die Sendung Moses," which commences with the argument that the founding of the Jewish state [*jüdischer Staat*] by Moses was one of the most important events in history because of its global implications.[84] By virtue of the Jews, belief in the one true God spread throughout the world, and thus not only did Moses's law form the foundation of the two religions that held sway over most parts of the world, but indeed "we should thank it for a significant part of the Enlightenment [*Aufklärung*] we enjoy today."[85] In this light, Schiller formulates a representative image of the Hebrews' role in history:

> When investigated from this standpoint, the Hebrew nation appears as an important people in world history. All of the ills traditionally associated with it, and all of the efforts of the wittiest of writers to disparage it, will not sway us from judging it fairly. The wretchedness and contemptuousness of this nation cannot undo the legislator's sublime calling, nor the great influence rightly attributed to this nation on world history. We must regard it as the conduit through which Divine Providence chose to transmit to us the dearest of values, the Truth. But Divine Providence broke this conduit after its calling was fulfilled."[86]

The Hebrew nation is, in this account, but a vessel entrusted with a precious treasure. Thus, the Hebrews play a decisive role in universal history, not through any intrinsic virtues or skills of their own but rather *despite* their vile, coarse character. According to Schiller, this is precisely what drove God to shatter this vessel once it had fulfilled its mission.[87] The Hebrew nation as such is worthless and acquires its significance only within the context of historical development. The particular element in Hebrew faith and culture is therefore that which retards historical development.

In all the descriptions cited thus far—despite their differing worldviews and emphases—the ancient Hebrews are posited as a people entrusted with the universal task of educating humanity. Despite their limitations, the Hebrews were those who carried the gospel of a universal rational religion that transcended regional differences to point to humanity's oneness. As George Gusdorf has argued, the scholars of the Enlightenment tended to exchange traditional, faith-centered, holy history for "the mytho-history of reason."[88] Denuded of its status as timeless, the biblical story of the Israelites' origin, a holy history existing in absolute time and interpreted allegorically and typologically, is now accorded a new meaning as one segment of the foundation of civilization's natural development. It had become a source, an *Ursprung*, a charged story from the dawn of mankind that testified to the origins of the modern era. The scholars of the German Enlightenment placed the Hebrews within the history of reason, according them a newfound role within the history of Enlightenment itself.

Notes

1. Johann Ernst Faber, *Archäologie der Hebräer* (Halle: Curt, 1773), 1–2.
2. See also: Jonathan Sheehan, *The Enlightenment Bible* (Princeton, NJ: Princeton University Press, 2005), 187–297; Todd Kontje, *German Orientalisms* (Ann Arbor: University of Michigan Press, 2004).
3. Johann Ernst Faber, *Diss. De animalibus, quorum sit mentio Zephan. 2, 14* (Göttingen: Barmeier, 1769); Johann Ernst Faber, *Diss. Historia Mannae inter Hebraeos* (Jenna: Fickelscherr, 1773).
4. Johann Ernst Faber, *Beobachtungen über den Orient als Reisebeschreibungen, zur Aufklärung der heiligen Schrift* (Hamburg: Bohn, 1772–1774).
5. For a biography and list of publications, see: Heinrich Döring, *Die gelehrten Theologen Deutschlands im achtzehnten und neunzehnten Jahrhundert: nach ihrem Leben und Wirken dargestellt* (Neustdat: J. K. G. Wagner, 1831), 390–391.
6. Carolus Linnaeus, *Systema Naturae* (Stockholm, 1758), 24.
7. Michaelis, however, claims that the troglodytes are the descendents of Esau; see: Johann David Michaelis, *De Troglodytis Seiritis* (Göttingen: Vandenhoeck, 1759).
8. Faber, *Archäologie der Hebräer*, 20–49.
9. He relies here on the travel accounts of Rauwolff (1535–1596), Schweigger (1551–1622), Billon (1517–1564), Tavernier (1605–1689), and Chardin (1643–1713).
10. Faber, *Archäologie der Hebräer*, 35.
11. Faber, *Archäologie der Hebräer*, 49–50.
12. Reinhart Koselleck, *Vergangene Zukunft* (Frankfurt am Main: Suhrkamp, 1979), 63.
13. Peter Hanns Reill, *The German Enlightenment and the Rise of Historicism* (Berkeley: University of California Press, 1975), 34–50.
14. On this, see: Asaph Ben-Tov, *Lutheran Humanists and Greek Antiquity: Melanchthonian Scholarship between Universal History and Pedagogy* (Leiden: Brill, 2009).
15. On the history of this genre, see: Heinrich von Srbik, *Geist und Geschichte vom deutschen Humanismus bis zur Gegenwart* (Salzburg: O. Müller, 1950), 1.70–71; Jörg Zbinden, "Heterogeneity, Irony, Ambivalence: The Idea of Progress in the Universal Histories and the Histories of Mankind in the German Enlightenment" *Storia della Storiografia*, 29 (1996): 21–45.
16. All English biblical passages are taken from the Authorized King James Version.
17. On the Christian conception of Abraham's chosenness, see, for instance: Amos Funkenstein, "Jews, Christians and Muslims: Religious Polemics in the Middle Ages," in *The Jews in European History*, ed. Wolfgang Beck (Cincinnati, OH: Hebrew Union College Press, 1994), 26–30.
18. Johann Friedrich Hochstetter, *Einleitung zu der Universal-History* (Tübingen: Schramm, 1740), 7.
19. Frank Manuel, *The Eighteenth Century Confronts the Gods* (New York: Atheneum, 1967), 128–130.

20. See: Nicholas Wickenden, *G. J. Vossius and the Humanist Concept of History* (Assen: Van Gorcum, 1993), 155–157.
21. On the Christian interpretations of the figure of Melchizedek, see: Bruce A. Demarest, *A History of Interpretation of Hebrews 7, 1–10 from the Reformation to the Present* (Tübingen: Mohr Siebeck, 1976), 16–18.
22. Benedict Spinoza, *Tractatus Theologico-Politicus*, trans. S. Shirley (Leiden: Brill, 1989), 89. On Spinoza's conception of chosenness, see, for instance: S. Leyla Gürkan, *The Jews as a Chosen People: Tradition and Transformation* (New York: Routledge, 2009), 49–55.
23. Ernst Cassirer, *Die Philosophie der Aufklärung*, (Princeton, NJ: Princeton University Press, 1951), 187–194.
24. See: Martin Mulsow, "Antiquarianism and Idolatry: The 'Historia' of Religions in the Seventeenth Century," in *Historia: Empiricism and Erudition in Early Modern Europe* ed. Gianna Pomata and Nancy G. Siraisi (Cambridge, MA: MIT Press, 2005), 181–211.
25. Johann Christoph Gottsched, *Erste Gründe der gesammten Weltweisheit* (Leipzig: Breitkopf, 1777), 18.
26. On the meaning of this term in the discourse of the Enlightenment, see: Michael M. Carhart, *The Science of Culture in Enlightenment Germany* (Cambridge, MA: Harvard University Press, 2007), 200–201.
27. Friedrich Andreas Walther, *Geschichte der Weltweisheit der alten Hebräer* (Göttingen: Victorinus Boßiegel, 1750), 18.
28. Voltaire, *La philosophie de l'histoire* (Geneva, 1765), 106–108.
29. The association of Abraham with Brahma already appears in the work of Renaissance orientalist Guillaume Postel (1510–1581) and continued in the centuries thereafter. See Paolo Rossi, *The Dark Abyss of Time* (Chicago: University of Chicago, 1984), 137.
30. Voltaire, "Juifs," in *Dictionnaire philosophique* (Geneva: Bruyset, 1756), 524.
31. Michael Carhart, *The Science of Culture in Enlightenment Germany*, 5. For a discussion on religious skepticism in the Enlightenment, see: James A. Herrick, *The Radical Rhetoric of the English Deists: The Discourse of Skepticism, 1680–1750* (Columbia: University of South Carolina Press, 1997), 2–3.
32. See: David Jan Sorkin, *The Religious Enlightenment: Protestants, Jews, and Catholics from London to Vienna* (Princeton, NJ: Princeton University Press, 2008), 129–139.
33. Michaelis also published his address there: "Von den herumziehenden Hirten in dem alten Palästina" *Göttingische gelehrte Anzeigen* 140 (November 1756): 1265–127.
34. Johann David Michaelis, *Commentatio de nomadibus Palaestinae* (Göttingen, 1759).
35. Anna-Ruth Löwenbrück, "Johann David Michaelis et les débuts de la critique biblique," i In *Le siecle des Lumieres et la Bible*, ed. Yvon Belaval and Dominique Bourel (Paris: Beauchesne, 1986), 114–115. See Michaelis's autobiography: Johann David Michaelis, *Lebensbeschreibung von ihm selbst abgefasst* (Leipzig, 1793), 32–34.
36. Fania Oz-Salzberger, *Translating the Enlightenment: Scottish Civic Discourse in Eighteenth-Century Germany* (Oxford: Oxford University Press, 1995), 229–233; Norbert Waszek, "Die Schottische Aufklärung in der Göttinger Wissenschaft vom Menschen," in *Die Wissenschaft vom Menschen in Göttingen um 1800: wissenschaftliche Praktiken, institutionelle Geographie, europäische Netzwerke*, ed. Hans Erich Bödeker, Philippe Büttgen, and Michel Espagne (Göttingen: Vandenhoeck & Ruprecht, 2008), 125–149.
37. On Kennicott, see especially: Sheehan, *The Enlightenment Bible*, 183–187.

38. Robert Lowth, *De sacra poesi Hebraeorum: notas et epimetra adjecit Ioannes David Michaelis* (Göttingen: Pockwiz u. Barmeier, 1758), 352.
39. Michaelis, *Göttingische gelehrte Anzeigen*, 1266.
40. Michaelis, *Göttingische gelehrte Anzeigen*, 1262.
41. Herder, "Hebräer". In: *Ideen zur Philosophie der Geschichte der Menschheit* (Riga & Leipzig: Hartknoch, 1784), 99.
42. Ibid, 3.
43. Reill, *The German Enlightenment and the Rise of Historicism*, 29–30.
44. *Deutsche Uebersetzung des Alten Testaments*, (Göttingen: Dieterich, 1773) 67.
45. Theodor Jakob Ditmar, *Geschichte der Israeliten bis auf den Cyrus* (Berlin: Maurer, 1788).
46. Ditmar, *Geschichte der Israeliten*, 8.
47. Wilhelm Martin Leberecht De Wette, *Lehrbuch der hebräisch-jüdischen Archäologie nebst einem Grundrisse der hebräisch-jüdischen Geschichte* (Leipzig: Vogel, 1830), 30, 190.
48. Josef Wiesehöfer and Stephan Conermann, eds., *Carsten Niebuhr (1733–1815) und seine Zeit* (Stuttgart: Franz Steiner, 2002).
49. Manuel, *The Broken Staff*, (Cambridge, MA: Harvard University Press, 1992), 252–262.
50. Thomas Thorowgood, *Jews in America or Probabilities That the Americans Are of That Race* (London: Brome, 1650).
51. Richard Popkin, "The Rise and Fall of the Jewish Indian Theory," in *Menasseh Ben Israel and his World*, ed. Yosef Kaplan and Richard Popkin (Leiden: Brill, 1985), 63–82.
52. William Penn, *Account of the Leni Lenape* (Somerset: Middle Atlantic Press, 1970), originally published in 1683.
53. Howard Eilberg-Schwartz, *The Savage in Judaism: An Anthropology of Israelite Religion and Ancient Judaism* (Bloomington: Indiana University Press, 1990), 40.
54. Eilberg-Schwartz, *The Savage in Judaism*, 37.
55. See: Nigel Penn, "Peter Kolb and the VOC Voyages to the Cape," in *Many Middle Passages: Forced Migration and the Making of the Modern World*, ed. Emma Christopher and Cassandra Pybus (Berkeley: University of California Press, 2007), 72–84.
56. Peter Kolbe, *Caput Bonae Spei Hodiernum* (Nürnberg: P. C. Monath, 1719), 22.
57. See: Peter Harrison, "'The Book of Nature' and Early Modern Science," in *The Book of Nature in Early Modern and Modern History*, ed. Klaas van Berkel and Arjo Vanderjagt (Leuven: Peeters, 2006), 1–26.
58. Johannes Fabian, *Time and the Other* (New York: Columbia University Press, 1983), 11, 26.
59. Ronald L. Meek, *Social Science and the Ignoble Savage* (Cambridge, UK: Cambridge University Press, 1976); John Greville Agard Pocock, *Barbarism and Religion: Barbarians, Savages and Empires* (Cambridge, UK: Cambridge University Press, 2005), 99–110.
60. Voltaire, "Juifs," 524.
61. On the transformation of the idea of "oriental wisdom," see: Andrea Polaschegg, *Der andere Orientalismus: Regeln deutsch-morgenländischer Imagination im 19. Jahrhundert* (Berlin: Walter De Gruyter, 2005), 102–143; Marchand, *German Orientalism in the Age of Empire: Religion, Race, and Scholarship* (Cambridge, UK: Cambridge University Press, 2009), 15–18; G. J. Toomer, *Eastern Wisdom and Learning: The Study of Arabic in Seventeenth Century England* (Oxford: Oxford University Press, 1996), 309–313; in a Hebraistic context, see: Manuel, *The Broken Staff*, 228; see also: Edward W. Said, *Orientalism* (New York: Vintage Books, 1978), 117–123.

62. Robert Lowth, *De sacra poesi Hebraeorum: praelectiones academicae Oxonii habitae, subjicitur metricae Harianae brevis confutatio et oratio Crewiana* (Oxford: 1753).
63. Stephen Prickett, *Words and the Word: Language, Poetics and Biblical Interpretation* (Cambridge, UK: Cambridge University Press, 1986), 114.
64. Moses Mendelsohn, "Robert Lowth, De sacra poesi Hebraeorum," in *Gesammelte Schriften* (Stuttgart: Friedrich Frommann, 1977), 4:20.
65. Rudolf Smend, "Lowth in Deutschland," in *Epochen der Bibelkritik* (Munich: Chr. Kaiser, 1991), 43–62.
66. Maike Oergel, *The Return of King Arthur and the Nibelungen: National Myth in Nineteenth-Century English and German Literature*, 68–70.
67. Christian Benedikt Michaelis, *Disputatio academica de Muhammedismi laxitate morali* (Halle: Henckel, 1708); Christian Benedikt Michaelis, *Dissertatio philologica de antiquitatibus oeconomiae patriarchalis* (Halle: Henckel, 1728).
68. Faber, *Archaeologie der Hebräer*, 5.
69. Johann David Michaelis, *Mosaisches Recht* (Frankfurt am Main: J. Gottlieb Garbe, 1775), 4:40, 5:198.
70. Michaelis, *Mosaisches Recht*, 1:293.
71. Michaelis, *Mosaisches Recht*, 1:13.
72. Johann David Michaelis, "Forster's Observations," in *Orientalische und Exegetische Bibliothek* 48 (1779):14–16.
73. Rolf Engelsing, "Die Perioden der Lesergeschichte in der Neuzeit," *Archiv für Geschichte des Buchwesens* 10 (1970): 945–1002.
74. Georg Lorenz Bauer, *Handbuch der Geschichte der hebräischen Nation von ihrer Entstehung bis zur Zerstörung ihres Staats* (Altdorf: Monath & Kussler, 1800), 108.
75. Reinhart Koselleck, "'Progress' and 'Decline': An Appendix to the History of Two Concepts," in *The Practice of Conceptual History: Timing Concepts, Spacing Concepts* (Stanford, CA: Stanford University Press, 2002), 219–235.
76. John Locke, *Second Treatise on Government* (London, 1690), 155.
77. Johann Gottfried Herder, *Vom Geist der Ebräischen Poesie* (Dessau: Buchhandlung der Gelehrten, 1782–1783), 1: 18.
78. Heinrich Ehrenfried Warnekros, *Entwurf der hebräischen Alterthümer* (Weimar: Hofmann, 1782), 11.
79. Ernst Breisach, *Historiography: Ancient, Medieval, & Modern* (Chicago: University of Chicago Press, 2007), 84–88.
80. Gotthold Ephraim Lessing, *The Education of the Human Race*, in *Theological Writings*, trans. Henri Chadwick (Stanford, CA: Stanford University Press, 1956), 83.
81. Jonathan Israel, *Democratic Enlightenment: Philosophy, Revolution, and Human Rights 1750–1790* (Oxford: Oxford University Press, 2011), 317–318.
82. Lessing, *The Education of the Human Race*, 83.
83. Lessing, *The Education of the Human Race*, 83.
84. Friedrich Schiller, "Die Sendung Moses," in *Schillers Werke: Nationalausgabe*, ed. Karl-Heinz Hahn (Weimar: Hermann Böhlaus, 1970), 17: 377–413.
85. Schiller, "Die Sendung Moses," 2.
86. Schiller, "Die Sendung Moses," 3.
87. Schiller, "Die Sendung Moses," 3.
88. Georges Gusdorf, *Les sciences humaines et la pensée occidentale* (Paris: Payot, 1973), 6: 379.

2 The Law and the People: Mosaic Law and the German Enlightenment

From the very inception of Christianity, its founders differentiated themselves from Jews by depicting the Old Testament as "the religion of the Law," as opposed to "the gospel of faith" founded by Christ. As far back as Paul's epistles, the Torah is referred to as *nómos* (the law), for instance, in Galatians 3:23: "But before faith came, we were kept under the law." In fact the term *nómos* refers not solely to the laws themselves but often also to Prophets or Genesis.[1] Hence, in Christian tradition, the scripture is identified more with the foundation of the law than it is with other elements such as poetry, narrative, or prophecy.

Despite the fact that post-Pauline Christianity undermined the validity of Old Testament law—and at times even revoked it outright—several influential Christian schools taught that, in his fallen state, man needed revealed divine law [*lex divina*] if he was to live in society. In Reformation thinking, the scripture played the part of Pope—an ultimate, incontrovertible source of authority regarding living custom.[2] This principle applied to biblical law in particular, although the Reformation's reading of this codex was complicated and contradictory.

In his earlier years, Luther regarded Mosaic law as a suitable substitute for Catholic canon law. Several princes and preachers who followed the reformer went as far as turning the biblical commandments into the only law that applied in the territories under their rule.[3] They believed that by bringing their subjects under the rule of Pentateuch law they were following the edict of *sola scriptura*. Some sought to abolish usury or ban the production of graven images. And in a different context, the rebellious German peasants in 1524 based their demands on the regulations governing offerings described in Numbers 18.[4]

A year later, as part of his turn against the peasants, Luther changed his stance on Mosaic law. He now stressed faith's absolute precedence to the law in keeping with Paul's assertion that "the letter killeth, but the spirit giveth life" (2 Corinthians 3:6), viewing Mosaic law as a particularly Jewish legal system to which the "heathen" were not beholden. Just like the medieval German legal codex *Sachsenspiegel*, he wrote, Mosaic law did not apply to other peoples—other than those cases in which it corresponds to natural law.[5] At this point he goes so far as to assert unequivocally that "Moses is dead" and that "his Law applies to us not."

We must therefore silence the mouths of those factious spirits who say, 'Thus says Moses,' and so forth. Here you simply reply: Moses has nothing to do with us. If I were to accept Moses in one commandment, I would have to accept the entire Moses. Thus the consequence would be that if I accept Moses as master, then I must have myself circumcised, wash my clothes in the Jewish way, eat and drink and dress thus and so, and observe all that stuff. So, then, we will neither observe nor accept Moses. Moses is dead. His rule ended when Christ came. He is of no further service.[6]

Despite these firm utterances, however, Luther maintains that Moses is an important teacher, who offers an approach to legal matters that Christians should adopt. In other writings, Luther's stance on the law is even more ambivalent. Although he believed that the law did not lead to redemption, he claimed that a fallen world could be sustained without it: if humans were left with only "human law" [*lex humana*], their ways would be corrupted as they had been before the Flood. In a world held in Satan's grip, God-given law was akin to the shackles placed on the hands of a man possessed lest he injure those around him.[7] And as the New Testament contained almost no laws at all, its divine law was largely identical to the *lex Mosaica*; Mosaic law, hence, helps us recognize divine will but cannot ever be fully applied. To further elucidate this proposition, Luther devised a distinction between those elements of the Torah worthy of being recognized as eternal divine law—headed, of course, by the Ten Commandments—and "ceremonial law" [*Ceremonialrecht*], which applied to Jews alone. Luther, however, never clearly laid out the distinction between the law's different elements, thus stirring a lively theological debate within the different Protestant denominations that fed into contemporary political developments associated with the complex relation between state law and religious law.

In this chapter, I survey the debate that raged throughout the eighteenth century on the scriptures' place within German law. Since the Reformation, the question of the status of the law [*Gesetz*] in religion and the state featured in a series of momentous conflicts that gripped the German-speaking space—from Luther's polemical dueling with his detractors in the 1520s and 1530s on the law's validity to debates between conservative theologians and liberal jurists that lasted well into the nineteenth century. The question of the law touched directly on one's relation to the Old Testament, projecting onto biblical exegesis and interpretation. This chapter will thus address the different standpoints adopted regarding the aims of Mosaic law—a question increasingly tied to historical inquiry into its origin. More specifically, I shall focus on the growing part played by ethnic and national concepts in legal interpretation.

The chapter will revolve around Michaelis's *Mosaisches Recht*, the most influential German text written about biblical law during the eighteenth century. The ethnographic aspect of the scholar's work, discussed in the previous chapter, will form the basis for a discussion of his juridical conception. I survey the influences on Michaelis's major work, as well as the roots of its conceptions and methods. In keeping with its title, *Mosaisches Recht* is first and foremost a legal treatise that divides the laws of the Pentateuch according to the categories of German *Landrecht*—administrative, civil, property, marital, criminal, commercial law, and damages. Unlike previous studies on this book, my discussion does not center on Michaelis's role in the history of anti-Jewish thinking, nor on his place in the history of biblical philology. I read *Mosaisches Recht*, as well as other works by Michaelis and his followers, mainly as a legal treatise relating to the juridical and political reality of Germany under the aegis of Friedrich II of Prussia and Joseph II of Austria.

The book will furthermore be placed within the context of the constitutional and theological debates regarding the validity of Mosaic law that took place in the German principalities from the Reformation onward. Jonathan Hess and others have noted that biblical law played a significant part in several European legal systems during Michaelis's time.[8] None of this research, however, has exhaustively investigated the scriptures' actual legal status.

While the legal aspect takes center stage, it is impossible to read Michaelis's texts on the law in a narrow legalistic context alone. Like other canonical writings of the period that influenced them, these texts comprise a cultural and historical investigation of Mosaic law—and the human environment from which it sprang— no less than they address a series of philosophical, anthropological, and theological questions. Indeed, strict disciplinary specialization among scholars was not yet entrenched by the end of the eighteenth century—neither in the universities nor in the larger "republic of letters."[9] Just as one would not regard Montesquieu's *De l'esprit des lois*—Michaelis's major source of inspiration—as a strictly legal treatise (it is no less a philosophical and ethnographic investigation), so *Mosaisches Recht* should not be read as a purely legal tract. The book adheres to an eclectic literary genre characteristic of the period—a legal treatise interwoven with an orientalist essay of a lexical nature that offers a wide variety of discussions and asides about other subjects. Throughout his career, Michaelis meandered between addressing concrete practical legal questions and engaging in cultural and historiographical investigation into the origins of language and religion. And even though his separate texts seemingly belong to distinct realms of knowledge, they all play a part in a single philosophical system, centered on the investigation and historical grounding of Hebrew law and its concomitant regime.

Michaelis's interpretation of biblical law is organized around the figure of Moses, and its origin is reconstructed according to the leader's political machinations as nation builder.[10] However, besides Moses, one cannot overlook another entity that is fleshed out in Michaelis's description: the Hebrew people. Thus, in keeping with the general framework of this investigation, I treat *Mosaisches Recht* also as a historical-ethnographic description of ancient Israel. In particular, I highlight the fundamental contradiction between universalism and particularity that runs throughout almost the entire book and is expressed above all in the distinction between law and custom, between Egypt and the Hebrew people, and between the legislator and his people.

Lex Mosaica in the Post-Reformation German Legal Systems

In 1689, Hohenzollern princess Marie Amalie von Brandenburg (1670–1739), sister of Frederick III, married Moritz Wilhelm, duke of Saxe-Zeitz (1674–1718). The marriage was an attempt by the Reformed House of Hohenzollern to buttress its power against the Lutheran princes of the German Reich. This match aroused fierce protest in Saxon clerical and aristocratic circles, mainly because of Duke Wilhelm's confessional affiliation. In the era following the Treaty of Westphalia (1648), interconfessional marriage raised mighty opposition, as it was seen as undermining the harmony of the family unit and a possible gateway to apostasy.[11] Within the aristocracy especially, it was feared that such marriages would undermine the Reich's fragile balance of power, just recently stabilized after the Thirty Years' War.

In that same year, Philipp Müller (1640–1713), a Magdeburg preacher and theology professor at the University of Jena, anonymously published an essay fiercely criticizing interconfessional marriage within the aristocracy. In his essay, widely disseminated among Reich jurists, he focuses on the biblical injunction against intermarrying with Canaanite women: "Take heed to thyself, lest thou make a covenant with the inhabitants of the land whither thou goest" (Exodus 34:12). Commenting on Luther's interpretation of this passage, Müller writes that "in this issue/God's fierce injunction of Exodus 34:12 and 32:14, commanding to desist from any covenant with the unbelievers/and especially marriage, as reiterated again in Deuteronomy 7:1–6, applies. And indeed Doctor Luther/further clarifies/when he says that a wife and bad company brings strife and the danger of divine wrath."[12]

We see here that Müller believed that God's Exodus prohibition applied to contemporary interconfessional relations. Following publication of the Magdeburg theologian's essay, Leipzig legal scholar Christian Thomasius (1655–1728) sprang to the defense of the Hohenzollerns, systematically disproving Müller's claims in a book entitled *Lutherischen und Reformirten Fürstlichen Personen Heyrath* [Lutheran and Reformed Princes' marriages]. A pioneer of the German Enlightenment, Thomasius was the foremost German proponent of the Natural Law School, a legal school devoted to the idea of a political sphere subject to universal, rational law rather than religious rule. This legal conception, whose roots go back as far as Thomas Aquinas, was developed in the seventeenth century by Dutch legal scholar Hugo Grotius (1583–1645) and then by Samuel Pufendorf

(1632–1694). It began to make a substantial impact among north German legal scholars at the end of the seventeenth century.

Thomasius's debate about marital law revolved around the status of divine law [*ius divinum*] in the German Reich. The meaning of this concept varies from one text to another in Christian history, but in many cases, it is identified with Mosaic law—scriptures' major positive legal system. In the German principalities, marital law was a common flashpoint between religious and civil law. One of the Reformation's fundamental impacts on the lives of Protestant believers was the transference of marriage from the aegis of canon law and the religious courts to the jurisdiction of the secular ruler.[13] But this development only served to strengthen biblical law: ever since the Peace of Augsburg (1555), individual sovereigns of the different Reich principalities were allowed to enforce "moral law" [*Sittenrecht*]—primarily meaning marital-related scriptural law—to ensure their subjects' "Christian life" as it pertained to the sovereign's church. And once the state had identified itself with the enforcement of marriage law, violation was tantamount to a rebellion against the crown; transgressions such as adultery and sodomy were thus conceived of as violations of state law.[14] However, the implementation of biblical law across the Protestant areas raised a wide array of difficulties and misunderstandings—especially since, unlike Catholic canon law, enforcement was not based on generations of tradition.

The *ius divinum* played an especially central role in Saxony, given the formidable influence that the Lutheran establishment exerted over law enforcement systems and the fact that religious law was often enforced by the civilian authorities. Thus, for instance, at least up to the 1680s, those convicted of adultery and bestiality were sentenced to death in keeping with Deuteronomy 20.[15] Leipzig legal scholar Benedikt Carpzov (1595–1666), the foremost Saxonian scholar of his time, developed a system that placed Mosaic law at the foundation of all state law. Carpzov, who boasted he had read the Bible from beginning to end fifty-three times, described Moses's laws as the font of all other directives.[16] His essays and rulings had a considerable impact on the German legislative system until well into the eighteenth century.

This legal situation began to change at the end of the seventeenth century with the growing influence of the Natural Law School, whose members viewed Mosaic law and its underlying principle of "an eye for an eye" [*lex talionis*] as a base and cruel legal form. The jurists and philosophers of this school also sought to restrict the application of Mosaic law to marital matters.[17]

In the final decades of the seventeenth century, a fierce debate regarding the validity of marital law raged in various European countries, sparked in part by the expansion of the continent's geographical horizons and a growing recognition of the diversity of marital arrangements and norms of sexual propriety in different societies.[18] In fact, there was a growing understanding toward the end of the seventeenth century that grounding moral principles in scripture was unsatisfactory. The distinction between "proper" and "improper" sexual practices became fluid, and was eventually replaced by a dichotomy of "natural" and "unnatural" acts, and an emphasis on the preservation of the social order. Many English and Scottish writers also highlighted the inferiority of legal prohibitions grounded in punishment—such as in the Old Testament—as opposed to sexual propriety grounded in the individual's pure conscience, following the example of Christ.[19]

In the German principalities, however, the transformation in this legal discourse proceeded particularly slowly.[20] Thomasius was the first German jurist to explicitly formulate a demand to restrict Mosaic law's validity in marriage. In his essay on the German princes, he addresses at length biblical law governing adultery, cohabitation, and marriage, stressing the distinction between the jurisdiction of law and theology, while simultaneously warning that a codex of laws grounded in scripture could be "especially harmful" if not used within "rational interpretation"—the only way to acquire "political wisdom."[21, 22]

Thomasius lavishes praise on the historical inquiry of law—a method he proceeds to apply to "Israelite marriage" law, where he makes a distinction between the divine laws handed down to all of mankind and those included only in the Jewish constitution. The latter include ordinances pertaining to the "Jewish polity" [jüdische Policey] and to "ceremonial law" [Ceremonial-Gesetz], which, according to Thomasius, neither applied to Christians nor served any of their needs after the advent of Jesus: "Ceremonial law came to an end with the coming of the Redeemer, and the administrative law given by God/applies to no other people besides the Republic of the Jews."[23]

In fact, he adds, Moses legislated ceremonial law to curtail the Israelites' penchant for foreign worship, giving them a form of worship distinct from that of Egyptians and other idol worshippers. His theory formed the basis for the justification of a prince's right to suspend unnecessary religious rituals [adiaphora], namely those that did not contribute to the salvation of the soul. Since the beginning of the seventeenth century, the Reformed princes of Brandenburg sought to curtail ceremonial elements they considered Catholic "superstition," such as icons and priests' vestments. They met with fierce opposition from Lutheran jurists such as Carpzov, who warned that reforms of this nature would shock the simple believer.[24]

Thomasius indeed claimed that curtailing ritual was the one distinguishing feature between Protestant Christianity, on the one hand, and Catholicism and Judaism on the other. The injunction against intermarriage with the Canaanite, Emorite, Jebusite, and other "peoples of the land" was identified with these ritual laws, now regarded as devoid of any divine or universal element; at any rate, Thomasius believed, Israelite marriage law had no bearing on the relations between Lutheran and Calvinist Christians.[25] In Thomasius's understanding, suspension of divine law and the establishment of a civil sphere under the jurisdiction of natural law would put an end to interconfessional political strife. While Miller interprets the injunction against intermarrying with the peoples of Canaan as an interdiction on forming unions with "unbelievers," Thomasius clearly translates this distinction into ethnic terms, stressing the difference between the citizens of the Hebrew republic and "other peoples."

These assertions stirred fierce opposition among Saxony's religious and political establishment. In fact, the publication of Thomasius's essay so irked the Prince of Saxony that he had him banished. Unsurprisingly, the writer fled to Brandenburg, where he enjoyed the support of the elector. He was likewise welcomed by the leaders of the Pietist movement in Halle, and especially by August Hermann Francke (1663–1727). The Pietists preached a Christianity centered on spiritual-mystic love of God, seeking to rid religion of legalistic dogma altogether. With the establishment of the University of Halle in 1691, Thomasius settled in the town, continuing to advocate the expansion of state law [*Staatsrecht*] jurisdiction at the expense of religious law.[26]

Within several years, however, Thomasius fell out of favor with the Pietist establishment and his teaching privileges in Halle were restricted. Yet this did nothing to diminish his influence on the development of German political and juridical thought in the eighteenth century. Furthermore, besides his influence on other jurists, Thomasius's innovations were also taken up by German Bible scholars. His essay on the marriage question marks a turning point in that discipline as well; from that point on, we find that critical investigation of biblical law and its placement within the concrete context of Hebrew history grew out of the project of establishing a civil legal sphere in Germany.

Michaelis's Historical Investigation of Marriage Law

Thomasius's innovative proposals, including the establishment of a legal system distinct from Mosaic law, gradually infiltrated the German legal system during the first decades of the eighteenth century. These ideas were especially well received in the new universities founded at that time, especially at the University of Göttingen. Established in 1734, this institution provided a secure institutional framework for scholars of a modern juridical frame of mind. As far as its founder, Gerlach Adolph Freiherr von Münchhausen (1688–1770) was concerned, Thomasius was the very embodiment of a perfect Göttingen professor. As opposed to traditional universities, mainly supported by the church, Göttingen rested on the power of the absolutist state, which appointed all its lecturers. All professors were accorded the title of "secret adviser" [*Geheimrat*] by regal decree to ensure that their interests accorded with those of the state. And to better serve the state bureaucracy, Göttingen's law department was significantly expanded until it outgrew the theology department.[27] Consequently, issues previously deemed to be entirely theological were now addressed by other faculties, using tools gleaned from classical philology and other disciplines such as ethnography and history.[28]

Another significant innovation introduced at Göttingen from its inception was the idea of teaching freedom [*Lehrfreiheit*]—the freedom which allowed lecturers to investigate and teach subjects that lay beyond their official area of expertise.[29] Indeed, the way research was conducted in the theology department changed, acquiring historical characteristics. Scholars at German universities now downplayed their confessional allegiance and steered clear of purely confessional scripture readings, seeking instead to lay the foundations for a critical, objective investigation of the text to be used by all Christians.

Michaelis's work is one of the most characteristic examples of this trend. Having never identified himself as a theologian, he relegated the discipline to a secondary role in his professional-academic array. He saw himself rather as a historian and civil educator, maintaining that the theology department should train good citizens through promoting debate of philosophical, historical, and linguistic questions.[30] A significant number of these questions concerned the existing legislature in the German Reich's legal system, derived from or based on biblical law. From this viewpoint, the title *Mosaisches Recht* should be understood literally; this is fundamentally a juridical essay, assessing Mosaic law—the biblical layer of the legal system—historically, in the same way that other essays address canon or Roman law. This is evident in the book's opening passage: "Although the laws of Moses are not obligatory on us, they nevertheless merit a fuller elucidation than they have hitherto received; or rather, they not only deserve to be known in their whole connection, by the philologist, who, occupied in study of oriental languages, regards them merely as a branch of Hebrew antiquities; but even to persons of other pursuits,—to the theologian, the lawyer, and the man who philosophizes on legislative policy, they ought not to remain so strange and Asiatic, as they have 'hitherto' been."[31] Far from a systematic doctrine on scripture, Michaelis's encyclopedic writings on the Bible use the text to debate and engage with a wide array of issues that arose during his own time—foremost among them being the question of the validity of biblical law. As we have seen, the issue of Mosaic marriage law, and especially incest and inbreeding law (Leviticus 18), was one of the most vexed juridical questions in post-Reformation Germany. Most reformers adopted a conservative line, remaining largely loyal to Leviticus. Luther and Melanchthon believed that prohibition of marriage should be maintained to the third degree of kinship at least, while Calvin determined that marriage should be prohibited to the fourth degree.[32] However, the issue of the sweeping prohibition of marriage continued to vex jurists and theologians. These restrictions placed real hardships on the population, and some claimed they were in fact impeding population growth, which at the time was construed to be in the state's interest. Simultaneously, the upholding of the prohibition gave rise to a lively trade in ecclesiastical dispensations for intermarriage.

A decisive turn in this situation occurred in 1740 with the coronation of Friedrich II. One of the first edicts the new king gave was the annulment of all marriage restrictions, "except those that can be clearly inferred from divine injunction" [wo die Ehe nicht klar in Gottes Wort verboten].[33] Originally intended to overcome the complications of the existing law, the edict ended up further complicating it, triggering opposition from the church and creating a need for biblical interpretation that would clarify which laws were generally valid prohibitions and which applied to Jews alone.

It was against this backdrop that Michaelis published *An Essay on Moses's Marriage Law* [Abhandlung von den Ehegesetzen Mosis] in 1755.[34] And given the controversial status of biblical marriage law within the legal discourse of the time, it is unsurprising that Michaelis's first comprehensive text on Hebrew law addressed the Mosaic marital corpus. Published fifteen years before the comprehensive *Mosaisches Recht*, this forgotten text already contains all the main elements of the writer's historical, interpretive, and legal understanding. It appears that he published it in the concrete context of the debate over the Prussian king's marriage edict. Indeed, Michaelis explicitly refers to it within the book.[35] Biblical law is no ethereal theoretical issue, he maintained, for it touches on questions that were high on the legal and political agenda of the German principalities. Michaelis states that Moses's marriage law serves as a foundation of "customary behavior rules" that persisted to his day.[36] He elaborates on this idea in *Mosaisches Recht*: "The real theologian must see that they [the Laws of Moses] can never serve as a model, or rule of direction, to other legislators; and he will, of course, refrain from blaming our rulers when their laws are contradictory to those of Moses; as, for instance, in the punishment of theft and adultery; and from thus exalting himself from a preacher to a legislator: a thing which happens more frequently than we are apt to imagine."[37]

In his 1755 essay, Michaelis favors the elimination of marriage restrictions not explicitly mentioned in the Bible, going so far as to claim that even the ten marriage restrictions mentioned in Leviticus are not derived from any rational moral philosophy [vernünftige Sittenlehre] or indeed from natural or divine law. From this standpoint, he seeks to forge a new path in the decades-long debate regarding Mosaic law's validity in a Christian state. In Michaelis's eyes, the public debates held on this legal system returned to the same arguments ad infinitum.[38] "Religious scholars" adhere to a strict reading of the validity of Mosaic law, while "legal experts" try to undermine its jurisdiction. Yet, asserted Michaelis, both sides lacked sufficient knowledge of oriental languages and were not even conversant in the forms of writing and thinking prevalent in Moses's time.

This is the aspiration Michaelis expresses with regard to other topics as well: to forge a new path in Old Testament interpretation beyond traditional debates through a new kind of objective investigation. Using novel methods, he seeks to resolve several questions: does Mosaic marriage law apply to the entire human race, or to the Israelites alone? What are the reasons for this law? And in what circumstances would civil authorities be permitted to declare a dispensation from these rules?

In fact, Michaelis claims that the laws prohibiting incest and interbreeding were not even legislated by Moses himself. The corpus known as "Mosaic marital law" was nothing more than a series of customs [*Herkommen*] already established before the legislator's time.[39] A significant part of the essay is devoted to characterizing the nomadic lifestyle, which included unwritten laws that were followed decades before the advent of Moses. As he does elsewhere, Michaelis proceeds to compare the customs of the Hebrews with those of the Greeks, the Arabs, and even the Native Americans, to whom he obviously feels no little sympathy.[40] Even more specifically, he references orientalist ethnographies, according to which each woman living in the region inhabited her own tent with her descendants. Michaelis claims such a situation encouraged both promiscuity [*Hurerey*] and the sexual exploitation of fourteen-year-old boys and girls, and that the laws barring marriage between siblings of the same mother were promulgated to prevent such incestuous relations.[41]

Here as elsewhere, Michaelis stresses the strangeness of the Hebrews' oriental sexuality. Biblical narratives that explicitly involved prostitution, adultery, and rape required interpretive mediation. Many Enlightenment writers voiced embarrassment at the erotic expressions in the books of Hosea and the Song of Songs. In his own translation of the Bible, Michaelis glaringly omitted the latter book in its entirety, since he regarded it as a secular love song rather than a holy text. He explains its blunt sexual imagery through an ethnography of the "oriental lifestyle"; the more oriental men are barred from meeting any unmarried woman and enjoined to inhabit all-male groups, he claims, the more their speech is free and coarse—unencumbered by "feminine blushing." Thus, biblical expressions are occasionally indelicate, even coarse, "to our ears"; in Europe, where men are free to spend time in the company of women, even the stanzas of Virgil may appear immodest.[42] Had a text like the Song of Songs been penned by a German poet, it would have rightly been construed as a lewd sexual poem; placed in the oriental context, it is to be understood otherwise.

Michaelis, then, seeks to "see through the eyes" of the Bible's oriental authors to overcome the text's foreignness. Having lived in a different climate, the Hebrews, in fact, wrote under the influence of different modes of expression and emotions, all tied to a different social structure and sexuality. He likewise invokes climate to explain "the polygamy of the Southern peoples." Through its effect on the sexual constitution, climate indirectly impacts political affairs.

Law, Custom and Mentality in *Mosaisches Recht*

In the introduction to *Mosaisches Recht*, Michaelis lays out his method of comprehensive interpretation of Mosaic law and elaborates on the difficulties the European investigator faces when seeking to understand it. Indeed, in the two decades after its publication, the chapter was to become the formative text of the historical-critical school of biblical interpretation, of which Michaelis is considered the founder. It opens with a declaration of his intent to investigate Mosaic law "through Montesquieu's eyes," and proceeds to maintain that although Mosaic law does not apply to his contemporary readers, it is worthy of their attention "as the law of a faraway land." To evaluate the law through Montesquieu's eyes one must regard the legal systems of other peoples—and the farther temporally and geographically removed these are, the better.[43]

Montesquieu's *De l'Esprit des lois*, translated into German in 1753, was very favorably received, mainly because of the writer's stance on the Germanic tribes, which he describes as a free people living independently in the forest.[44] From that point onward, the writings of this French philosopher rather ironically exerted a major influence on the intellectual camp that sought to highlight Germany's unique identity and distinguish it from France. The book's idea of the separation of powers was skeptically received on the other side of the Rhine, but German political thinkers passionately adopted its focus on "local traditions" and the "national character," as fashioned by climate, religion, and other variables. According to Montesquieu, all laws share a universal essence, which is, however, historically contingent on concrete conditions and on the "spirit of the nation" [*l'esprit de la nation*].[45] Michaelis speaks of the same essence as the national concept [*Nationalbegriff*] or the national spirit [*Nationalgeist*].

Montesquieu's stance on Mosaic law was itself ambivalent; he terms the penalties applied to many offenses as "fairly harsh" [*bien rude*] and refutes any link between commandments such as the prohibition of work on the Sabbath and natural law.[46] But he then goes on to state that this deviation from natural law stems from the influence of popular customs and the Israelites' wild nature. Mosaic law is thus understood as preferable, which is in fact Montesquieu's interpretation of the verse "Wherefore I gave them also statutes that were not good" (Ezekiel 20:25). In other instances, he claims that Mosaic law is "very wise" and commends the way Moses unified religious custom and state law.[47]

Michaelis employs Montesquieu's method when dealing with the unwritten stratum of custom [*Herkommen*]. Custom, he finds, is the major obstacle to be overcome if one is fully to understand Hebrew law in its correct context. Most of the customs underlying the law are implicit to biblical law and thus remain unrevealed to a scholar who employs traditional textual interpretation methods. Michaelis, therefore, proposes a new path toward understanding of the Israelites' customs: "The ancient traditionary law which Moses sometimes adopted, and sometimes improved, I find to be principally Nomadic, that is, suited to the state of free wandering herdsmen, such as were Abraham, Isaac and Jacob, the ancestors of the Israelites. And hence the reason why it receives so much light from the manners of the wandering Arabs, the descendants of Abraham."[48]

The idea that biblical law is built on a more ancient layer of pre-Mosaic law given to the patriarchs—and perhaps even to Adam—is an ancient one, originating in the apocrypha. In the Christian tradition, this law was often identified with universal natural law. Another theory prevalent among Christian theologians was that the source for much of Mosaic law was the set of ancient laws of the Israelites from their idolatrous days. One of the more popular forms of this argument was adopted by Christian Hebraists relying on Maimonides, who, in *The Guide for the Perplexed*, claimed that Abraham was raised among the Sabians, an idolatrous people also mentioned in the Koran. The Jewish philosopher relates that "the meaning and causes of many laws became fully clear to me only when I studied the beliefs, views, actions, and methods of worship of the Sabians."[49] According to Maimonides, Abraham in fact legislated many ritual laws to supersede Sabian law, which governed many of his own people's actions, thereby precluding an overly violent upheaval in their customs.

As Jonathan Elukin has shown, this theory was adopted by many early modern Christian interpreters seeking to explain the sources of obscure sections of Mosaic law.[50] It was most widely disseminated by English Hebraist John Spencer (1630–1693), who, in *De Legibus Hebraorum,* interprets each of Moses's laws according to Sabian law, which he considered equivalent to Egyptian law. Spencer held that Moses used a canny political tactic to create a system of commandments actually based on ancient religious practices such as animal sacrifice, a custom that originates in human needs and desires.[51]

Michaelis was well acquainted with Maimonides, so it is safe to assume that his theory of ancient custom is based on the Jewish philosopher's work or on a later variation of it. However, he imbues the debate about pre-Mosaic law with essentially new content, characterizing the pre-Mosaic period *culturally* rather than theologically or juristically. As Carhart shows, Michaelis's book is a clear expression of the ascendancy of *Kultur* as a theoretical category during the final third of the eighteenth century.[52] Michaelis sought to show that culture, namely that aspect of society encompassing its "customs" [*Sittenlehre*], was always more powerful than any particular legislator.

Michaelis's historical conception of the sources of Hebrew law is most clearly enunciated in his interpretation of blood feud law, which the author celebrates as Moses's greatest work of art. His discussion of this section makes for some of the richest and most complex writing in all of *Mosaisches Recht*, in which he formulates several anthropological and historiographical insights implicit in his other writings.

As he did when addressing marriage and chastity law in the preceding chapters of the book, Michaelis begins his debate on blood feud law by explaining that this is so fundamentally foreign a custom, and so alien to the European reader, that it requires some interpretive mediation. He notes that the blood avenger [Bluträcher], described in Deuteronomy 19:6 as a relative of a victim who is permitted to kill whoever murdered his kin after trial by the community, is a juridical entity "almost unknown in our law, but very prominent in the Hebrew one."[53]

To arrive at a deeper understanding of the law beyond the sparse information the biblical text itself provides, Michaelis compares the customs to which it applies with those of the Arabs—in this case, with the Arab notion of the blood avenger. He finds that in Arab society honor and glory rest entirely on the blood feud, hence their customs provide more pertinent evidence toward understanding this concept than do the few biblical chapters that actually address it. Indeed, ethnographic comparison to Arab custom constitutes Michaelis's basic method of biblical interpretation. However, his interpretation of the blood feud is augmented by further, philosophical-historical discussion, which appears in paragraph 132, entitled "The Origin of the Kinsmen Redeemer in the Natural State."

As opposed to customs such as polygamy and circumcision, Michaelis states, the fact that Hebrew and Arab blood revenge customs are "so alien to us" (that is, to Europeans) is *not* a matter of climactic difference; their foreignness derives, he maintains, from "these peoples' pronounced ancientness." To clarify this argument, he proceeds to present his basic anthropological understanding: "Nations, how remote soever in their situation, yet resemble each other while in their infancy, much in the same way as children in every country have certain resemblances in figure and manners, proceeding from their age, by which we can distinguish them from adults and old people; and of this infancy of mankind, or, to speak more properly, of that state of nature, whence they soon pass into the state of civil society, the blood-avenger seems to me to be a relic."[54]

What is this "state of nature" of which the blood feud is a "relic"? Fundamentally, it appears to be that primordial, prepolitical, and prehistorical state described in the philosophical models of thinkers such as Hobbes. Indeed, Michaelis does not initially place the natural state in any concrete historical reality, but rather employs it as a theoretical model. When human beings led a lawless existence and no courts were at hand to impose punishments on murderers, they had no choice but to enact blood revenge to punish offenders.[55]

In the philosophical spirit of the social contract, the blood feud custom is conceived to be a necessary political outgrowth of human nature—a form of "the war of all against all" of the natural state. Yet unlike those thinkers who used the state of nature as a mere philosophical instrument, Michaelis seeks to find it in the biblical description itself, claiming that the human race could hardly be imagined to have existed in a more complete state of nature than that which prevailed in the era directly after the Flood, when only Noah and his three sons lived on the earth. The father being too old to enforce his authority, the sons spread throughout the world, each a master unto himself, not subject to a common state.

Michaelis's identification of the state of nature with the state of humanity after the Flood is by no means unique; the same notion appears, albeit slightly differently, in Locke, Rousseau, and others.[56] According to the German writer, during that era, the blood feud was a fundamental divine commandment that served to protect human life, remaining in place until humanity established "civil ties" [*bürgerliche Verbindung*] through legislation and the appointment of rulers, thereby providing greater security for the populace. Michaelis, however, by no means idealizes this state of nature, describing at length the inhumanity and cruelty of the nomadic Arabs' blood feud customs.

Michaelis holds that when Moses began leading the Israelites, they were close to the American "savages" in their primordial natural state, and that they too practiced an unchecked custom of blood revenge. By way of proof, he notes that Moses treats the blood avenger as an "intimate personage" that requires no description. The fact that the biblical text does not offer a detailed account of the custom, claims Michaelis, indicates that both the legislator and the law's subjects (that is, the people) were well acquainted with an unwritten, customary system of justice going back to the precivil state of nature. And even though Moses and the later scribes sought to cover up remnants of prelegal customs wherever they could, Michaelis identifies these characteristics of the natural state in the early chapters of Israelite history, in particular in the patriarchal stories.

Having presented a political theory of the blood feud's evolution from a state of nature, Michaelis proceeds to employ a different interpretive method, based on ethnographic observation. While on some occasions he speaks of the blood feud as a universal custom of humanity when still in the state of nature, in other contexts he regards it as a "national concept" [*Nationalbegriff*]. He asserts that in Arab culture "the most august poetry is devoted to the blood-avenger," and that, in fact, these poems highlight "the national spirit" [*Nationalgeist*].[57]

National "mentality" is here presented as the primary characteristic of a people—stronger than law and religion. Thus, Michaelis claims that Mohammed's prohibition of the practice of blood revenge failed to overcome the Arabs' "lust for revenge." An Arab raised on the "national concept of honor" [*Nationalbegriffe von Ehre*] would, so he insists, be more inclined to violate religious law than have his honor slighted.

Judging by his arguments up to this point, it emerges that Michaelis understood the blood feud to be a custom that invariably appeared among peoples at a lower stage of development. He identifies this stage, *historically*, with humanity's state after the Flood; but also *geographically and ethnographically* with the condition of certain contemporary Arab societies, in which people still lived "close to the state of nature." However, a remnant of this state of nature was still to be found in the more "developed" nations of Europe itself in the guise of a popular custom there, namely the duel. "Customary among us," the duel played the same role in Europe that the blood feud played for the Arabs: both were based on "national concepts of honor."[58]

While valid in the natural state, both these customs became obsolete when a nation reached the level of civil society and established legal institutions. Here Michaelis voices a reservation common among many Enlightenment thinkers; in the eighteenth century, the duel was seen as an aristocratic privilege, and even though it had reached the height of its popularity in the seventeenth century, many intellectuals regarded it as a feudal relic. Several French and English philosophers even described it as a medieval, barbaric custom that had no place in the new Age of Progress.[59] Comparison to the duel thus rendered the ethnographic-theoretical discussion of the blood feud as a timely debate touching on social reform of entrenched defects unbefitting to a modern state. And since these customs—the blood feud and the duel—originated in those primordial "national concepts," simple legislation would not suffice to combat them. Indeed, Michaelis rules out the simple solution of banning the practice of the duel, arguing that such a prohibition "would have very little impact on the entrenched national conception of honor"; those who proposed such a course of action showed "very limited understanding of the human heart."[60]

Here Michaelis reaches the crux of his entire interpretive project: an explanatory basis for the justification of Mosaic blood feud law. Even had he wished to do so, Moses could not have eradicated the custom; he sought, rather, to minimize the harm done by the blood avenger. According to Michaelis, the solution that Moses devised allowed the custom to persist while mitigating its effect, as manifested in the two novel provisions that appear in Numbers 35: a trial before the congregation and the establishment of cities of refuge for unintentional killers. These ordinances did not altogether avert the shedding of innocent blood, as civil law cannot prevent every kind of moral wrongdoing; but they did ensure that this would occur only in exceptional circumstances. Thus did Moses fully achieve the goal he had set himself; the blood avenger was, in fact, subsumed under the state's law enforcement apparatus. The seeking of revenge and unchecked ideas of honor had become institutional instruments.

Michaelis seeks to situate the blood feud in an exotic geographical and chronological space, as far removed from his European readers as possible.

In fact, he claims, revenge-seeking was a dominant feature "in the characters [*Gemüthsbildung*] of the peoples of the south."[61] Although he does not employ the precise term, Michaelis can be said to characterize the blood feud as a primitive custom befitting a primordial developmental stage of human society. However, even when highlighting the fundamental differences between peoples, Michaelis does not indulge in the kind of dichotomous distinction between a "lowly Orient" and a "developed Occident" so prevalent in orientalist writing from the end of the eighteenth century onward. While he construes the Arabs and the Hebrews to be closer to the state of nature, he discerns remnants of their customs in contemporary Europe. His comparison with the custom of the duel highlights that there is no need to return to the ancient Orient: the very persistence of this murderous tradition in Europe itself—despite the state's attempts to eradicate it—proves the power of ancient custom.[62] In this sense, the power of entrenched traditional customs was not a phenomenon peculiar to the peoples of the Orient or the south.

Under the influence of Montesquieu, Michaelis makes ethnographical distinctions between various peoples, taking into account local variables, above all climate. Yet as Reill shows, these distinctions serve to indicate the relativity of all laws, and to demonstrate that they are suited to the conditions of their legislation.[63] Every legal system is preceded by the entity that establishes and facilitates it: the people themselves. And no less important than his attempts to identify the characteristics of oriental mentality, Michaelis seeks to demonstrate the signs of national mentality or more generally, the traces of *the people* in the law: "It is necessary that I here notice the particular mode of life, on which the whole Mosaic polity is founded, and show, at the same time, how its laws bore upon other modes of life. For neither the form of the Israelitish government, nor what I have already said concerning its fundamental principles, can be fully understood, unless we are acquainted with the *people*, or, in other words, with the material of which the state is composed."[64]

During the 1750s and 1760s, in the wake of the Seven Years' War, German writers—headed by Johann Heinrich Gottlob Justi (1717–1771) and Friedrich Karl von Moser (1723-1798)—began to engage in discussion of the German national spirit.[65] The debate—as embodied in Moser's essay *Von dem deutschen Nationalgeist* of 1756—revolved around the question: does this spirit in fact exist?[66] Michaelis himself took part in this debate by publishing a review in the *Göttingische gelehrte Anzeigen*.[67] The term "national spirit" was initially closely bound up with the ethnographic discourse on the differences between peoples, especially between those of the old and new worlds.[68] In this sense, Michaelis's writings are typical of this liminal phase between the time when the notion of "national spirit" was used as an ethnographic category and the period in which it became a positive political ideal.

Summary: The Concept of Nation and the Question of the Law's Validity

For many Protestant biblical interpreters of the late eighteenth century, Michaelis's interpretive project represented a resurgence of the Reformation—a return to the Lutheran spirit and a rebirth of the Bible itself. In his eulogy to Michaelis, Johann Eichhorn—his foremost disciple and a leader of the critical biblical scholarship school—asserted that his mentor's project meant that: "with him, the Germans have returned to being interpreters in their own right; they have returned to decipher the meaning of Scripture as during the Reformation, through grammatical exegesis, and then historically according to the spirit of antiquity—according to ancient history, customs, views and ways of thought."[69]

In fact, as I have shown in this chapter, Michaelis's investigation into Mosaic law, on the one hand, featured novel research methods and the use of modern historical, ethnographic, and philological tools; while on the other, it in fact continued the Reformation's fundamental thrust as well as Luther's interpretation of Paul's writings.

In *German, Jews and the Claims of Modernity*, Jonathan Hess shows how Michaelis dubs Mosaic law an "oriental" codex that lags behind Christianity and does not fit the spirit of modernity. He goes so far as to present Michaelis's life's work as an attempt to "purify" European legislation of the primitive, oriental influences of biblical law.[70] Yet the chapters of *Mosaisches Recht* discussed above show that Michaelis's engagement with the Bible was far more nuanced. As we have seen in his treatment of blood feud law, he portrays Mosaic law as an ethical revolution, a shining example of intelligent legislation and social reform. Although some commandments (such as circumcision) are considered oriental customs suited to warm climates, others (such as the blood feud) are touted as primitive solutions for grave social problems that no European legislator has yet been able to solve.

Therefore, contrary to Hess, I believe it is mistaken to claim that Michaelis viewed biblical law as having merely "archival value" and nothing more. In fact, the German scholar's interpretation oscillates between the biblical world and European society of his own time. In the comparisons and analogies he draws, biblical customs are compared with Arab—and also European—ones. Biblical law is not necessarily interpreted as an "archeological remnant" of a different time and place; the dilemmas raised by biblical law are at times debated as issues on contemporary European and German society's agenda. Biblical exegesis serves here as a medium for debating timely questions; investigation into Mosaic law becomes a sort of debate on social reform in which Moses is construed as siding with enlightened social reformers. In fact, Mosaic law is touted as the model of a legal codex perfectly adapted to the "national concept" of its subjects. Michaelis's analysis of the blood feud and the duel revolves around general principles regarding the relation between popular custom and state law.

Philological research into popular custom and law does not necessarily entail positing the subject of the investigation as a "total other." Interpretive tracts similar to *Mosaisches Recht* were written in Germany regarding ancient Germanic tribal law. As early as the late eighteenth century, many German scholars labored to reconstruct the popular roots of German law, as well as the ancient past shared by all Germans—even though this ancient Germanic people was generally portrayed as no less (and in some cases, more) savage than the ancient Israelites.

Like other scholars working in the newly founded German universities of the period, Michaelis contributed to the establishment of a new civil discourse and the consolidation of a new discipline of political science placed at the service of the centralized, bureaucratic principality administration. Göttingen University trained members of the legal and administrative apparatus of a modern state, guided by an ideology of a unified, rational law. Historical-philological research of ancient law and administration was recruited to enhance the state's knowledge of legislation and enforcement history. In the final account, this academic endeavor served a project of social reform that sought to replace social institutions regarded as ossified with universal-rationalist ones.

The biblical text that Michaelis addressed was laden with meanings for him—to him it was not just a Protestant "meta-narrative," but a legally binding codex, as well. And in *Mosaisches Recht*, Michaelis in fact addresses a stratum of German law. The text about which he writes in many ways structured the social reality of his own times and gave them meaning; it was woven into innumerable ordinances, rituals, and practices that were still in effect in the Christian German society of his time.

One of the major projects of the Enlightenment was to describe the world in a novel manner that correlated with new authoritative sources of knowledge. Michaelis's project is lexical; *Mosaisches Recht* is a kind of ethnographic study, and some of his other works, such as *Geographiae Hebraeorum* (1767), are actual lexicons. As Homi K. Bhabha put it, orientalist knowledge is "a static system of 'synchronic essentialism,' a knowledge of 'signifiers of stability' such as the lexicographic and the encyclopedic."[71] Michaelis sought to establish a clear distinction between the interpreted object and the society in which he lived—to transform the biblical text into a static "ancient landscape." The imagined oriental space constructed by the orientalist essays is, however, a mirror image of the German social, political, and religious system—that of the universities in particular, and of the absolute monarchy in general.

Furthermore, the move to weed out Hebrew law from the legal codex governing Christians was not, in fact, Michaelis's own original idea. The distinction between absolutely valid Christian gospel and relatively valid Mosaic law forms the very basis of the Protestant understanding of the New Testament's relation to the Old Testament. Paul himself, in Galatians, restricts the law's validity to the Jews alone: "Wherefore then serveth the law? It was added because of transgressions, till the seed should come to whom the promise was made" (Galatians 3:19). He also chronologically distinguishes between pre-Revelation time, when the law was still valid, and the post-Revelation period, when it became superfluous, since "the law was our schoolmaster to bring us unto Christ, that we might be justified by faith. But after that faith is come, we are no longer under a schoolmaster" (Galatians 3:24–25). In Christian tradition, this chronological distinction is correlated with a bifurcation between the Father's harsh and cruel "age of the Law" and the Son's "age of Grace," beginning with the advent of Christ.

In Luther's writing, this theological distinction between the temporary and the eternal, that is, between valid and already invalid law, rests on an interpretive method that contains the germ of historical research. While he initially adhered to the traditional Christological interpretation of the Old Testament—which sees it as an allegory of Christ's life—in his later work he veered toward initial form of historical interpretation.[72] Thomasius and other Protestant Enlightenment jurists of the early eighteenth century developed this germ into actual critical-historical investigation that distinguished between Mosaic law's universal moral elements and its political and ritual components. There is, however, another facet to Protestant treatment of the Old Testament; it severs the Old Testament from the Bible as a whole and then recontextualizes it historically as a stand-alone book, thereby conferring on Hebrew history an autonomous ontological status.

The historical investigation undertaken by interpreters of the critical-historical school preserved a similar dualism. Michaelis's interpretive project distinguishes between universal legislative principles and the particular elements of popular Hebrew custom. This distinction reveals a new layer of the Old Testament: its ethno-cultural facet. Stripped of its universal validity, Mosaic law is inscribed with new meaning as an august example of particular legislation adapted to the *Volk*'s national "concept." In this way, Michaelis also solved the problem of biblical law's status. Although Mosaic law doesn't apply to Christians, they are duty bound to learn from Moses how to legislate a "civil law" [*bürgerliches Gesetz*] best suited to the people's needs.[73]

Pauline theology—and Enlightenment universalism thereafter—sought to ascertain the law's validity on an absolute scale. Michaelis, conversely, introduces an element of relativity in suggesting that it is mediated through a particular nation. The major novelty of the biblical exegesis of Michaelis and his disciples is precisely the idea that the *Volk* is the stuff of the state—a conception based, inter alia, on the innovations of political science in the second half of the eighteenth century. The state is never an abstract creation—it is the creation of the *Volk*.

By contrast to earlier accounts, which tended to generalize the Hebrew regime into a political-philosophical model, Michaelis stressed the historical dynamics of the Hebrew state, paying special attention to the relation between government and culture. Thus, although it is a distinct fruit of the Enlightenment, Michaelis's biblical interpretation already references the national aspects of the Bible. As shown by Wolf-Daniel Hartwich, the Montesquieu-like qualities that Michaelis attributes to Moses's legislation in asserting that his laws suited his people's customs and traditions corresponds with the criticism German scholars leveled against Enlightened absolutism and the centralist rule they termed *Josephism* following the judicial reforms undertaken by Kaiser Joseph II (1741–1790).[74] German political thinkers such as Justus Möser (1720–1794) decried the administration's efforts to unify the legislation and institutions of the German Reich and recoiled from what they saw as the truncating of historical continuity and local custom. Simultaneously, opposition grew to the forced enactment of Roman Law throughout the Reich.

Johann Stephan Pütter (1725–1807), Michaelis's colleague at Göttingen, sought to recreate original German law [*Gewohnheitsrecht*], which in his view drew its vitality and authority from the people's customs and traditions.[75] In his account, this organic, natural law was in harmony with German national character [*Nationalcharacter*] and had regrettably been supplanted by abstract, universalist, and ahistorical Roman law. This concept is reminiscent of the clannish traditional layer of Hebrew law as depicted by Michaelis. As we shall see, this idea was later developed by other German writers and especially by Herder.

Notes

1. For a debate on the concept of the law in Paul, see: Heikki Räisänen, *Paul and the Law* (Tübingen: Mohr Siebeck, 1987), 15–23.
2. See, for example: Roy A. Harrisville and Walter Sundberg, *The Bible in Modern Culture* (Cambridge, UK: Erdman, 1995), 21–22.
3. Ditlev Tamm, "Reformation, Rechtstudium und Rechtwissenschaft," in *University and Reformation*, ed. Leif Grane (Leiden: Brill, 1981), 67–68.
4. Siegfried Raeder, "The Exegetical and Hermeneutical Work of Martin Luther," in *Hebrew Bible / Old Testament: The History of Its Interpretation: From the Renaissance to the Enlightenment*, ed. Magne Saebo, 363–406 (Göttingen: Vandenhoeck & Ruprecht, 2008), 385; Brooks Schramm, *Martin Luther, the Bible, and the Jewish People: A Reader* (Minneapolis, MN: Fortress Press, 2012), 93–94.
5. Martin Luther, "Eyn Unterrichtung, wie sich die Christen yn Moses sollen schicken," [1525], in *Werke* (Weimarer Ausgabe), Weimar, 1883, 16:363–393.
6. Luther, "Sermon: How Christians Should Regard Moses," in Schramm, *Martin Luther, the Bible, and the Jewish People*, 96–97.

7. Luther, "Außlegung der Epistel St. Pauli an die Galater." [1531], in *Werke*, (Weimarer Ausgabe) 40, no. 1, 480–490. Weimar, 1883.

8. Hess, *Germans, Jews and the Claims of Modernity*, (New Haven, CT: Yale University Press, 2002), 60.

9. On this issue, see, for instance: Carhart, *The Science of Culture in Enlightenment Germany*, (Cambridge, MA: Harvard University Press, 2007), 52–53.

10. Legaspi, *The Death of Scripture and the Rise of Biblical Studies*, (Oxford: Oxford University Press, 2010), 130–131.

11. See: Dagmar Freist, "One Body, Two Confessions: Mixed Marriages in Germany," in *Gender in Early Modern German History*, ed. Ulinka Rublack (Cambridge, UK: Cambridge University Press, 2002), 275–305.

12. Philipp Müller, *Der Fang des edlen Lebens durch frembde Glaubens-Ehe* (N.p., 1689), 45–46.

13. See: John Witte, *Law and Protestantism: The Legal Teachings of the Lutheran Reformation* (Cambridge: Cambridge University Press, 2002), 199–214.

14. On this, see: Philip Gorski, "Calvinism and State-Formation in Early Modern Europe," in *State/Culture: State-Formation after the Cultural Turn*, ed. George Steinmetz (Ithaca, NY: Cornell University Press, 1999), 147–181; Isabel V. Hull, *Sexuality, State, and Civil Society in Germany, 1700–1815* (Ithaca, NY: Cornell University Press, 1996), 66.

15. See: Ludwig von Bar, *A History of Continental Criminal Law* (Boston: Little Brown, 1916), 229–230.

16. Bar, *Continental Criminal Law*, 236.

17. The most comprehensive survey of the legislation of marital prohibitions is still Heinrich Wilhelm Josias Thiersch, *Das Verbot der Ehe innerhalb der nahen Verwandtschaft, nach der heiligen Schrift und nach den Grundsätzen der christlichen Kirche* (Nördlingen: Beck, 1869), 135–166.

18. A prime example can be found in England during the inheritance battle between Charles I's brothers and his mistress's sons. See: Faramerz Dabhoiwala, *The Origins of Sex: A History of the First Sexual Revolution* (Oxford: Oxford University Press, 2012), 103.

19. Dabhoiwala, *The Origins of Sex*, 93.

20. Dabhoiwala, *The Origins of Sex*, 99.

21. Christian Thomasius, *Erörterung von der Lutherischen und Reformirten Fürstlichen Personen Heyrath* (Leipzig: Renger, 1689), 4.

22. Thomasius, *Erörterung von der Lutherischen*, 289.

23. Thomasius, *Erörterung von der Lutherischen*, 31.

24. Thomas Ahnert, *Religion and the Origins of the German Enlightenment: Faith and the Reform of Learning in the Thought of Christian Thomasius* (Rochester, NY: University of Rochester Press, 2006), 48–56.

25. Ahnert, *Religion and the Origins*, 51–52.

26. See mainly: Ian Hunter, *Rival Enlightenments: Civil and Metaphysical Philosophy in Early Modern Germany* (Cambridge, UK: Cambridge University Press, 2001), 60–64.

27. Thomas Albert Howard, *Protestant Theology and the Making of the Modern German University* (Oxford: Oxford University Press, 2006), 104–106.

28. On this development, see: Legaspi, *The Death of Scripture*, 31–33.

29. Legaspi, *The Death of Scripture*, 44; Luigi Marino, *Praeceptores Germaniae: Göttingen 1770–1820* (Göttingen: Vandenhoeck & Ruprecht, 1995), 70–90.

30. Legaspi, *The Death of Scripture*, 44.
31. Johann David Michaelis, *Commentaries on the Laws of Moses*, trans. Alexander Smith (London: Longman, 1814), 1:1.
32. Joel F. Harrington, *Reordering Marriage and Society in Reformation Germany*, (Cambridge, UK: Cambridge University Press, 1995), 85–96.
33. Christian Friedrich Hempel, *Königlich Preußisches allgemeines Processual-Lexicon* (Halle: Bauer, 1749), 3. See too: Claudia Jarzebowski, *Inzest: Verwandtschaft und Sexualität im 18. Jahrhundert* (Cologne: Böhlau, 2006), 292–293.
34. Johann David Michaelis, *Abhandlung von den Ehegesetzen Mosis welche die Heyrathen in die nahe Freundschaft untersagen* (Göttingen: Vandenhoeck, 1755).
35. Michaelis, *Abhandlung von den Ehegesetzen Mosis*, 327–330.
36. Michaelis, *Abhandlung von den Ehegesetzen Mosis*, 2.
37. Michaelis, *Commentaries on the Laws of Moses*, 1:5–6.
38. Michaelis, *Abhandlung von den Ehegesetzen Mosis*, 1.
39. Michaelis, *Abhandlung von den Ehegesetzen Mosis*, 68–70.
40. Michaelis, *Abhandlung von den Ehegesetzen Mosis*, 193.
41. Michaelis, *Abhandlung von den Ehegesetzen Mosis*, 71–72.
42. See, for example, the notes to Lowth in Robert Lowth, *De sacra poesi Hebraeorum … notas et epimetra adiecit, Ioannes David Michaelis* (Göttingen: 1758), vii.
43. Lowth, *De sacra poesi Hebraeorum* (Göttingen: 1758), 1.
44. Charles de Secondat Montesquieu, *De l'Esprit des lois* (Geneva: Barillot & Fils, 1749), 1:194.
45. Montesquieu, *De l'Esprit des lois*, 1:484.
46. Montesquieu, *De l'Esprit des lois*, 1:417–418.
47. Montesquieu, *De l'Esprit des lois*, 2: 208.
48. Michaelis, *Commentaries on the Laws of Moses*, 1:13.
49. Maimonides, Moses, The Guide for the Perplexed. Trans. Chaim Rabin (Indianoplois, IN: Hackett, 1996), 179.
50. Jonathan Elukin, "Maimonides and the Rise and Fall of the Sabians: Explaining Mosaic Laws and the Limits of Scholarship," *Journal of the History of Ideas* 63, no. 4 (2002): 619–637.
51. John Spencer, *De legibus hebraeorum ritualibus et earum* (Cambridge, UK: Chiswel, 1685). Regarding Maimonides's influence on Spencer through his Sabian theory, see: Guy G. Stroumsa, *A New Science: The Discovery of Religion in the Age of Reason* (Cambridge, MA: Harvard University Press, 2010), 95–98.
52. Carhart, *The Science of Culture in Enlightenment Germany*, 48–49.
53. Johann David Michaelis, *Mosaisches Recht* (Frankfurt am Main: J. Gottlieb Garbe, 1775), 2:287–320.
54. Michaelis, *Commentaries on the Laws of Moses*, 1:195.
55. Michaelis, *Mosaisches Recht*, 2:350.
56. On this topic, see: Helen Thornton, *State of Nature or Eden? Thomas Hobbes and His Contemporaries on the Natural Condition of Human Beings* (Rochester, NY: University of Rochester Press, 2005); Ronald L. Meek, *Social Science and the Ignoble Savage* (Cambridge, UK: Cambridge University Press, 1976), 73–79.
57. Michaelis, *Mosaisches Recht*, 2:322.
58. Michaelis, *Mosaisches Recht*, 2:325.

59. Dena Goodman, *The Republic of Letters: A Cultural History of the French Enlightenment* (Ithaca, NY: Cornell University Press, 1994), 94–97; Armstrong Starkey, *War in the Age of Enlightenment, 1700–1789* (Westport, CT: Praeger, 2003), 79–82.

60. Michaelis, *Mosaisches Recht*, 2:328.

61. Michaelis, *Mosaisches Recht*, 2:331.

62. Michaelis, *Mosaisches Recht*, 2:333.

63. Peter Hanns Reill, *The German Enlightenment and the Rise of Historicism* (Berkeley: University of California Press, 1975), 134–135.

64. Michaelis, *Commentaries on the Laws of Moses*, 1:206–207.

65. On this trend, see: Nicholas Vazsonyi, "Montesquieu, Friedrich Carl von Moser, and the 'National Spirit Debate' in Germany, 1765–1767," *German Studies Review* 22, no. 2 (May 1999): 225–246.

66. Friedrich Carl von Moser, *Von dem deutschen Nationalgeist* (Franz Varrentrapp, 1765).

67. Michaelis, *Göttingische Anzeigen von gelehrten Sachen* 98 (August 1965) 785–787.

68. Vazsonyi, "'National Spirit Debate' in Germany," 229–231.

69. Johann Gottfried Eichhorn, *Allgemeine Bibliothek der biblischen Litteratur* (Leipzig: Weidman, 1791), 3:885.

70. Hess, *Germans, Jews and the Claims of Modernity*, 12, 58–62.

71. Homi K. Bhabha, "The Other Question: Stereotype, Discrimination and the Discourse of Colonialism," in *The Location of Culture* (New York: Routledge, 2004), 66–84.

72. See: Raeder, "The Exegetical and Hermeneutical Work of Martin Luther," 380.

73. Michaelis, *Mosaisches Recht*, 1:19–20.

74. Wolf-Daniel Hartwich, *Die Sendung Moses: von der Aufklärung bis Thomas Mann*. (Munich: Fink, 1997), 68–69. On Michaelis's conservative tendencies. See also: Legaspi, *The Death of Scripture*, 140–141.

75. See, for example, Johann Stephan Pütter, *Beiträge zum deutschen Staats-und Fürstenrecht*, (Göttingen: Vandenhöck, 1777), 2:85; Reill, *The German Enlightenment*, 180–187.

3 The Eighteenth-Century Polemic on the Extermination of the Canaanites

IN HIS BOOK *Moses the Egyptian: The Memory of Egypt in Western Monotheism*, Jan Assmann traces the emergence of the symbolic antagonism in modern European thought between two biblical peoples—the Israelites and the Egyptians.[1] He shows how radical Enlightenment thinkers sought the rehabilitation of the ancient Egyptians, one of the most disgraced peoples in the biblical tradition. In the eighteenth century, Assmann maintains, two opposing intellectual camps evolved, both of which subscribed to the antagonistic concepts of "Israel" and "Egypt." This conflict became an ideological battleground, as the memory of the Egyptian enslavement and the Exodus was constantly revised and rewritten.

At the center of the present chapter stands another conflict, which plays no less important a role in the biblical narrative. This is the war of the Israelites against the peoples of Canaan. Like the Israelite/Egyptian duality, the Israelite/Canaanite pairing serves, within European memory, to represent a war between revealed religion and idolatry; yet the description of the conflict with the Canaanites in the books of Deuteronomy and Joshua reveals that it is constructed out of different elements and raises distinctly different questions. The war against the Canaanites is the flip side of the Exodus—not a "leaving of" but rather an "invasion of"; rather than the story of an enslaved people's revolt and liberation, it relates a battle between two peoples vying for the same territory.

While the Exodus narrative is an epic of enslavement and liberation, the story of the conquest of Canaan is a chronicle of occupation and extermination. The commandments "Thou shalt save alive nothing that breatheth" (Deuteronomy 20:16) and "but thou shalt utterly destroy them" (Deuteronomy 20:17) lay at the center of the modern polemic concerning the Canaanite question. Unlike other controversial biblical passages, whose authenticity began to be questioned in the early seventeenth century, the description of the Canaanite extermination obliged commentators to address questions of ethics and *iure belli*.

This chapter discusses the ways in which eighteenth-century European writers treated the biblical account of the conquest of Canaan by the Israelites and the extermination of its inhabitants. It surveys the attacks made by anticlerical philosophers on the morality of Moses's extermination decree and proceeds to focus on attempts made by conservative adherents of the Bible to affirm its legitimacy. It demonstrates how rationalist theologians and Bible scholars, especially those of the German Historical-Critical School, were forced to devise novel legal and theoretical tools in order to justify the conquest of the land in terms of modern reasoning.

"The right of the Israelites to Palestine has been a Gordian knot, whose loosening was often held as the most accurate touchstone for scholars' acumen," wrote the Bible scholar Johann Gottfried Eichhorn (1753–1827).[2] Indeed, it would be no exaggeration to say that the legitimacy of the Canaanite extermination was among the most controversial historical–theological questions in the Enlightenment's "republic of letters." Almost no major thinker of the period could afford to ignore the subject, with Hugo Grotius and John Locke addressing it as early as the seventeenth century. The eighteenth century witnessed an animated scholarly polemic concerning the extermination of the Canaanite peoples; launched by English deists, it was taken up by Voltaire and other anticlerical writers. They all protested the infringement of the Canaanites' rights, as well as the immoral aspects of their expropriation.

These protests were, in turn, answered by conservative churchmen such as John Leland in England and Augustin Calmet in France. In particular, all the major German Bible scholars of the era—among them Johann Friedrich Wilhelm Jerusalem, Johann David Michaelis, Johann Ernst Faber, and Johann Gottfried Herder—aligned themselves with the Hebrew conquerors: almost every treatise issued by these scholars on ancient Jewish or Hebrew history contained an elaboration of the topic.[3]

Scholars in German universities—the center of Bible research in Europe during the second half of the eighteenth century—went out of their way to dispel deist and *Freidenker* claims, while at the same time wrangling among themselves over the most appropriate means to justify the conquest. However, this extremely rich polemic—and the manifold questions it raises—has not received the scholarly attention it deserves.[4]

In the Bible itself, the story of the Canaanite extermination appears first as a commandment—in Deuteronomy, and then as a narrative—in the book of Joshua. Unlike ancient Egypt, which was extensively depicted in classical literature, the Canaanites figured in European consciousness almost exclusively by dint of the biblical narrative. The biblical characterization of the seven peoples of Canaan is extremely succinct, found mostly in three verses in Deuteronomy: "But of the cities of these people, which the Lord thy God doth give thee for an inheritance, thou shalt save alive nothing that breatheth; but thou shalt utterly destroy them; namely, the Hittites, and the Amorites, the Canaanites, and the Perizzites, the Hivites, and the Jebusites; as the Lord thy God hath commanded thee; that they teach you not to do after all their abominations, which they have done unto their gods; so should ye sin against the Lord your God" (Deuteronomy 20:16–18).

The exclusionary religious ideology expressed in these lines, which was fashioned, according to contemporary Bible scholarship, by the intellectual elite of the Kingdom of Judah in the seventh century BCE, retained much of its vitality in those monotheist religions that sought to inherit the biblical religion of Israel—and not least in Christianity.[5] A part of the foundational text of European-Christian culture, this extermination commandment, attributed to Moses, retained its status as holy decree up to the eighteenth century, even if interpreted in divergent ways. The eighteenth century saw the rise of alternative readings of the conquest story—readings that presented the Israelites and Moses's commandments as dark elements alien to enlightened Europe.

Deist Criticism of the Extermination Commandment

Substantial reservations concerning the legitimacy of the takeover of Canaan by the Israelites were voiced already in the second century CE by the heretic theologian Marcion and subsequently, by other early adversaries of the Old Testament.[6] However, it was only at the end of the seventeenth century, as rationalist philosophers began to challenge the moral and religious validity of the Bible, that the conquest of Canaan and the extermination of its inhabitants became the center of a fierce controversy.

The commandment calling for the eradication of all the peoples of Canaan and the seizure of their land was perceived by radical commentators as an extreme expression of the contradiction between biblical commandments and natural law. These anticlerical attacks simultaneously objected to the cruelty with which the Canaanites (particularly women and children) were treated and questioned the Israelites' fundamental right to appropriate another people's land.

French priest Jean Meslier (1664–1729) was arguably the first Enlightenment writer to explicitly criticize the Israelites' conquests on moral grounds.[7] In his *Le testament*, he describes God's divine promise to Abraham as simple fraud, wondering how the French would react if a German or Swiss man declared that God had promised him and his progeny the entire territory of France, from the river Rhine to the Ocean.[8] Due to its controversial content, Meslier's essay did not gain a wide audience until it was published by Voltaire in 1762—more than thirty years after its author's death.[9] Thus, the first widely circulated criticisms of the Canaanite extermination were those issued at the beginning of the 1730s by the English deists.

The deist movement was nourished by the relative religious freedom that characterized England after the Glorious Revolution of 1688, which facilitated criticism of traditional structures and dogmas.[10] Although different deist writers diverged in their views and motivations, one common feature of their writings was their endeavor to undermine the authority of the Bible and institutionalized religion.[11]

The deists saw themselves as proponents of moral and religious universalism and resistance to coercion in religious matters. It is unsurprising, then, to learn that these writers strongly opposed the biblical ideas of the chosen people and the Israelites' aloofness from idolatrous peoples, especially in their manifestation as a war of persecution against idolatry.[12]

The first English deist to systematically address the question of the conquest was Matthew Tindal (1657–1733). His *Christianity as Old as the Creation* (1730) is considered the "deist Bible," and an influential manifesto in support of the principle of natural religion.[13] Tindal claimed that the Canaanites were exterminated even though they had done almost nothing to harm the Israelites.[14] According to Tindal, such cruelty and fanaticism could not be justified in any way: "Tell me how you can account to the conduct of the Jews, in invading, and that too without any Declaration of War, the Canaanites, a free and independent nation, and against whom they had not the least cause of complaint; and on Pretence of their being Idolaters, destroying not only the Men and Women, but Infants incapable of Idolatry, or any other Crime?"[15]

The attack on the Israelites' morality forms the basis for a more general attack on the morality of the Bible and the God of Israel as described in the Old Testament. Thomas Morgan (d. 1743), author of *The Moral Philosopher*, offers a more focused attack on "the seed of Abraham," namely the Israelites themselves. The annihilation of the Canaanites is presented not only as a theological paradox; its significance is extended to characterize the "Hebrew shepherds" and their leader, Moses: "They were not only left at Liberty, but encouraged and directed by Moses himself to extend their Conquests as far as they could, and to destroy by Fire and Sword, any or every Nation or People that resisted them, and that would not submit to become their Subjects and Tributaries, upon Demand: The Inhabitants of Canaan were to be utterly destroy'd Root and Branch without Mercy, not sparing or leaving alive Man, Woman or Child."[16]

The deists' arguments were principally aimed at contesting the Bible's moral authority and undermining the religious criteria employed to differentiate between various peoples. In these anticlerical essays, the case of the Canaanite extermination is offered as philosophical–rhetorical support for undermining the relevance of scripture and the authority of institutional Christianity. However, their contempt for the Jews surpassed the requirements of a purely rationalist Bible critique. Tindal and Morgan depicted the Hebrews as ferocious conquerors, whose actions provided an unfortunate source of inspiration for future religious violence.[17]

The Conquest of Canaan as Colonial Precedent

One of the recurring rhetorical tropes in deist writing from Tindal onward is the comparison of the Israelites' doings in Canaan to the Spaniards' slaughter of the American peoples. A number of seventeenth- and eighteenth-century writers denounced the Spanish conquest of the Americas as barbarous and inhumane.[18] Radically anti-Catholic, the English deists were especially virulent in their condemnation of Spanish cruelty. In this context, they depicted the Israelites' invasion of Canaan as a precedent that had far-reaching, grave implications: "Wou'd not people, if like the Children of *Israel*, they were destitute of an habitation, be apt to think what the *Israelites* did to the *Canaanites*, a good Precedent? . . . And I question whether the *Spaniards* would have murdered so many Millions in the *Indies*, had they not thought they might have used them like the *Canaanites*."[19]

A similar argument, frequently cited by later writers, served Lord Bolingbroke (1678–1751), who even more explicitly compared the ancient Israelites to the Spanish *conquistadores*: "In order to make good his grant to Abraham of the land of Canaan, he orders the posterity of this patriarch to conquer it, and to exterminate the inhabitants. Just so the leaders of Huns, of Goths, and Vandals, might, and did, make good their promises with the people who followed them. Just so the Spaniards made good the decree of Alexander the sixth, when they conquered America. Pizarro was not more cruel than Joshua."[20]

Since its very inception, the colonial takeover of the Americas was based on religious legitimacy that was couched in terms of the distinction between Christian and non-Christian peoples. This legitimacy was based in great measure on the conquest of Canaan by the Israelites. Spanish theologians regarded the Spanish as "the new Israelites," often comparing the Pope's conquest decree issued to the Spanish king to the equivalent commandment issued by Moses to Joshua.[21]

In this respect, deist criticism pertaining to the "precedent" of the Canaanite extermination was to a large extent justified. However, it was not only the Spanish who made such use of the biblical text but the English as well. The depiction of the conquest of Canaan served as a major source of legitimacy for conquests in the New World, and constituted a formative element of colonial ideology, which linked territorial expansion with purity, homogeneity, and ethnic exclusivity.

Paul Stevens defines the colonial discourse of the early modern era as *Leviticus thinking*—an exclusively Christian discourse based on the settlers' embodiment of the biblical "holy nation."[22] He maintains that the narrative of Canaan's conquest plays a major role in almost every colonial text of the seventeenth century—not merely as an arbitrary image, but as a religious imperative to be followed. In many such texts, the English, and especially the

Puritans, depicted themselves as a chosen people engaged in implementing, through their war against the American peoples, a divine plan to combat idolatry.[23]

The advocates of colonization argued that the same divine right that had justified the conquest of Canaan could be applied to the conquest of America by England. By the eighteenth century, the English became less inclined to employ religious rhetoric to justify the subjugation of indigenous American populations, partly because of the English colonists' desire to distinguish themselves from their Spanish counterparts. Consequently, English deists often compared Joshua's exploits to the Spanish-Catholic conquest of America but shied away from contemplating the actions of the English-Protestant settlers.

The Israelites' cruelty toward the peoples of Canaan was depicted by the deists as a form of barbarous savagery. Bolingbroke assigned Spaniards, Jews, and Huns to the same category of bloodthirsty barbarians. Beyond mere criticism of the carnage, his arguments were intended to transform the received image—to defrock the Jews of their chosen people status and show them to be more barbarous than the Canaanites.

Criticism of the Canaanite Extermination in Germany and France

Studies conducted over the past decade have cast doubt on the scale of the deist movement in England, as well as on its actual impact on public opinion in their homeland.[24] Yet, however limited the support for the deists' views may have been, their claims undoubtedly provoked considerable uproar among the clergy and conservative writers.[25]

The deist arguments appear to have had a stronger and longer-lasting impact within the German territories than in England itself—generally in a polemical context. By the time German scholarly interest in the deist writings reached its apex, deism had, more than a decade earlier, virtually ceased to exist in England itself. As shown by Christopher Voigt, deism posed a challenge to German religious Enlightenment writers, the terms *Deismus* and *Freigeisterey* subsequently becoming the key target of their polemic endeavor.[26]

Concurrently with the strengthening of commercial and intellectual ties between England and the northern German principalities, German translations of deist antibiblical works began to appear in the 1730s.[27] The first translations were accompanied by apologetic treatises, in which the freethinkers' arguments were countered. This format was probably employed in light of the authorities' censorship of anticlerical publications.[28] A case in point is the publication of Tindal's book by Johann Lorenz Schmidt (1702–1749), a Wolfenbüttel librarian who translated several controversial works on the Bible.[29]

Nevertheless, a few German writers did approve of the English deists' views, and in some cases, this led them to step up their vilification of the Old Testament. One of the first writers outside of England to issue a comprehensive rationalist attack on the Bible was Johann Christian Edelmann (1698–1767), rightly regarded as the most radical German critic of the Bible in the eighteenth century.[30]

An erstwhile Pietist turned worshiper of the "Divinity of Reason," Edelmann sought to purify Christianity of those elements he perceived as being opposed to reason, most notably the Old Testament. His most comprehensive attack on the Bible is contained in his major work, *Moses with Unveiled Face* [*Moses mit aufgededeckten Angesichte*], the first three volumes of which were published in 1740.[31] The book's publication sparked an uproar, and copies of it were burned in Hamburg in 1750. Edelmann was condemned in German theological and scholarly circles as a Spinozist, a *Freidenker*, and even an apostate.[32]

Directly after describing the Bible as nothing more than a bunch of "fictions" [*Histörchen*], Edelmann proceeds to engage in a contemptuous attack on the Bible's central figures, as well as on the Jews in general.[33] Like the English deists, the one event he finds most repugnant is the extermination of the Canaanites. He labels Moses as "diabolical" for having ordered the killing of women and children as well as "the extermination of entire peoples, along with their Gods and places of worship."[34] The cruelty of the conquest serves as the basis for Edelmann's most scathing attack on the Old Testament, and furnishes him with distinct proof of the book's moral worthlessness.

Another radical German writer who virulently condemned the morality of the conquest was Hermann Samuel Reimarus (1694–1768), the head of a Hamburg gymnasium who persistently throughout his *Apologie oder Schutzschrift für die vernünftigen Verehrer Gottes* sought to refute the Old Testament altogether. Parts of his *Schutzschrift* were published posthumously during the 1770s by Gotthold Ephraim Lessing (1729–1781), to become known as the *Wolfenbütteler Fragmente*. The section on the conquest of Canaan was only published after Lessing's death, in 1787.[35] Along with other accusations leveled at Moses and Joshua, Reimarus refuted the characterization of the Canaanites as shameless idolaters. He accused the Israelites of practicing far more abhorrent forms of idolatry than the peoples they massacred.[36]

A no less passionate debate on the legitimacy of the Israelites' deeds in Canaan was held in France, with Voltaire taking the leading role. Under the entry "Jews" in his *Dictionnaire philosophique* (1764), Voltaire launched a contemptuous assault on the moral standards underlying the extermination of the Canaanites.

Voltaire describes the people as a collection of desert nomads who looted Canaan and mercilessly massacred its residents.[37] He interprets the extermination as human sacrifice, depicting the Israelites as lowly ignorant savages, akin to Native Americans. In his *Essai sur les moeurs*, Voltaire presents the face-off between Israelites and Canaanites as a conflict between "a trading, industrious, and learned people, settled from time immortal" and "a wandering people" bereft of knowledge and industry, "subsisting solely by rapine."[38]

Back in the *Dictionnaire philosophique*, Voltaire goes so far as to compare the Israelites to "American cannibals." In this context, he ironically recounts the story of a Jesuit priest in Canada, who in a sermon described Moses's edicts: "exterminate without mercy all the poor inhabitants of the Land of Canaan, who did not know these laws; cut their throats, massacre the whole lot, men, women, old people, children, animals, for the greater glory of God."[39]

Voltaire goes on to recount that, following the sermon, one of the French settlers cried out with horror, "But those are the cannibals' rules!," whereupon one of the local "cannibals" rose up in protest, countering that Native Americans had never possessed such cruel laws. This would seem to be an ironic variation on Montaigne's famous *Des cannibales*, which praises the human flesh-eaters for their simplicity, casting Europeans' belief in the supremacy of reason over ignorance in an absurd light.[40] However, Voltaire's aim was to portray the Hebrews as total savages, who even outdid the cannibals. By doing so, he sought to undermine the special status that Christianity accorded the chosen people and the Old Testament, presenting Christianity's Urtext as barbarous and savage.

Apologetic Writings in Defense of the Israelites

Apologetic explanations of the conquest of Canaan were offered by the early church fathers. The most prominent was that provided by Epiphanius, in the fourth century, who justified the takeover of Canaan by claiming that the land had been granted to Shem and his descendants by Noah after the Flood.[41]

As the question resurfaced during the Enlightenment, major thinkers were drawn into the discussion, in keeping with the skeptical atmosphere of the period. John Locke, for instance, maintained that the promised land was God's kingdom, and thus, the destruction decree hinged on the fact that the the adoration of other gods in that country constituted "an Act of High Treason."[42]

However, it was the English deists' harsh antibiblical excoriations—as well as those of their German and French counterparts—that turned the issue of the conquest of Canaan into an urgent challenge to conservative theologians and writers, thus generating the emergence of wide-ranging apologetic writing on the subject by English clergymen and Bible scholars.[43]

Most such apologies invoked the theological legitimacy of the conquest and sprang to the defense of the extermination commandment. This type of apology can be found in the writing of John Leland (1691–1766), a Presbyterian theologian who authored the first systematic argument against deism in England.[44] In fact, Leland's works gained a wider audience than that of the deists' books themselves and thus contributed substantially to the propagation of their ideas in England and on the continent. Less than a year after the publication of Leland's book on Tindal, an extensive review was published in a German periodical, and his refutation of the arguments of other deist writers subsequently appeared in German translation.[45]

Seeking to defend the Israelites, Leland claims that God's right to punish humans and people who have sinned gravely is incontestable. He argues that the sins of the Canaanites—sacrificing their children to Moloch, incest, sodomy, and bestiality—are crimes that "in all civiliz'd countries deserv'd death."[46] He goes on to assert that in other biblical instances, God Himself had exterminated individuals and groups that perpetrated such acts, for instance, by celestial fire (in Sodom and Gomorrah), plague, or other forms of punishment. Extermination at the hands of the Israelites was thus nothing but another instrument in God's hands to enforce punishment.

Inasmuch as the deists sought to undermine the religious legitimacy of the divine commandment, Leland and similar writers strove to buttress and strengthen its authority. On both sides of the dispute, the question of the conquest of the land and of the extermination of its inhabitants presented a *theological* challenge within the framework of the debate regarding Revelation. In this type of religious apologetics, the moral-political dimension is negligible; since we are dealing with one of God's commandments, there is no reason to censure the Israelites for carrying out the deeds.

Within the framework of this apologetic argument it was stressed that this divine mandate was something unique and should therefore not be invoked as justification for similar actions. An early instance of this interpretive restriction is to be found in the writings of Francisco de Vitoria (1483–1546), one of the "founding fathers" of international law. This Spanish theologian claimed that the Israelites had slaughtered the residents of Jericho in good faith (Joshua 6:21) because they were commanded to do so by God—but that such commandments belonged only to biblical times and should not be emulated thereafter.[47] Hugo Grotius (1583–1645) took a similar stance, claiming that the extermination of the seven peoples of Canaan was carried out in accordance with a special mandate from God [*speciale mandatum dei*] issued only for this specific purpose.[48] Other versions of this theological-jurisprudential theory appeared in many eighteenth-century commentaries. Leland's essay, for example, refers to arguments made by Thomas Paine (1739–1809), who used the biblical precedent to castigate the crimes of the Spanish in America: "I shall only say, that if no Nation undertakes to exterminate another, and possess their Country without as evident Proofs of a divine Commission, as the Israelites had, we need not be afraid of any ill Consequences that may be drawn from this Example . . . if there had been no such Thing ever done, as the Extirpation of the Canaanites by the Israelites, The

Spaniards wou'd have done what they did, which was evidently owing to their own Ambition, Avarice, and Cruelty."[49]

While this strategy continued to uphold the scriptures' validity and sanctity, it removed the extermination issue from human history, thereby defusing its volatility as a moral problem and a dangerous political precedent.

Michaelis: The Nomads' Historical Right

Despite the fact that the translation of the deists' texts into German left a noticeable mark on German Bible scholarship, instances of blanket condemnation of the morality of the Old Testament remained marginal within the German scholarly milieu. Edelmann's outright denunciation defined the boundaries of acceptable scripture criticism within the German states. His book was banned, and his outlook remained anathema to theologians and scholars of religion. It is not surprising that Reimarus refrained from publishing his book during his lifetime.

According to Jonathan Israel, the German Enlightenment was split between an informal, underground network of radical freethinkers such as Edelmann and Reimarus, and a more conservative intellectual elite.[50] With respect to the Bible, the major project of mainstream Enlightenment was not to undermine the text but to establish its validity through the vehicle of historical criticism, a methodology that was primarily designed to serve as an antidote to religious skepticism.[51] The proponents of this method, who developed it to its ultimate refinement, were the members of Göttingen's historical-critical school.

Faced with the freethinkers' allegations regarding the cruelty of the Israelites, leading German Bible scholars energetically engaged themselves in defending the righteousness [*Gerechtigkeit*] of the occupation as well as the Israelites' right to the land. Upholding the Israelites' righteousness, in this context, is one of the major themes in Michaelis's work.

Michaelis's arguments on this theme recur throughout his work—in at least five different essays.[52] *Mosaishces Recht* devotes an especially comprehensive section (running to more than sixty pages) to the question of "Recht der Israeliten in Palästina," a topic debated at greater length than any other single issue in the book.[53] Michaelis begins the debate by presenting the difficulty that Moses's laws on this subject present: "How Moses, therefore, should have declared war against a nation that had never attacked the Israelites and, should have, in the name of God, made a gift of their country to his people, appears somewhat incomprehensible, and in fact much of a piece with the Pope's generosity to the Spaniards, in making them a present of America. Nor has indeed the opportunity been overlooked of attacking Christianity in this quarter, as founded on the Mosaic dispensation, and of representing the war which Moses authorized, as in the highest degree unjust."[54]

Michaelis, here, fosters the arguments of Christianity's detractors, including their recurring comparison between the commandment to conquer Canaan and the Pope's license to the Spanish to conquer America.[55] He was, however, loath to adopt the deists' claims against the Israelites. In his historical criticism, Michaelis sought to reaffirm the credibility and authenticity of the Old Testament by positioning it within the ancient context in which it was written. As Daniel Weidner has shown, Michaelis conceives Moses to be both the historical figure described by the biblical text and the author of the text itself.[56] And since Moses is the lawgiver, the authority of those laws is contingent on the authority of the text. Accepting Moses as a diabolical criminal and acquiescing to the undermining of the moral stature of his rules would hence severely dent the historical credibility of the text he wrote. The desire to defend the discipline of biblical history and reassert the historical validity of scripture thus entailed defending the moral integrity of Moses's commandments.

Several German university scholars of the period who addressed the extermination of the Canaanites, such as theologian Johann Friedrich Wilhelm Jerusalem (1709–1789), reiterated the traditional arguments centering on their vices and idolatry.[57] Michaelis followed a different path. He took great pains to describe the history of the Hebrews within the context of the general history of nations rather than within the traditional salvation narrative. The challenge he faced was to explain the commandment to exterminate the peoples of Canaan and to justify it solely on historical grounds, without recourse to theological anchoring. As mentioned above, the principal argument that theologians and clergymen had employed to justify the war of extermination was that, in punishing the Canaanites for their sins, the Israelites were merely pawns in the hands of providence. But this argument was incompatible with the rationalist thinking of German Enlightenment writers.

In Michaelis's terms, the fact that all military conquests, indeed all earthly occurrences, are directed by God does not justify war: "Every country which a people conquers by force of arms, is given into their hands by Providence; and even their victories are its gift: and the same Providence may punish a guilty nation by the hands of its enemies, be their cause just or unjust, as it may; but then this is no argument for the justice of war, otherwise we must admit, with all its consequences, the principle, that *whatever is, is right*."[58]

With this philosophical argument, Michaelis upheld the honor of religion and of providence's role in the world; but by extending the scope of providence to cover every human action, he removed the issue from the historical debate concerning the motives and justifications of the Hebrews' deeds. Given their newfound status, that of a regular historical entity, the actions of the Israelites could not be justified teleologically, that is, as the implementation of the divine plan through the vehicle of history. Michaelis further clarified his objection to the divine commandment purely on grounds of religious tolerance; a war of extermination based on the argument that "that's what God decided" would be harmful to religion, and might even be used by the Pope as grounds for abrogating his agreements with the Protestants, declaring that they must all convert or be damned.[59]

In keeping with this assertion, Michaelis justified the conquest of Canaan on juridical grounds, invoking the Israelites' legal and historical right to the land. This claim was one of Michaelis's first innovations, published as early as 1756, in his lecture to the *Königliche Gesellschaft der Wissenschaften* on the topic of "the nomadic shepherds of ancient Palestine."[60] Michaelis claimed that the land later called Canaan had belonged to the Mesopotamian nomads from whom Abraham's forefathers sprang. Therefore, Abraham's family had possessed the right to the land long before the birth of the patriarch himself. A condensed version of this claim is highlighted in *Mosaisches Recht*: "Palestine had from time immemorial been a land of Hebrew herdsmen; and the Israelites who had never abandoned their right to it claimed it again of the Canaanites as unlawful possessors."[61]

To prove this point, Michaelis developed a theory according to which the Canaanites were actually later, transient "settlers" [*Colonisten*]. Taken at face value, this assertion would appear to contradict the description in Genesis, which cites several towns—such as Hebron, Shechem, and Be'er Sheba—as already extant in the patriarchs' time. Subsequently, most scholars agreed that the Canaanites were the first people to settle the land after the Flood—the stance taken, for example, by the writers of the English *Universal History*.[62]

Citing certain textual evidence, Michaelis offered an alternative narrative. The Canaanites, he asserted, had originated from a territory on the shores of the Red Sea, but they had overstepped their boundaries, infiltrated the land and had gradually appropriated it: "The Canaanites were nothing but Colonists . . . the Phoenicians originally lived on the sea shore . . . in Abraham's time the land was still owned by Mesopotamian tent-dwellers, and whoever wished to adopt that lifestyle immigrated there."[63]

Palestine was the "tent-dwellers' homeland," and therefore, the battle waged against the Canaanites who lived on the West Bank of the Jordan was justifiable and lawful. The Canaanites, on the contrary, are described as colonists who exploited the patriarchs' hospitality.[64]

The Israelites' right to their "fatherland" having been proved, there remained the question of why their war of conquest had to be prosecuted in so murderous a fashion. Like earlier biblical apologists, Michaelis attributed the extermination to the Canaanites' "loathsomeness."[65] In *Mosaisches Recht*, Michaelis claimed that the Canaanite "extermination" [*Vertilgung*] was a "natural outcome" of a war fought by a people seeking to settle a land and work it, and had hence been forced to "kill" [*todtschlagen*] the farmers already settled there.[66]

Despite its many weaknesses, Michaelis's theory of the Hebrews' natural right to the land proved so expedient that it was readily adopted by the greatest German scholars of the time. In the 1761 edition of his *Universalhistorie*, Johann Christoph Gatterer (1727–1799) followed his Göttingen colleague in describing the Canaanites as "foreign settlers" from the shores of the Red Sea, who had usurped the land formerly in the possession of Abraham's forefathers, the nomadic shepherds. "The justifiability of the Israelites' war against the Canaanites in the West Bank of the Jordan was based on the fact that the Israelites, who roamed as tent-dwellers from place to place, were still the rightful owners of the land from time immemorial; as opposed to the Canaanites and Phoenicians, who were no more than newcomers and colonists, recently arrived from the Red Sea."[67]

Gatterer concluded that the Israelites had "the fullest right" to "uproot" [*entrisen*] the "illegal settlers" through war. Accusing the Canaanites of illegal settlement of the land is also the perfect response to the arguments pertaining to the conquest's cruelty: "The charge of this war's cruel means can thus be rejected on the grounds that anyone who did not resist, but simply vacated the land they had illegally taken over, was shown mercy."[68]

The attempt to justify the conquest of Canaan by employing nonreligious arguments gave rise to another theory that gained some popularity in Germany. Indeed, Johann Ernst Faber (1745–1774), Michaelis's disciple and subsequent rival, devoted an extensive chapter to it in his *Archäologie der Hebräer*, published in 1773.[69] Like Michaelis, Faber expounded on the traditional justifications for the extermination of the Canaanites and proceeded to rule them out one by one.[70] However, he likewise rejected Michaelis's thesis, according to which the Canaanites had stolen Abraham's family's ancestral homestead, calling it a "monstrous inconsistency."[71]

The argument that Faber formulated in response to the *Freygeisters*' charges is quite different: since the Israelites were forced to flee Egypt and, as no option was open to them, their invasion of Canaan must be regarded as legitimate and lawful. "Every people enjoys an equal right to any other on our Globe. If it were not tolerated somewhere, it cannot be blamed when it came to the first and best place it could have come by. And when that was not to be got by good, it tries to conquer it by force. A people so exiled could not have been expected to leave the world, and indeed crossing into another planet is not so simple. Thus, it has the right to establish itself in another land, either through beneficent means or through force."[72]

The right to the land is here not a function of some earlier right of ownership but of the "state of emergency" [*Notrecht*] in which the people found themselves after having been forced to flee Egypt, where they had, in turn, been subjected to "tyrannical oppression." And Canaan was also the land in which the Israelites had evolved into a people, and hence it was to be considered their homeland above any other land: "Since this land was the place where they originally arose, it could rightly consider it its homeland, since its forefathers herded their sheep in its expansive pastures. . . . What other land but Canaan can one name, to which the Israelites had a justified claim?"[73]

Faber, moreover, informs his readers that, in fact, most of the Canaanites were not actually exterminated but rather fled to Africa and settled there.[74] He relies here on sixth-century historian Procopius's claim, according to which two marble columns found in Tangiers bear the Phoenician inscription "we have fled the robber Joshua."[75]

Herder: The War of the Semites and the Hamites

While Michaelis's theory of the Hebrews' historical right to the land predominated among German scholarly circles, some Bible scholars employed different reasoning to justify the extermination of the Canaanites, invoking the supremacy of the Israelites over the native peoples. In this version, the war of conquest is presented as a campaign of extermination waged against lowly "hordes." Such is the pathetic description provided by Johann Gottfried Herder (1744–1803), perhaps the Hebrews' most ardent supporter within the circle of Enlightenment thinkers, in his *Vom Geist der Ebräischen Poesie*.

Herder's argument combined the traditional justifications for the conquest of Canaan with new, ethnographic explanations. Alluding to Michaelis's theory, he claimed that the Canaanites had "usurped the land" from the sons of Abraham. He termed the Israelites' war a zealous "holy war" unparalleled by later-era combat. And this was a war over territory, whose *casus belli* was "the Fatherland": "Israel fought *pro aris et focis patrum*, for from this country they came, and there lay the bones of their fathers. There was many a grove, and altar, sacred to the God of their fathers; every thing, which among ancient nations was denominated the family sanctuary, was to be sought there."[76]

However, stressing these rights does not in itself explain the commandment issued by Moses to exterminate the inhabitants of Canaan. The duty to exterminate the peoples of Canaan was linked to their characteristics. Clearly, claimed Herder, the Israelites could not have dwelt among them because of the jarring contrast between their lifestyle and that of the locals:

> These nations were warlike hordes, and Israel was to be a peaceful, agricultural people. A part of the inhabitants of the country were troglodytes, dwellers in caves, and we know how debased and hateful these were in the eyes of Nomad tribes. . . . They must be expelled from the country on account of their savage mode of life, the promiscuous intercourse of the sexes, and other vices among them. The Hamitic superstition, however, was the blackest of all, for human sacrifices existed among them, and how could this coexist with the Mosaic economy and political constitution? Only one means remained of attaining the end, the sad but commonplace right of war, as it existed in those times. They must leave the country or be destroyed!![77]

Herder used two exclamation marks to justify extermination of the Canaanites—cave dwellers [*Troglodyten*] whose lifestyle was base and abhorrent and whose sexual practices were "unnatural."

Herder's configuration of these "base" human groups is still not fully distinguishable from the more traditional characterization of the idolatrous peoples who inhabited the ancient world prior to the election of the Israelites as the chosen people. Idolatry was linked to "crudity" [*Rohheit*] and "sensuality" [*Sinnlichkeit*], but these were religious characteristics, more distinctly identified with moral corruption than with primitiveness.

However, Herder endows the term *base* [*niedrig*] with a new, modern meaning, linked to the primordial characteristics of the Canaanite peoples. Eutyphron, one of the protagonists in Herder's dialogue, who in fact generally represents Herder's stance, proceeds to explain to his friend why the Hebrews and the Canaanites could not live in the same land, and why Moses commanded their extermination with such "fervor": "It could not have occurred to [Moses] that the two peoples live together in the same land. The Semites regarded the Hamites as a slave-people [*Knechtsstamm*], with whom even the temperate Abraham ruled out any assimilation . . . marriage to a Canaanite woman was considered a slight to the tribe's honor—in short, the two peoples differed not only religiously, but also in the sense of their living environment, their customs and their ways of thought; fraternity between the two was inconceivable."[78]

Seemingly just another variation on the traditional Christian apology for the Canaanite extermination based on their idolatrous religion or base customs, Herder's explanation, in fact, introduces a new element to distinguish Hebrews from Canaanites, namely the attribution to "tribe" [*Stamm*]. While the Hebrews are Semites [*Semiten*], the Canaanites are sons of the Hamitic tribe [*Chamiten*]. The contrast and the animosity between the Semites and the Hamites are portrayed as primordial and profound.

Herder goes on to extol the supremacy of the Semites' language and religion, as well as their conception of human moral obligations. He believes that the Hamitic religion is saturated with "dark idolatry," whereas the Semites' religion is sacred, simple and nonsensual.[79] From the antediluvian world, the sons of Shem carried with them "the purest ideas about religion and Creation."

This description is explicitly based on the curse that Noah cast on Canaan, son of Ham, that is, "A servant of servants shall he be unto his brethren" (Genesis 9:25). Ever since the sixteenth century, the biblical tradition pertaining to Canaan's curse served as a major source of legitimacy for the enslavement and colonization of African peoples.[80] Here, Herder employs it to justify retroactively the war of extermination against the Canaanites themselves.

As in other aspects of his treatment of Hebrew history, Herder's work here signifies a turning point in the debate on the Canaanite extermination. His contrasting of the Semite and Hamitic elements shuns the allegedly rational historical approach of Michaelis and his Göttingen circle. He furthermore infuses the debate with protoracist concepts regarding the link between *Stamm* and *Kultur*.

No less importantly, Herder views the Hebrews' triumph over the Canaanites as a pivotal, necessary stage in the expansion of pure religion and the idea of the oneness of God. Thus, the Canaanite extermination fits into a universal process of "world enlightenment" [*Weltaufklärung*] or of the "education" [*Erziehung*] of the human race. However, within the German conception of the Enlightenment, this historic process of overcoming ignorance hinges no less on belief than it does on reason, that is, on the development and expansion of a religion of revelation. According to this conception, as articulated most succinctly in Lessing's *Die Erziehung des Menschengeschlechts*, God chose the Israelites to spread the true belief among the idolaters so that "the future educators of the human race" may arise from this people.[81]

Summary: Biblical Extermination as a Modern Problem

Defending the legitimacy of the Canaanite campaign and the extermination of its population became a hallmark of German Bible scholarship of the historical-critical school. It was the vitriolic nature of the deists' and other freethinkers' attacks on the Bible on this issue that aroused German conservative scholars to spring to the defense of the Israelites, considering this a crucial element in their argumentation.

Nevertheless, the historical methodology employed by these German Bible scholars fundamentally transformed the image of the biblical past, signifying a break from traditional readings of scripture. This shift was well reflected in the debate over the conquest of Canaan. The arguments offered by Michaelis and his followers in defense of the land's conquest were based on the assumption that within the bounds of a modern, rational debate, this campaign of conquest could no longer be justified by the religious excuse of holy war.

The focal point of the debate shifted from the question of legitimacy of a religious war to the issue of historical rights to a territory and the link between a people and a tract of land. The brutality of the Canaanite peoples' extermination, as described in scripture, engendered harsh attacks on the Israelites by detractors of the Bible. But by the same token, it forced its apologists to formulate ever more rigorous defenses of these deeds and in so doing, to take modern ethnic categories to their very extremes.

When the deists condemned the "extermination ideology" underlying the commandment to annihilate the peoples of Canaan, they were attacking not only the biblical story itself but also a more broadly based ideology symbolized by this commandment—an ideology of a purifying violence that justified annihilating entire populations because of their religion. This was the same ideology that was fully realized with the conquest and extermination of the indigenous peoples of the Americas. Criticism of the Canaanite extermination was thus part and parcel of the decline of the religious war ideology in the Enlightenment era.

The conservative German scholars could not repudiate Moses, since doing so would mean rejecting the Bible as a whole. They thus had to formulate a new defense of the Canaanite extermination, or, in broader terms, a new defense for killing off a population that would not involve divine intervention.

Apologetic justifications for the extermination of the Canaanites have been offered throughout the history of Christian theology. The novel component introduced by the historical-critical school was the attempt to justify the massacre in terms of juridical and political concepts. No longer regarded a unique, theological event of the miraculous past, it was now proclaimed to be a political act legitimized by particular circumstances.

In this fashion, Michaelis, Herder, and their peers formulated one of the earliest justifications for genocide on ethnic grounds. Once perceived as an extraordinary outburst of divine violence, the Canaanite extermination was now normalized and naturalized, portrayed as a predictable and even necessary outcome of human nature. The religious opposition between Christian Europe and non-European idolatrous peoples, encrypted into the biblical extermination commandment, did not vanish with the secularization of European thought. Rather, it was transformed into a new, no less extremist, and dangerous kind of antagonism.

Notes

1. Jan Assmann, *Moses the Egyptian: The Memory of Egypt in Western Monotheism* (Cambridge. MA: Harvard University Press, 1997).

2. Johann Gottfried Eichhorn, *Allgemeine Bibliothek der biblischen Litteratur* (Leipzig: Weidmann, 1787), 1261–1262.

3. The relevant essays are discussed later in this chapter.

4. Two recent works deal with the figure of Joshua in Judaism and in Christianity. See: Thomas R. Elssner, *Josua und seine Kriege in jüdischer und christlicher Rezeptionsgeschichte* (Stuttgart: W. Kohlhammer, 2008); Cornelius Houtman, "Josua im Urteil einiger Freidenker," in *The Land of Israel in Bible, History, and Theology: Studies in Honour of Ed Noort*, ed. Jacques van Ruiten and J. Cornelius de Vos (Leiden: Brill, 2009), 339–355. The story of Canaan was used extensively in the English colonialist project in America. See in particular: Paul Stevens, "'Leviticus Thinking' and the Rhetoric of Early Modern Colonialism" *Criticism* 35 (1993): 441–461. For an essay that addresses the conquest of Canaan from the perspective of the Israeli-Palestinian conflict and the theological context, see: Nur Masalha, "Reading

the Bible with the Eyes of the Canaanites: Neo-Zionism, Political Theology and the Land Traditions of the Bible (1967 to Gaza 2009)," *Holy Land Studies* 8 (2009): 55–108.

5. Nadav Na'aman, *Canaan in the 2nd Millennium B.C.E.* (Winona Lake, IN: Eisenbrauns, 2005), 377–78; Lori L. Rowlett, *Joshua and the Rhetoric of Violence: A New Historicist Analysis* (Sheffield: Sheffield Academic Press, 1996), 30–49.

6. Tertullian, *Adversus Marcionem* (Oxford: Clarendon, 1972), 2:18, 4:23; See: Heikki Räisänen, "Marcion," in *A Companion to Second-Century Christian "Heretics,"* ed. Antti Marjanen and Petri Luomanen (Leiden: Brill, 2008), 108–109.

7. See: Houtman, "Josua im Urteil einiger Freidenker," 339–344.

8. Jean Meslier, *Le bon sens du curé J. Meslier, suivi de son testament* (Paris: Anthropos, 1970), 1:193–194.

9. Regarding the book's surreptitious publication, see: Jonathan I. Israel, *Enlightenment Contested: Philosophy, Modernity, and the Emancipation of Man 1670–1752* (Oxford: Oxford University Press, 2006), 726.

10. James A. Herrick, *The Radical Rhetoric of the English Deists: The Discourse of Skepticism, 1680–1750* (Columbia: University of South Carolina Press, 1997), 2–3.

11. See: David S. Katz, *God's Last Words: Reading the English Bible from the Reformation to Fundamentalism* (New Haven, CT: Yale University Press, 2004), 116–153; Diego Lucci, *Scripture and Deism: The Biblical Criticism of the Eighteenth-Century British Deists* (New York: Peter Lang, 2008), 56–58.

12. Frank Manuel, *The Broken Staff: Judaism through Christian Eyes* (Cambridge, MA: Harvard University Press, 1992), 187–188.

13. See, for instance: Magne Saebo, *Hebrew Bible / Old Testament: The History of Its Interpretation* (Göttingen: Vandenhoeck & Ruprecht, 2008), 864.

14. Matthew Tindal, *Christianity as Old as the Creation* (London: W. Innys, 1730), 84.

15. Tindal, *Christianity as Old as the Creation*, 245.

16. Thomas Morgan, *The Moral Philosopher: In a Dialogue between Philalethes a Christian Deist, and Theophanes a Christian Jew* (London, 1738), 28.

17. Todd M. Endelman, *The Jews of Georgian England, 1714–1830: Tradition and Change in a Liberal Society* (Ann Arbor. University of Michigan, 1999), 96–97.

18. Laura M. Stevens, *The Poor Indians: British Missionaries, Native Americans, and Colonial Sensibility* (Philadelphia: University of Pennsylvania, 2004), 123–130; Colin Haydon, *Anti-Catholicism in Eighteenth-Century England, c. 1714–1780: A Political and Social Study* (Manchester: Manchester University, 1993), 136.

19. Tindal, *Christianity as Old as the Creation*, 239.

20. Henry St. John Bolingbroke, *Philosophical Works* (London: J. Whiston, 1754), 5: 376.

21. Luis N. Rivera, *A Violent Evangelism: The Political and Religious Conquest of the Americas* (Louisville, KY: Westminster/John Knox, 1992), 236–237.

22. Paul Stevens, "'Leviticus Thinking,'" 441–461.

23. William Alexander, *An Encouragement to Colonies* (London: W. Stansby, 1624), 152; Robert Gray, *A Good Speed to Virginia* (London: William Welbie, 1609); William Bradford, *History of Plymouth Plantation, 1620–1647* (Boston: John Bellamie, 1650).

24. S. J. Barnett, *The Enlightenment and Religion: The Myths of Modernity* (Manchester: Manchester University Press, 2003), 105.

25. Jonathan Sheehan, *The Enlightenment Bible: Translation, Scholarship, Culture* (Princeton: Princeton University Press, 2005), 38.

26. Christopher Voigt, *Der englische Deismus in Deutschland: Eine Studie zur Rezeption englisch-deistischer Literatur in deutschen Zeitschriften und Kompendien des 18. Jahrhunderts* (Tübingen: Mohr Siebeck, 2003), 11.

27. Jan van den Berg, "English Deism and Germany: The Thomas Morgan Controversy," *Journal of Ecclesiastical History* 59 (2008): 48-61.

28. Paul Spalding, *Seize the Book, Jail the Author: Johann Lorenz Schmidt and Censorship in Eighteenth-Century Germany* (West Lafayette, IN: Purdue University Press, 1998), 184-185.

29. Matthew Tindal, *Beweis, daß das Christenthum so alt als die Welt sey, nebst Herrn Jacob Fosters Widerlegung desselben. Beydes aus dem Englischen übersetzt* (Frankfurt, 1741).

30. On Edelmann, see: Rüdiger Otto, "Johann Christian Edelmanns' Criticism of the Bible and its Relation to Spinoza," in *Disguised and Overt Spinozism around 1700*, ed. Wiep van Bunge and W. N. A. Klever (Leiden: Brill, 1996), 171-191; Thomas P. Saine, *The Problem of Being Modern, or, The German Pursuit of Enlightenment from Leibniz to the French Revolution* (Detroit. MI: Wayne State University Press, 1997), 205-210.

31. Johann Christian Edelmann, *Sämtliche Schriften in Einzelausgabe* (Stuttgart: Frommann-Holzboog, 1987).

32. Saine, *The Problem of Being Modern*, 206.

33. Edelmann, *Sämtliche Schriften*, 7: 124.

34. Edelmann, *Sämtliche Schriften*, 7: 133.

35. Hermann Samuel Reimarus, *Uebrige noch ungedruckte Werke des Wolfenbüttlischen Fragmentisten* (1787).

36. Reimarus, *Uebrige noch ungedruckte Werke des Wolfenbüttlischen Fragmentisten*, 171-172.

37. Voltaire, *Dictionnaire philosophique*, Vol. 19 of *Oeuvres* (Paris: Granier, 1879), 524.

38. Voltaire, "Philosophical Dictionary," in *The Complete Romances of Voltaire* (New York, Walter J. Black, 1927), 378.

39. Voltaire, *Political Writings*, ed. David Williams (Cambridge, UK: Cambridge University Press, 1994), 23.

40. Michel de Montaigne, "Des cannibales," in *Les Essais: Oeuvres complètes*, ed. Maurice Rat and Albert Thibaudet (Paris: Gallimard, 1962), 1:31.

41. Epiphanius, *Panarion*, trans. Frank Williams (Leiden: Brill, 2009), 32-33.

42. John Locke, *A Letter Concerning Toleration*, ed. Ian Shapiro. (New Haven: CT, 2003 [1689]), 240.

43. See, for example: John Leland, *An Answer to a Late Book Entitled, Christianity as Old as the Creation* (Dublin: S. Powell, 1733), 428.

44. Lucci, *Scripture and Deism*, 256.

45. Voigt, *Der englische Deismus in Deutschland*, 89-90, 130.

46. Leland, *An Answer to a Late Book*, 429.

47. Elssner, *Josua und seine Kriege*, 277-279.

48. Hugo Grotius, *De Jure Belli Ac Pacis* (Paris: Buon, 1625), 35.

49. Leland, "An Answer," 437.

50. Jonathan Israel, *Democratic Enlightenment: Philosophy, Revolution, and Human Rights, 1750-1790* (Oxford: Oxford University Press, 2011), 172-178.

51. Michael C. Carhart, *The Science of Culture in Enlightenment Germany* (Cambridge, MA: Harvard University Press, 2007), 5-9; Sheehan, *The Enlightenment Bible*, 182-218.

52. For instance, Johann David Michaelis, *De nomadibus Palaestinae* (Göttingen: Vandenhoek, 1759); Johann David Michaelis, *Mosaisches Recht* (Frankfurt am Main: J. Gottlieb Garbe, 1775), 1:95-156.

53. Michaelis, *Mosaisches Recht*, 1:95–156.
54. Johann David Michaelis, *Commentaries on the Laws of Moses*, trans. Alexander Smith (London: Longman, 1814) 1:113.
55. Michaelis, *Commentaries on the Laws of Moses*, 97.
56. Daniel Weidner, "Politik und Ästhetik: Lektüre der Bibel bei Michaelis, Herder und de Wette," in *Hebräsiche Poesie und jüdischer Volksgeist: Die Wirkungsgeschichte Johann Gottfried Herders im Judentum Mittel-und Osteuropas*, ed. Christoph Schulte (Hildesheim: Olms, 2003), 43–44.
57. Johann Friedrich Jerusalem, *Briefe über die Mosaischen Schriften und Philosophie* (Braunschweig: Waisenhaus, 1783), 69.
58. Michaelis, *Commentaries on the Laws of Moses*, 115.
59. Michaelis, *Commentaries on the Laws of Moses*, 153.
60. Michaelis, "Die herumziehenden Hirten in dem alten Palästina," *Göttingische Gelehrte Anzeigen* 140 (1756): 1265–1271.
61. Michaelis, *Commentaries on the Laws of Moses*, 153.
62. George Sale, George Psalmanazar, Archibald Bower, George Shelvocke, John Campbell, and John Switnon, *An Universal History from the Earliest Account of Time* (London: Osborne, 1747), 2:193–194.
63. Michaelis, "Die herumziehenden Hirten," 1266–1267.
64. Michaelis, "Die herumziehenden Hirten," 1268.
65. Michaelis, "Die herumziehenden Hirten," 1268.
66. Michaelis, *Mosaisches Recht*, 125.
67. Johann Christoph Gatterer, *Handbuch der Universalhistorie nach ihrem gesamten Umfange* (Göttingen: Vandenhoeck, 1761), 188–189.
68. Gatterer, *Handbuch der Universalhistorie nach ihrem gesamten Umfange*, 189.
69. Johann Ernst Faber, *Archäologie der Hebräer* (Halle: Johann Jacob Curt, 1773), 70–100.
70. Faber, *Archäologie der Hebräer*, 78–80.
71. Faber, *Archäologie der Hebräer*, 86.
72. Faber, *Archäologie der Hebräer*, 95.
73. Faber, *Archäologie der Hebräer*, 96–97.
74. Faber, *Archäologie der Hebräer*, 100.
75. In German: "Wir sind dem Räuber Iosua dem Sohne Nave entflohen"; Procopius, *de bello Vandalico*, 2: 10.
76. Johann Gottfried von Herder, *The Spirit of Hebrew Poetry*, trans. James Marsh (Burlington, VT: Edward Smith, 1833), 2:140.
77. Herder, *The Spirit of Hebrew Poetry*, 139.
78. Johann Gottfried Herder, *Vom Geist der Ebräischen Poesie* (Dessau: Buchhandlung der Gelehrten, 1782–1783), 294.
79. Herder, *Vom Geist der Ebräischen Poesie*, 295.
80. For the early vicissitudes of this tradition, see: David M. Whitford, *The Curse of Ham in the Early Modern Era: The Bible and the Justifications for Slavery* (Farnham, UK: Ashgate, 2009), 77–105.
81. Gotthold Ephraim Lessing, *Die Erziehung des Menschengeschlechts* (Berlin: Christian Friedrich Voss, 1780), 13–14. And see chapter 1 of this book.

4 "Is Judah Indeed the Teutonic Fatherland?" The Hebrew Model and the Birth of German National Culture

THE SECOND PART of Georg Wilhelm Friedrich Hegel's early essay, *The Positivity of the Christian Religion* [*Die Positivität der christlichen Religion*, published in 1795], bears the intriguing title "Is Judah indeed the Teutonic Fatherland?" [*Ist denn Judäa der Thuiskonen Vaterland?*]. In this section, Hegel noted that the Germanic peoples had their own heroes, whom they extolled in their poems and folk celebrations and worshipped in their sacred groves, that is, until the arrival of Christianity in Germany: "Christianity has emptied Valhalla, felled the sacred groves, extirpated the national imagery as a shameful superstition, as a devilish poison, and given us instead the imagery of a nation whose climate, laws, culture, and interests are strange to us and whose history has no connection whatever with our own. A David or a Solomon lives in our popular imagination, but our country's own heroes slumber in learned history books".[1]

Hegel decried the erasure of the German people's original folk fantasy by Christianity, claiming it had been replaced by the fantasies and heroes of the Hebrews—a foreign, alien people who had nothing to do with the Germans. Hegel's objection to the Bible's excessive influence on German national culture expressed a resentment that was growing in German literary circles at the turn of the eighteenth century. Johann Wolfgang von Goethe likewise derided the "Biblical Flood" that had inundated German poetry prior to his own appearance on the literary scene, criticizing the poets of the time for drawing inspiration from "Jewish shepherd songs."[2] Although clearly serving their own cultural projects, the criticism voiced by these two commentators echoed a real phenomenon, namely great excitement over the Bible and intensive engagement with Hebrew poetry during the formative era of modern German culture. Indeed, writing about and under the influence of Hebrew poetry may be considered one of the initial trends in the effort to establish and define a unique German cultural identity.

In this chapter, I discuss the discourse on Hebrew poetry and the Hebrew cultural model in eighteenth-century German literature. In contrast to those scholars who associate reverence for the ancient Hebrews exclusively with Herder's work,

I seek to place this approach within a wider context. Reference to Hebrew poetry was a common practice of German literature of the period, especially among the writers of the mid-eighteenth-century *Sturm und Drang* circle. Furthermore, the Hebrew model allowed the German literature of the period to differentiate itself from the neoclassical literature of France, and to develop its own styles and themes. Years before Herder, this tendency characterized Friedrich Gottlieb Klopstock (1724–1803), a pioneer of German patriotic poetry and one of the fathers of modern German poetry. I furthermore tie German literary Hebraism to two contemporaneous cultural-conceptual developments. The first context is a novel conception of the Hebrew language and of Hebrew poetry as a natural, primary, and sublime language. Imitation of the Hebrews thus became a prominent feature of the *Sturm und Drang* poets' sentimental style, which was inextricably linked to Pietist Protestant ideology. Another, no less important context was the adoption of the ancient Hebrew model as an alternative cultural–political one to the dominant Greek-Roman model.

Baroque Theories of the Hebrew Source

As early as the mid-seventeenth century, German poets tended to portray their work as having descended from the poetry of the Bible. Many of these poets held to a theory according to which the biblical patriarchs had invented or developed the art of poetry itself.[3] As the Old Testament is so much richer in poetry than the New Testament, the "Hebrew poets" were seen as providing theological "legitimacy" to poetry.

Referencing Hebrew poetry to gain legitimacy was a function of German poetry's unique status during the Baroque period, when it sought legitimacy on two different fronts. On the one hand, these ancient poets were recruited to underpin the very act of writing poetry on a theological basis. This was effected chiefly by portraying poetry as a holy art, firmly entrenched in the history of redemption by way of associating it with divine speech and the language of the patriarchs. To gain legitimacy for their craft, poets pointed to the primordial nature of their art, citing a list of biblical poets. Greco-Roman poetry was, in this context, portrayed as a mere imitation of biblical poetry.

Besides claiming theological legitimacy, German poets also invoked the authority of biblical verse in order to defend German poetry vis-à-vis other European poetic languages. The relatively brief history of German poetics (compared to that of its French, Italian, and Spanish counterparts) led them to trace a genealogy that linked German to the language of the Bible, a tongue which the church fathers had decreed to be the language of Adam. This was intended to refute claims that German was a barbaric, parochial, and coarse tongue.

To this end, poets adopted a popular theory during the Baroque period, according to which Hebrew had given birth to German. One of the pioneers of this hypothesis was grammarian Justus Georg Schottel (1612–1676), who claimed that the Celts, allegedly the forefathers of the Germans, had brought the Hebrew language with them on their westward peregrination following the fall of the Tower of Babel.[4] The invention of a direct link between German and Hebrew, "the mother of tongues," released German writers from Greek poetic rules governing meter and syllables. Thus, for instance, Enoch Hanmann (1621–1680) could write as follows in a volume of the poetry of Martin Opitz, which he published in 1658: "Therefore it is known that our forefathers, the ancient Germans, received their poetry from the Hebrews / and before they knew how to read or write / already rhymed / and their rules / rights and religion they captured in short verses and chants."[5]

Speculation concerning the Hebrew origins of German began to appear as early as the sixteenth century. Chroniclers of the time claimed that the Germans were descendants of Ascenas (the son of Gomer and grandson of Japhet), and that their mythical ancient father Tuisco (who is mentioned by Tacitus) lived during the time of Abraham. Some even sought to link biblical Ascenas with the Askanier Saxon dynasty of Sachsen-Anhalt. A more circumspect version of the theory, according to which "Germano-Celt" and Hebrew were sister tongues of the same origin, began to circulate in the seventeenth century.

As late as the early eighteenth century, German philologists were still attempting to find etymological connections between Hebrew and German. But influential thinkers such as Gottfried Wilhelm Leibnitz (1646–1716) were beginning to undermine Hebrew's privileged status as the mother of tongues. Dutch orientalist Albrecht Schultens (1686–1750), for example, claimed in 1724 that Hebrew was not a divine language that was given to Adam but rather an offshoot of the Arab languages. Schultens indeed laid the groundwork for a methodical orientalist interpretation of the Bible based on the use of Arabic. Simultaneously, he and other orientalists refuted the theory regarding the Celts' Hebrew origins. Voltaire (1694–1778) had already dismissed the idea as "one of the greatest follies of the human spirit."[6]

The accumulation of knowledge in the fields of European and oriental philology that resulted in the historicization of linguistic inquiry led to the rejection of this genealogical linkage between German and Hebrew—and to a different approach to biblical history in general. European and oriental peoples were now portrayed as belonging to different genealogies, and ethnographic descriptions and accounts resulted in a reclassification of the Bible and the Hebrew language in an "oriental" context.[7]

"A Beautiful Country Girl": Hebrew as a Poetic Ideal

Even after the demise of the Hebrew source theory, interest in the Hebrew language and in Hebrew poetry did not wane. In fact, it can be said to have intensified. Although Hebrew was dethroned from its seat as the mother tongue of the human race, claims of Hebrew's primacy persisted and were recontextualized. Hebrew poetry served as the ideal for the *Sturm und Drang* poets, headed by Klopstock, as well as for theologians Herder and Hamann and critics such as Johann Jacob Bodmer (1698–1783) and Johann Jacob Breitinger (1701–1776). In these writers' works, biblical themes formed the basis for developing a Christian sentimental style that sought to distinguish itself from French neoclassical stylistic influences.[8]

The mid-eighteenth-century project of founding a national German literature was characterized by an effort to distinguish it from other European literatures that had previously served as models for German poets and writers. First and foremost, German poets sought to buttress the status of the German language itself as a literary tongue, especially vis-à-vis the French. This aspiration formed the background to a literary feud between German and French poets that reached its apex in midcentury; a feud defined by literary scholar Jürgen Fohrmann as "the quarrel of nations." Unlike the earlier "quarrel of the Ancients and the Moderns" [*Querelle des Anciens et des Modernes*], which was waged mainly in France and questioned the ability of the moderns to measure up to the ancients, the later feud had a synchronic character. The poets of both nations faced off, each camp drawing its legitimacy from a different ancient source.[9]

German literary history attributes the new aesthetic values of the *Empfindsamkeit* (sentimentalism) and *Strum und Drang* movements to the rise of a new bourgeois class of German readers who were alienated from the restrained, courtly aesthetics of the classicist style. Many poets of the period sought to distance themselves from the influence of the French classicist style as represented in Germany by Johann Christoph Gottsched (1700–1766), favoring alternative sources of influence like Shakespeare and Edward Young.[10]

German poets and playwrights who strove to formulate a cultural identity unfettered by religious association sought literary continuity with an ancient, privileged tradition. This, however, presented a difficulty, since classical—and especially Latin—poetry was identified with French poetry and the French language in general. Distinguishing themselves from classicism necessitated choosing separate themes and searching for alternative sources of inspiration. Antiquary and critic Johann Joachim Winckelmann (1717–1768) proposed that Greek poetry and art serve as a model for German culture.[11] In the decades that followed, this ideal fed Weimar classicism, the literary movement led by Goethe and Friedrich Schiller (1705–1805), which took ancient Greece as its source of inspiration. Yet, while they followed Winckelmann, another camp of German poets and writers extolled a different model during the midcentury, namely that of the Hebrews. One of the pioneers of this group was Johann Georg Hamann, who called on poets and men of letters not to forgo the ancients but, indeed, to move further back into history than the Greeks to whom Winckelmann and his peers clung. He used the biblical expression "broken cisterns" [*durchlöcherten Brunnen*, Jeremiah 2:13] to describe the Greek sources, calling the Hebrew texts "the most vibrant source of ancient times."[12]

No one responded to this call to return to the Hebrew source more enthusiastically than Johann Gottfried Herder, Hamann's friend and disciple. His early essay of 1769, *The Archaeology of the Hebrews* [*Archäologie der Hebräer*], heralded an intellectual–interpretive project that posited the Hebrews as an aesthetic and political ideal. While Herder commended Winckelmann for his approach to the ancient world, he criticized the exaggerated importance that the latter attached to the Greek contribution. Following Hamann, he proposed an alternative to the idolization of the classical world in the form of "pilgrimages to the East" [*Wallfahrten nach den Morgenländern*]. As conceived by Herder, the "Orient" [*das Morgenland*] had preceded the Greeks, and thus offered a more primary source of culture in general—and of poetry in particular.[13] Although he did not clearly demarcate a cultural–geographic unit, to him, the document that embodied the orient above all others was the Bible, which he consistently referred to as "Hebrew poetry."

This reawakening of interest in biblical themes was not confined to theology and interpretation, but extended to German poetry and theater as well, and the Old Testament consequently became a far more popular theme than the New Testament.[14] The upsurge in biblical interest was fed by a new aesthetic sensibility, which also emerged in England and Scotland at around the same time. Unlike during the Renaissance and the Baroque—when Hebrew was lauded as a perfect language with no blemishes, an ideal that transcended the faulty languages born after the confusion of tongues that began with the fall of the Tower of Babel—during the mid-eighteenth century, theologians, poets, and critics began to find a new quality of naturalness, sublimity, and emotionality in Hebrew speech and poetry.

The most substantial development within this trend was the publication by Michaelis, in 1758, of the lectures of English bishop Robert Lowth (1710–1787).[15] Through its wide impact, this book turned Hebrew poetry into a major theme in the German aesthetic-poetic discussion. As shown in the first chapter, Lowth depicted the Hebrews as an oriental nature-people and read the Bible as a majestic poetic creation that preserved primary and natural modes of expression. According to Lowth, the biblical text was a noble expression of natural forces themselves, an unmediated overflowing of majestic powers, a tempestuous manifestation of the primeval soul. When Lowth's claims appeared, they stood in stark contrast to those prevalent in the period's "republic of letters." Enlightenment philosophers tended to depict Hebrew poetry as coarse, unclear, and vague, created under the influence of the Orient's hot climes. Even those scholars who did not question the Bible's authority generally agreed that its beauty fell short of that of classical poetry, since it did not abide by Aristotelian poetic principles for a start.[16]

Lowth, by contrast, rehabilitated oriental poetry: he described Hebrew poets as natural bards who gave their feelings free rein. This depiction of Hebrew as the natural language was formulated most succinctly by Herder in his *The Spirit of Hebrew Poetry*. In this work's imagined dialogue, Alciphron, the more critical of the two interlocutors, begins by describing Hebrew as "a poor, barbaric tongue" and goes so far as to compare it to the languages of the Huron Native Americans.[17] Herder's view is articulated by Euthyphron, who does not deny that Hebrew is simple and unrefined, but claims, on the contrary, that it is these very qualities that grant it its singular character. According to Euthyphron, Hebrew should be compared to "a poor but beautiful and pure country girl" [*schönes und reines Landmädchen*].[18] Indeed, he proceeded to maintain, the fact that the Hebrew language was poor in nouns and rich in verbs rendered it a more vibrant, poetic, and younger language than its European sisters. "Even should I admit that for an abstract reasoner the Hebrew language may not be best, still it is, in regard to this active form of it so much the more favourable to the poet. Everything in it proclaims 'I live and move and act. The senses and the passions not abstract reasoners and philosophers were my creators. Thus I am formed for poetry, nay my whole essence is poetry'"[19]

Herder, who failed to secure a position at a university, used Hebrew to formulate the antagonistic stance of a *Sturm und Drang* Hebraist. Hebrew, according to him, may not be conducive to abstract thought but is, for that very reason, the language of poets. This kind of reading constituted a novel form of self-orientation vis-à-vis the biblical text. It situated the book's meaning on an aesthetic plane and thereby rendered it immune to attacks on its descriptive credibility. This was a paradigmatic shift in assessing the Old Testament, which made a significant impact on Herder's contemporaries. Simultaneously, the biblical prophet-poet was now described as a medium—a man firmly entrenched in a people through whom the popular spirit flows.

David versus Pindar: Klopstock as a Hebraist Poet

In his biography of Klopstock (which he wrote when his subject was still a young man), Bodmer described the poet's childhood and noted the decisive influence the Bible had exerted on Klopstock's personality ever since he came across it in his Lutheran preacher father's library.[20] This library indeed contained only several prayer books and ten copies of scripture—but not a single Latin or Greek book of poetry. The young boy was drawn to scripture from an early age, "less because of his father's preaching than from his own inner taste." Bodmer goes on to describe: "While still in his childhood, he was so well acquainted with the forms of the Hebrew language, and the figurative way of representing things, which he found in them, that he used them, unintentionally, wherever he would express anything with earnestness."[21]

This description, so characteristically *Sturm und Drang* in its aesthetic, well conveys the poetic ideal prevalent in mid-eighteenth-century literary circles: that of a great poet raised on the lap of Hebrew poetry and from whose writing its forms flow as if it were his very own tongue. Bodmer proceeds to describe how Klopstock was moved by the expressive natural images he found in the books of the Prophets and in Job. In the mornings, when he woke from his sleep, the boy would read aloud entire passages of these books. Hebrew poetry is depicted as having been firmly impressed on the poet's soul; his poetic expression was entirely bound up with the spirit of the Bible—especially on the subject of nature. According to Bodmer's description, the young Klopstock would identify natural phenomena according to the expressions he knew from the Bible: on gazing on a natural scene, he would exclaim that "he had already seen it in the Psalms or the Prophets."[22] "There is no precedent for Klopstock's poetry," Bodmer wrote at the time, "if it exists—it is to be found in the Prophets."[23]

Indeed, as Bernadette Malinowsky asserts, Klopstock signified a paradigm shift in the German lyrical tradition with his portrayal of the poet as a modern prophet.[24] The poetry of the Hebrews inspired an attempt to break free from rigid poetic rules and to express strong emotion and mysterious forces. This relation to poetry in general, and to biblical poetry in particular, was closely linked to the Pietist reading of the Bible.[25] A popular movement, Pietism's worldview denied that the educated critic was in any way superior to the common believer. The movement was based on emotional identification, tying understanding to emotion and the individual's psychic experience.

Within Pietist ideology, the depiction of religious–sentimental poetry as prophecy was no metaphor—it was understood literally. Contrary to orthodox Lutheran doctrine, which determined that the gates of prophecy had been sealed after the time of the apostles, Pietism maintained that Revelation was possible in the present, and that the present was in fact a continuation of holy history. It was in this vein that Klopstock claimed that the poet's task was not to imitate the prophets but rather to walk in their footsteps and "further develop what Revelation has taught us."[26] Gerhard Kaiser has written that Pietist ideology achieved a dialectical sacralization of the poet and secularization of prophecy itself. Both trends are to be found simultaneously in the work of Klopstock. The poet is sacralized and the prophet undergoes secularization.[27]

During the first half of the eighteenth century, radical Pietist circles produced several "inspired men" [*Inspirierten*]—individuals who were prone to public fits of twitching ecstasy and who claimed to be prophets speaking in God's name—who operated either individually or in groups.[28] Klopstock's poetic practices are reminiscent of the *Inspirierten*'s proclamations; witnesses who saw him read his poems aloud remarked that he used bodily gestures "as if speaking in a vision."[29]

The prophetic ideal and its concomitant self-conception were also manifested in his style. Literary critic Katrin Kohl has shown that the free-rhyming form—the most influential innovation that Klopstock introduced into the tradition of German poetry—drew its inspiration from biblical poetry and especially from the Psalms.[30] Her understanding differs from the commentaries of earlier scholars, who identified the source of this influence in Greek poetry, and especially in Pindar. As Kohl herself mentions, her assertion rests on the declarations of Klopstock himself, who proclaimed that he preferred "David's poetry" to that of Pindar. Contemporary critics indeed regarded Klopstock as a disciple of the biblical poets, especially because of his free style. In his *Aesthetica in Nuce*, Hamann extols Klopstock's virtues, citing him as a positive example of how to imitate the Hebrews: "The free construction which Klopstock, that great restorer of lyric song, has permitted himself is presumably an archaism, a happy imitation of the mysterious mechanics of sacred poetry among the ancient Hebrews."[31]

According to Hamann, Klopstock's biblical archaism embodied a renewal of the scriptural source that would promote a revival of poetry itself. We find even greater adulation of Klopstock's biblical poetry in Herder, who addressed the poet as "you Assaph of our people" [*du Assaph unsers Volks*].[32] Herder commends Klopstock for rediscovering the Hebrews' poetic tradition and passing it on to the German nation. This gift was not merely of aesthetic value but had encouraged the Germans to develop a form and style of their own, thereby ending their futile mimicking of neighbor nations. He likened Klopstock's appearance to the resurrection of David, a moment of redemption for German poetry. A diachronic return to holy history constituted the foundation for the nation's rebirth in the present, as it freed itself from foreign influences.

This merging of past and present formed the basic structure of the Hebraist stream in contemporary German literature, the preeminent representative of which was Klopstock. His poetry is laden with biblical motifs and Hebrew words. Many of his poems depict oriental, quasi-biblical landscapes.[33] His ode "Siona" (1764) is addressed to a poetic muse of that name, described as a Hebrew harp player dwelling in a palm grove and dancing by the source of the Jordan River:

Play for me, palm grove harpist
Playmate of the Psalms of David![34]

Siona, who is also David's muse, would appear in other Klopstock poems, sometimes named *die Siontin* or *Sulamith*. This muse, who appeared on the "palm hill" [*Palmenhöh*] and awarded Klopstock "the purple wreath of Sharon," transformed him into the likeness of the poet of the psalms.[35]

During this period Klopstock depicted a rich biblical environment. His German text is rife with Hebrew words, which he used to create a world of Hebrew imagery to rival that of classical mythology—replete with heroes, landscapes, trees and deified forces of nature. The poems were joined by Klopstock's three biblical dramas, *David* (1772), *Salomo* (1764), and *Der Tod Adams* (1757). These are religious plays that took the genre of sentimental-biblical drama to its apex. Klopstock's work and especially his epos *The Messiah* (*Der Messias*), on which he spent twenty-five years, naturally contains many New Testament themes. In its relation to the Old Testament, however, his brand of Christianity differed considerably from the Protestant rationalism of the likes of Gotthold Ephraim Lessing (1729–1781), Michaelis, and Johann Salomo Semler (1725–1791). While these rationalist theologians sought to displace the Old Testament to the very periphery of Christianity—the more extreme among them even endeavoring to "cleanse" Christianity of its Old Testament–derived elements to turn it into a rational, universal religion—Klopstock considered his sentimental creed to be a renewed flowering of the Old Testament. The savior in *Der Messias* frequently appears as a warring deity, a fighting hero with armor stained with his enemies' blood, bringing to mind the description of God's revenge on the nations in Isaiah 63.[36] Klopstock once again employs the image of a bloodstained warrior in his depiction of Teutonic warrior Hermann in his ode "Hermann and Thusnelda" of 1752.[37]

Although his work clearly reflects the influence of the classical tradition, Klopstock raises the banner of resistance to the Greeks' excessive influence on German poetry. In some of his odes, he portrays German or Germanic heroes and myths—from Hermann through Luther and even Leibniz. In other poems he wrote during that period, Klopstock posits the Hebrew source as an alternative to imitation of the Greek classics. "Aganippe und Phiala," the title of an ode he wrote during this period, refers to poetry's two mythic sources: the former is the spring that lies at the foot of Helicon, the muse's mountain and the latter was considered the source of the Jordan.[38] The German poet lies soundly asleep on the bank of the Rhine as the two rivers flow through his dream. It is, however, not the Greek river that rouses "the grandson of Tuisco" from his slumber, but rather Hebrew poetry and the music of Siona's (or Sulamith's) harp heard near the Jordan, the Kishon River, and Mount Gerizim. In the poetic space created by these lines, the Jordan flows into the Rhine. A similar "Greece versus Judah" structure is evident in other poems, in which Klopstock proclaims the shepherd David's poetic supremacy over the Greek bard Pindar, likening the struggle between the two sources to a duel of sorts. "God's poet" is also the war hero who triumphed over the Philistine god Dagon.

In his sentimental poetry, Klopstock created a poetic-theological synthesis between German identity, Protestant belief, and a passionate allegiance to the Old Testament and the Hebrew model. While rational Protestantism sought to supersede the Old Testament in order to bring Christianity closer to the "natural religion," Klopstock, on the contrary, extolled the virtues of a German Christianity in which Hebrew myth played a decisive role. In this form of Protestantism, the poetic substances that imbue Christianity with its meaning are actually the Hebrew—rather than the universal—ones. Klopstock thus recruited the Old Testament to posit German Christian identity opposite both classicism and the Enlightenment. This form of Christianity could therefore be construed as a reaction to the Enlightenment, while at the same time encompassing the novel element of national pride and patriotism.

Klopstock's two-volume edition of odes, published in 1796 by Georg Joachim Goeschen, included engravings crafted according to the writer's specific instructions. The first volume's frontispiece displays an engraving of the figure of the biblical muse Siona standing in a palm grove and clutching a harp. The second volume is illustrated with the Germanic muse Teutona, shown standing in an oak wood. Together, Siona and Teutona succinctly represent the aesthetic and political value system of Klopstock and other writers of the *Sturm und Drang* stream.

"National Hymns": Political Readings of the Book of Psalms

The Seven Years' War, which began in 1756, provided the backdrop to the first stirrings of modern national sentiments in Germany.[39] As far as its actual strategic development was concerned, this was still very much an *ancien régime*-style, absolutist monarchical war. But seen from the vantage point of the discourse it sparked within intellectual circles, in Frederick the Great's war against Austria, France, and Sweden, one may discern certain similarities to the national wars of the nineteenth century. Historian Hans-Martin Blitz, for instance, claims that certain discourse structures of a national character, which originated in the Baroque period, came into sharp relief under the influence of this war.[40] According to Blitz, Prussia's transformation into a major European power "electrified" the educated elites, generating an aggressive and chauvinistic patriotic mobilization. Blitz further argues that, given the cosmopolitan image enjoyed by the German Enlightenment, scholarship of this period has largely disregarded the "patriotic cult" [*Patriotismus-Kult*] that existed in its midst.

One of the characteristics that Blitz identifies within German patriotic writing is the use of biblical themes and metaphors to describe the war, as in Klopstock's patriotic and bellicose hymns. Indeed, contemporary poets went so far as to view Klopstock's battle hymns as modern equivalents of the biblical psalms or the Song of the Sea.[41] Influential poems by Johann Ludwig Gleim (1719-1803) similarly praised a pseudobiblical god for striking Prussia's foes at the Battle of Lowositz with lightning.[42] In their study of the reception of the book of Psalms in German literature, Inka Bach and Helmut Galle point out that Prussian poets sought to confer legitimacy on Frederick's battle strategy by describing the hostilities as an archaic holy war waged by an elected king and a chosen people.[43] Although the Prussian king himself derided Pietism, the movement exercised considerable influence on his army, and the greater part of the military chaplains was inducted from the ranks of Halle's Pietist educational institutions.[44] Prussian theologians and preachers operating in Berlin fashioned their combative sermons into biblical molds while glorifying the king as a present-day David, king of the chosen Prussian people. According to Blitz, this version of the "national choice idea" prefigured the exclusivist nationalist discourse that would emerge in full force during the Napoleonic wars.[45]

It bears mentioning in this context that Moses Mendelssohn (1729–1786) employed biblical metaphors almost identical to those used by the Protestant preachers of his time in the context of a sermon he delivered in German to the Jewish community of Berlin after the Prussian triumph in the battle of Leuthen in 1757.[46] In that sermon, the oldest known text of a Jewish sermon in the German language, Mendelssohn compared Frederick's triumph to the Israelites' passage through the Red Sea. God himself had apparently come to the rescue of the beloved king, who was "chosen by our Lord" for salvation and granted a miraculous victory.[47]

The burgeoning national discourse of the period directly following the Seven Years' War also provided the context within which the young Herder's nationalist ideas evolved.[48] In his earlier essays, penned in the years directly after the war, Herder enthuses about the patriotic poems published at the time, calling them "national hymns" [*Nationalgesänge*] filled with Prussian patriotism in which, for the first time, "a German poet sings for his German homeland in German."[49]

One gains this impression not only from Herder's writings about political affairs, but from his biblical scholarship as well. At the end of the chapter dedicated to the psalms in his *The Spirit of Hebrew Poetry*, Herder added a contemporaneous text—the only cited text in the entire book not derived from the Bible. This was a long poem entitled "The War: A Holy Hymn" ["*Der Krieg: ein heiliger Gesang*"] written in 1758, at the height of the Seven Years' War, by the poet Johann Heinrich Schmied. Herder noted that he did not know who had penned the poem but extolled its grace, beauty and purity, which he claimed were "unparalleled in our tongue."[50] Comprising dozens of motifs from the Psalms and the Books of Prophets, its first section is largely dedicated to glorifying Jehovah, "God of the Christians," through a plethora of biblical expressions:

> From Zion where your Spirit through David's pious harp
> the laudable silver tone put forth/inspire me you alone, Jehovah
> and attend my entreaty."[51]

In the following stanzas the poet proceeds from glorifying God to a warlike hymn glorifying the king. The king and his people, God's elect, call out their

God's name and scatter His enemies. The military campaign is portrayed as a biblical battle, and the hymn closes with an impassioned address to the "Lord Sabaoth" [*Herr der Zebaoth*]. In its original form, the poem included the name *Friedrich*, but Herder deleted it and replaced it with the word *king* [*König*].

A nationalistically oriented reading of biblical poetry, and especially of the psalms, forms the foundation for Herder's Hebraist political project in *The Spirit of Hebrew Poetry*. He asserts that the Hebrews' lyrical poetry had reached its zenith during David's reign, when most of the verses were written or collected. The mighty king's reign served as the backdrop to Hebrew poetry's "classical" period, and the hymn collection was, in effect, the nation's hymnal [*Liederbuch der Nation*].[52] Throughout the text, Herder buttresses his claims with assorted excerpts from the book of Psalms, edited to resemble choral oratorio pieces.

The book's central section, comprising several chapters devoted to the psalms, deals with the hymns addressed to the king [*Königs-Psalmen*]. The power of these poems, which originated at the time of David, derives, according to Herder, from the fact that they were addressed to a "national god" [*Nationalgot*], a major component of Herder's Hebraist conception that would influence poets and theologians in the generation that followed him. Herder illuminated the "national sentiment" [*Volks-Gefühl*] that characterized these poems, as well as the local and concrete context in which they were written, namely David's wars. He rejected all the allegorical and spiritual interpretations of the psalms that had surfaced throughout Christian history. In fact, he claimed, these poems were written to serve a simple cause: to rally the people during the king's wars.

The psalms—whose long interpretive tradition in Christianity extends back to the church fathers themselves—were now reclassified as "national hymns" or "patriotic hymns." The traditional, mystical or symbolic interpretations of the psalms were, according to Herder, the result of alienation from the national sentiment. Herder located the biblical psalms' original context in an imagined popular gathering attended by all the tribes and estates of the "free nation." He maintained that the existence of such national rituals was an important element the Germans could learn from the Hebrews. He likewise interpreted the Hebrews' Three Pilgrimage Festivals as national holidays [*Nationalfeste*]—as distinct from Christian holidays, which he regarded as being purely religious events.

Herder emphasized the aesthetic and poetic elements of the Hebrews' regime no less than its political character. Singing and hymns formed a major component of that regime. The festivities, so full of music, singing and dancing, generated, according to Herder, a sense of brotherhood among the tribes and a national pride [*Nationalstolz*], which enabled the people "to rejoice communally and feel themselves to be God's people" [*Gottesvolk*]. The hymns lay at the very core of the celebration, and they commemorated both the people's origin and the history of the ancient fathers [*Altväter*]. At this point Herder turns his attention to his own people:

> When we use the words, sacred feast, temple, festivals, Psalms, we either form no clear conception, or at least, a cold, cheerless and lifeless one, because we have ourselves no national festivals, and songs of public rejoicing, no temple associated with the glory of our fathers, no law for the universal security of our national freedom. Hence, the Psalms, which are filled with this spirit, are so often contemplated by us without emotion or sympathy. No people can have a national poetry that has not objects of general pride and rejoicing, in which all have a community of interest.[53]

According to Herder, in their current condition, the Germans were unable to grasp the Hebrews' poetic conceptions, since these revolved around the national holidays, the temple, the glory of the fathers, and national freedom. Because they lacked communal sources of pride and joy, they were unable to create a national poetry. And since the psalms are steeped in a national spirit, they were interpreted, mistakenly, as sad, cold creations. In a later essay, Herder wondered why German poetry shied away from public issues while the Hebrews' poetry was "totally patriotic" [*ganz patriotisch*].[54]

Interestingly, in 1784, about a year after the publication of *The Spirit of Hebrew Poetry*, poet Friedrich Schiller (1759–1805) articulated almost identical ideas—but replacing Hebrew festivals with Greek theater. In a lecture he delivered in Mannheim on the subject of national theater [*Nationalbühne*], Schiller claimed that it was this institution that had brought the dispersed Greeks together, by virtue of the "patriotic content" of its dramatic poetry. Comparing the society of the ancient Greeks to that of contemporary Germany, Schiller proclaimed that "when it does come to pass and we have our own national theater, then we shall become a nation."[55]

The ideal of a national Hebrew poetry was thus bound up with German intellectuals' quest for a culture and ritual around which the nation could coalesce. Herder never ceased to be amazed at the way Moses was able to fashion an entire people through his poetry alone.[56] And since poetry was portrayed as the major political medium, poets became popular leaders. Small wonder, then, that in the comparisons Herder and his followers drew between the biblical world and their present circumstances, Moses and David were likened to poets such as Klopstock, rather than to kings such as Frederick or Joseph II. The Hebrew state was adopted as a model for a poetic-religious political regime.

This idea also had a hermeneutic side to it. Herder's method assumed that the principal problem that confronted Bible interpreters was to overcome their temporal and spatial remove from the author of the text. Since he maintained that nationhood lay at the core of Hebrew poetry, it followed that this poetry could only be understood from the viewpoint of the nation. In other words, as long as the Germans had no nation of their own and were yet to create their own national poetry, they would never really be able to understand biblical poetry. Herder's interpretation of biblical poetry was therefore transformative; by redefining its object of study, it simultaneously transformed the reading subject itself.

The Rehabilitation of the Hebrew Theocracy

In his reading of the psalms, Herder posits the Hebrew state as a model of poetic-religious politics, within which the nation coalesces around religious poetry. Herder marvels at the great influence that Moses's poetry exerted on the souls and customs of his people, which equaled that of his law. Similarly, David's glory was buttressed by his psalms just as much as by his military conquests.[57] Contrary to other Enlightenment figures, Herder does not view ancient oriental poetry as an inferior phase in the development of human consciousness but rather finds in it the origin [*Ursprung*] of all of culture's future development. He discerns in the ancient text a creative element that cannot be achieved through modern, cerebral writing; ancient poetry contains elements that only modern-day scholars could develop and imbue with meaning.[58] Nor does Herder forgo the traditionally religious dimension of Hebrew poetry, which is "saturated with the spirit of God."[59] He goes on to claim that the Hebrews' poetry enjoys a significant advantage over other "national poetries" [*Nationalpoesien*] in that it was a form of divine poetry sung in the temple.[60]

This nostalgia for national religion and ancient Israel's public worship expresses a yearning for the era that preceded the separation of religion from the public-political sphere.[61] In this context Herder also addresses the matter of Hebrew theocracy—one of the more controversial issues that arose in Bible readings of the eighteenth century. The English deists as well as Spencer, Voltaire, and other critics of orthodoxy portrayed Hebrew theocracy as a cruel, tyrannical form of government—the first in a long line of such corrupt religious regimes. In fact, this theocracy was frequently linked to "Oriental despotism."[62] As with other questions pertaining to the Bible, Herder seeks to salvage the honor of the Hebrew regime in the face of the deists' mocking. He confesses discomfort at using the term *theocracy* [*Theokratie*], which by that time had become a derogatory expression, and prefers to refer to the Hebrew regime by the German term *Gottesregiment*. At the same time, he vociferously defends the maligned regime, indeed, elevating it above all others:

> And the god-regime, which garnered so much scorn? I wish only that at our level of culture we could produce one such; since it is what all men aspire to, and all wise men desired, but only Moses, at such an early time, was courageous enough to fulfill—that the Law governs, rather than any ruler; that a free nation

accept it voluntarily and uphold it by choice; as well as [agreeing to] be bound together by a benign, sentient and invisible force, not by shackles and chains. Such was Moses' vision; and I know none that is purer or more august.[63]

This is perhaps Herder's most impassioned apology on behalf of the Hebrew state. He laments the fact that Moses's political idea, as well as all the institutions built on it, came into being "three and even four thousand years too early," adding that even if it were to appear six thousand years hence it would still be ahead of its time. He enumerates three principles which, so he asserts, inform the basic form of the Hebrew state: tribal honor, equal national rights [*Nationalrechte*], and liberty.[64] Submission to God's rule is what ensures the maintenance of these principles. Underlying Moses's law is the notion of creating a free people, subjugated to nothing but the law. Thus, God himself assumes the role of "legislator, safe-guarder of the law and king."[65]

Herder conceives the Hebrew theocratic constitution—the same constitution maligned by contemporary philosophers as a contemptuous example of anachronism and subjugation—to be an egalitarian, communalist regime, in which the worship of God fosters brotherhood among the population and where law and custom replace tyranny. Herder posits this model as an alternative to the absolutist state's despotism and militarism.

It bears noting that Herder is aware of certain blemishes in his ideal of the Hebrew state. He highlights the inequality between the tribes as the source of the Hebrews' misfortunes. The stronger tribes took the lion's share of the land, bringing about a de facto rift within the people. This inequality eventually led to the division into two weak kingdoms, constantly at battle with each other and surrounded by powerful neighbors. It is no wonder, then, that the kingdoms of Assyria and Babylon conquered them almost effortlessly.[66]

Yet Herder attributes this calamity to the weakness displayed by the Hebrew leaders that followed Moses rather than to any shortcomings of the constitution authored by the nation's founder. On the contrary, maintains Herder, this constitution transcended the different clans' conflicts of interests through the single unifying element of religion. Herder portrays Moses as a leader who devised a political solution to the problem of unifying "twelve free and independent republics into one people."[67]

According to his understanding, the federative model was inextricably linked to the theocratic system: the kingdom's unity depended on the subjugation of all the Israelites to the rule of Jehovah. When King Jeroboam inaugurated the worship of foreign gods to liberate the residents of his kingdom from the rule of Jehovah, he in effect precipitated its secession from the union.[68]

Herder was one of the first writers of the eighteenth century to conceive of religion as a national and essentially public phenomenon, rather than a spiritual experience residing in the individual believer's soul.[69] He implores his readers to discard any suspicions they may harbor regarding the *regime of God* [*Gottesregierung*], which had become a pejorative term. Theocracy was not an oppressive regime of priests but a form of national integration through communal worship. At any rate, it was not a state church but rather a national religion linked to territory, custom, and popular ritual. By invoking the "regime of God," Herder clearly does not envisage a certain church taking over the entire kingdom, but a popular religion to be based on new texts and rituals, with national poetry as its cornerstone.

If we wish to understand the way contemporaneous writers established the Bible as myth, we must bear in mind that this myth was created only after images of the Hebrews as a savage oriental people had been firmly entrenched. Only once they had been transformed into a story, an ancient fiction, could the biblical texts become a national mythology. The mythic dimension is therefore precisely that which Herder employs to bridge the faraway world of the oriental Hebrews and that of his contemporary reader, transforming the Bible's "oriental" character from a negative into an admirable attribute.

Biblical poetry was the national myth of the ancient Hebrews; but the German nation could profit from it only by reinterpreting it—along the lines of the poetry of Klopstock and Herder's own essays. More than any other text, the Hebrews' poetry posited a model for the relation between a people and its national literature, according to which the community and the nation were constructed around its poetry and under the guidance of poets.

The National God and the Hebrew Nation

Hebrew poetry and the history it represents are posited, in *The Spirit of Hebrew Poetry*, as an ideal model of a people's national life. As Barnard and others have noted, this work contains some of Herder's most comprehensive political texts, which fully elaborate his political conceptions.[70] But our understanding of his political conception of the Hebrews' regime must take into account a major theological idea he develops, that of the Hebrews' "national god" [*Nationalgott*]. To my mind, this concept plays a key role in Herder's political theory, but it has been neglected in historical scholarship since it is buried among his theological writings.

The concept of the "national god" began to appear in various eighteenth-century rationalist texts that addressed biblical criticism. As noted previously, deist and radical writers derided Old Testament conceptions of God as childish, coarse, and sensual—as opposed to the New Testament's universalist "God of love." Jehovah is described as a jealous national god, basically no different than the idols of more ancient peoples. Indeed, many Enlightenment-era thinkers took up this topic as part of their intensive engagement with the question of the origins of idol worship. In his *Education of the Human Race*, Lessing describes the Hebrews as a link in a chain between the age of ignorance and rational Christian belief. According to this understanding, the Israelites were chosen by God as an instrument for the edification of the entire human race precisely *because* they were such a coarse people, virtually incapable of abstract thinking. Thus, given the people's mental limitations, God first presented himself to them only as "the God of their father"—that is, as Jehovah, the mightiest of all gods.

Like Johann Salomo Semler (1725-1791) and other rationalist Bible scholars, Lessing claimed that for a large part of their history the Hebrews entertained a childish, sensuous idea of a jealous "national god," which was "not the right concept that we should have of God."[71] Only gradually did their ideas become more refined as they learned to recognize "their Jehovah" as the only God. The distinction between *Jehovah* and *God* is pivotal to the rationalist theology of the Enlightenment and is very close to the distinction between a national-particular god and the universal God of all mankind. According to Lessing, the farther removed that Moses's law was from the national religion and the particular history of Israel, the closer it came to comprehending the abstract essence of God.

Other writers of the period adopted the stance that the "national god" was a "childish" theological idea. Among them was philosopher and avid Freemason Karl Leonard Reinhold (1757-1823), renowned as one of the early disseminators of Kant's critical method. In 1788, he published a Masonic essay titled *Die Hebräischen Mysterien, oder die älteste religiöse Freymaurerey* under the pseudonym Brother Decius, in which he claims that the religion founded by Moses was nothing other than the most ancient form of Freemasonry.[72] Reinhold adopts Lessing's ideas, claiming that the Israelites had lived in "the deepest ignorance" when Moses began his bid to free them from Egypt; thus he presented his people with "the god of their fathers," that is, "the sheltering god" [*Schutzgott*] or "a special guardian spirit of their people."[73] Lurking in the shadow of this figure of the national god was the god of nature, the Masons' cosmic deity.

While Reinhold's essay was read mainly within Masonic circles, it exerted a wider influence through the mediation of his friend Friedrich Schiller, whom he met in Jena. Schiller's essay "Die Sendung Moses" rested heavily on Reinhold's ideas, albeit stripped of their visibly Masonic elements.[74] Schiller, too, believed that God had initially been "a matter of blind faith" for the Hebrews.[75] Like other ancient peoples, the Hebrews had labored under a superstition regarding a special national divinity that watched over them. Moses learned of the secret existence of a single god from the Egyptian priests, but since the Hebrews were incapable of fathoming the idea of a "philosophical god," he dressed him up as "the national God of the Hebrews" [*Nationalgott der Hebräer*], the only type of god in which his people could believe.[76]

A similar notion of the national god appears in Herder's earliest writing. In drafts for an unpublished essay on Moses, apparently written in 1769, he laconically references the Exodus from Egypt. "God speaks: it is a national god—stronger than those of the Egyptians—who politically oversees the Israelites and no other nation on earth, willing in fact to harm any party that would challenge or oppress his people."[77]

This description comes across as critical of biblical belief—the political worship of a god who takes vengeance on other peoples. The concept subsequently appears in his essay "The Human Race's Oldest Document" (1774), a poetic commentary on the Creation story in Genesis. Interpreting Genesis 2:2 ("and He rested on the seventh day from all His work which He had done"), Herder paints an exotic image of an oriental day of rest. Like the stereotypical "orientals" [Morgenländer] or a dozy eastern despotic ruler surrounded by hundreds of awe-stricken servants, God rests from his work under the palm tree. "Thus rests God the Creator, Maker of all Things by Word, luxuriating in the tranquility of a sacred Sabbath … it is not our God … and indeed he is not the happy god reflected in his one, eternal thought of completeness: it is the god of the Orientals—the national god!"[78]

The national god is portrayed here as a mythical entity, a figment of the oriental lifestyle and imagination. This mythic image, so close to paganism, is at odds with abstract conceptions of God as omnipotent ruler or as contemplative philosopher. "This is not our god," Herder proclaims, although he later invites the reader "to delve into Oriental nature" and to approach it with empathy for the "popular sentiment" [Völkergefühl] this image engenders.

In this text, the national god appears as a poetic element within the colorful oriental myth. However, in *The Spirit of Hebrew Poetry*, published a decade later, the national god is portrayed in a political context. Surveying the elements of Moses's constitution, Herder highlights its most important element: "What all ancient legislators tried to achieve—tying their people by sentiment to the land of their fathers—Moses achieved in the most meaningful way through local law and through the national God of his forebears."[79]

The building blocks of Moses's philosophy, then, are not its universal edicts but rather its particular elements: the national God and the decrees connected to the land. Herder develops this idea in his interpretation of the psalms. There, Herder claims, the national God assumes an especially important role. In David's poetry, the national God appears as "the defender and founder of the Jewish state" [Schutzherr und Urheber des Jüdischen Staats].[80] The psalms are directed at a god who is judge and king of the nation. In a later religious essay, he identifies Jehovah's role in Hebrew religion as "national God and supreme king," who turned the Hebrews into "a free people."[81] In the Hebrew regime, God is the founder of a political entity and safeguards the people's liberty. For this very reason the prophets abhorred the golden calves in Dan and Bethel, which signaled the demise of the one unified nation.[82]

Another idea that Herder discusses in conjunction with the national god is one he finds in Mosaic law and Hebrew poetry, namely, God's special providence of the Israelites. When bestowing his law on the slave people that emerged from Egypt, Moses entrusted it to the care of "the most special local providence."[83] This concept, he explains, requires clarification since it has attracted so much criticism, in the form of assertions prevalent within Enlightenment authors' writings regarding the provincialism of Jewish and Hebrew religion and its claims that God was the people's personal protector. According to Herder, however, the Hebrew god's local providence over the promised land was designed to attach the people to a homeland. Rather than a mere superstition, this concept portrays the people's spirit as being inextricably tethered to the rules of the fathers and the land.[84]

As in other points throughout his book, Herder explicitly claims here that the denigrated religious and political principles associated with the national spirit of the Hebrews, and especially the idea of a private providence, should serve to guide "us"—although he never specifies exactly which collective he is referring to.

Like Schiller and others, Herder's argument bears clear imprints of Lessing's rationalist theory, which held that the national god was nothing more than a fictional being, a kind of "noble lie" that Moses invented to achieve a political goal. This approach highlights Herder's modernity and cunning; rather than asking whether the national god *exists*, he examines the functionality of the idea for the establishment of the nation.

Summary: The Bible and German Cultural Identity

In his book *The Enlightenment Bible*, historian Jonathan Sheehan maintains that the main thrust of biblical research during the Enlightenment sought a separation between the Old and New Testaments.[85] While the Old Testament was commended for its affective power and sublime style, the New Testament was associated with truth and morals. The political reading examined above, however, situated the text in a different framework. In many cases, while bringing the poetic components of the Bible to the fore, it placed them in a national context. This reading was bound up with the prominent features of the coalescing German nationhood, and stressed the link between religion, culture, and nationality. As a patriotic poet who wore the mantle of a biblical prophet, Klopstock embodied in his writing a German Protestantism that celebrated Christianity's Old Testament components.

Herder's writing on Hebrew nationalism was part of an emerging discourse within the circle of German literature following the Seven Years' War, which eschewed the Enlightenment's universalist political stance and revolved around the new concept of a national literature [*Nationalliteratur*]. Read according to its function and the political structure woven around it, the Hebrews' poetry was now construed as the supreme example of a national poetry—especially after orientalist Bible scholars had denuded it of the universalist layers heaped on it by traditional exegesis. While the Old Testament's characterization as a work of poetry or mythology was originally intended to undermine its authority, it simultaneously played a role in removing the barriers separating sacred and secular texts; and in this vein it laid the groundwork for a new poetics that imbued poetry with paradigmatic values previously reserved only for scripture.

The use of biblical rhetoric in a political context for the purpose of forming communal identities bestowing royal legitimacy was prevalent in almost all European nations in the early modern period. In German Protestant culture—as in its Dutch and English equivalents—one finds a tradition going back as far as the sixteenth century of a political Hebraism, that is, the use of a biblical vocabulary to galvanize the community against external enemies. In contrast to Catholic societies, Lutheran communities were constantly comparing themselves to the Israelites within a metaphysical conception of collective sin and divine retribution. Indeed, as early as the sixteenth century, German Evangelicals were already describing themselves as "the new Israelites."[86]

By comparing the Hebraist ideology of Herder and his disciples to the different forms in which political Hebraism appeared throughout modern European history, we are able to identify its unique characteristics. First and foremost, this is a thoroughly modern form of Protestant biblical discourse, as opposed to the English Puritans' or Dutch Calvinists' Hebraist rhetoric. In England, a marked decline in the use of biblical images in sermons and speeches was recorded after the accession of the Hanover Dynasty in 1714. As Ihalainen has shown, the idea of "the new Israel" fell out of favor as an appropriate rhetorical device to promote the consolidation of the nation.[87] In the Netherlands, too, biblical election rhetoric all but disappeared after the death of William IV in 1751.[88]

In opposition to those political phenomena of the seventeenth century that are sometimes described as forms of nationality *avant la lettre*, Herder's political Hebraism was already predicated on the vocabulary of nationalism and of modern political philosophy.[89] One is struck by his recurrent use of the word *national*, which appears dozens of times and in different combinations in *The Spirit of Hebrew Poetry*—*Nationalverfassung, Nationalstoltz, Nationaltempel, Nationalfeste*, and even *Nationalgott*. This is particularly evident in Herder's analysis of the political element in the books of Prophets. He seeks to show that the prophets were not megalomaniacal and delusional, but always based themselves on Mosaic law: "With all the prophets we know of, we can clearly see that in political matters the Law of Moses is always at the base of their judgment ... those who find the term 'the Spirit of Jehovah' [*Geist Jehovahs*] irksome may replace it with the more fashionable 'public spirit.'"[90]

The term *public spirit* had appeared in German political discourse several years beforehand, with the translation of Adam Ferguson's (1723–1816) *Institutes of Moral Philosophy* into German.[91] An intellectual debate regarding the correct translation of the term—as well as its applicability to German political culture—raged in the years thereafter. Herder himself engaged in the debate, and it would appear that he acerbically refers here to the "fashionable" use of this philosophical term. Yet he implicitly incorporates a radical argument into this utterance. The distinction between the biblical term *spirit of Jehovah* and the contemporary political term is purely semantic; despite its alleged religiosity, biblical politics has lost none of its relevance to the modern world. Following Herder, other scholars agreed that "in God's state this spirit [the public spirit] is godly."[92]

Writers of the mid-eighteenth century still treated the category of *nation* as a nebulous definition involving belonging, language, and kinship.[93] It was during the last decades of that century that the concept acquired a specific, political meaning in the European languages.[94] The emergence of a patriotic discourse following the Seven Years' War augmented the emotional resonance of the concept. German Bible scholars could no longer read scripture without addressing the national dimension, and many issues arising from Hebrew history—and particularly those pertaining to the relations between culture, religion, and nationality—became uniquely relevant to the political constellation of nascent German nationalism.

As we have seen, German Enlightenment scholars clung to the traditional concept of redemption history, albeit clothing it in different garb, with the Hebrews accorded the role of educators of mankind. This conception emerges in the works of Lessing, Schiller, and some lesser writers, who claimed that despite their limitations, the Hebrews had ultimately spread the gospel of universal rational religion, overcoming regional differences and pointing toward the oneness of humanity. This is the conception that Herder promotes in his earlier writing. In the historical scheme presented in *Auch eine Philosophie der Geschichte* (1774), he posits the Hebrews, to whom he refers by the general term *Morgenländer*, as the first disciples of providence on the path of human progress and refinement. It was precisely their "tender childish sense" that opened their hearts to divine authority even before humanity had matured sufficiently in the form of the Phoenicians, the Egyptians, and the Greeks.[95]

Like other German Enlightenment theologians and philosophers, Herder frequently anchors the meaning of Hebrew history to the pivotal role it played in the development of the monotheistic religions, and to its indirect contribution to the enlightenment of all of humanity [*Weltaufklärung*]. However, this book offers a different, and almost entirely novel, view of the Hebrew people. The Hebrews' singularity, that which made them a worthy role model, was *not* their role as disseminators of a universal religion but rather their *national* religion and *national* culture. The same national fervor that Lessing and Schiller associated with the parochial, base element of the Hebrew religion was now celebrated by Herder as that culture's most valuable and creative asset.

Herder was also the first major thinker of the eighteenth century to place myth at the center of his social and cultural theory. His essays on the subject are the first to formulate explicitly the ideas implicit in Hamann, Rousseau, Montesquieu, and others.[96] Herder made use, for his own purposes, of the rationalist historical theories of David Hume and Göttingen classicist Christian Gottlob Heyne (1729–1812) regarding myth formation, which portrayed myth as a crude, sensual form of thinking characteristic of savage peoples.[97] Contrary to those scholars, Herder values myth, emphasizing its close link to the people it serves. He regards myth as a people's valuable store of images and memories, and a vital element of its formation and existence.[98]

Differentiating himself from all other scholars of his time, Herder adopted a novel approach that focused on the *use* of myth. He elaborated this idea in an early essay written in 1767, "Vom neuern Gebrauch der Mythologie," in which he calls for the revitalization of modern literature through the use of myth. As Karl Menges has pointed out, this idea was extraordinary at the time of its appearance against the backdrop of the period's dominant rationalist stance on archaic belief.[99] Herder asserts that the correct study of stories of heroes and gods would enable poets to create myths of their own. He sidesteps the question of veracity, calling on artists to realize the poetic creation's sensual-aesthetic—but no less so, its political—value. The poet "creates the people around him," and possesses the power "to lead the souls" into the world he sees in his mind's eye.[100]

To understand the way contemporary writers established the Bible as myth, we would do well to remember that this myth was created only *after* the image of the Hebrews as a savage oriental people had already been set. Only after it was transformed into a *story*, into an *ancient fiction*, could biblical text morph into national mythology. The mythic category was therefore the interpretive means by which Herder bridged the problem of estrangement of the world of the oriental Hebrews from the world of the contemporary German reader. He uses it to turn the Bible's exotic nature from a liability into an advantage.

Biblical poetry is the national myth of the ancient Hebrews; and the German nation could only derive value or benefit from it by its reinterpretation, as in the case of Klopstock's poetry and the essays of Herder himself. More than any other text, the poetry of the Hebrews posits a model for the relation between a people and its natural literature—a model in which a community, a nation, a people is constructed around poetry, and led by its poets.

Notes

1. Georg Wilhelm Friedrich Hegel, "The Positivity of Christian Religion," in *Early Theological Writing*, trans. T. M. Knox (Chicago: University of Chicago Press, 1948), 146–147.

2. Johann Wolfgang von Goethe, *Aus meinem Leben: Dichtung und Wahrheit*. Vol. 9 of *Werke. Hamburger Ausgabe*, ed. Erich Trunz (Hamburg: Wegner, 1959), 272.

3. Joachim Dyck, *Athen und Jerusalem: Die Tradition der argumentativen Verknüpfung von Bibel und Poesie im 17. und 18. Jahrhundert* (Munich: C. H. Beck, 1977).

4. William J. Jones, "Early Dialectology, Etymology and Language History in German Speaking Countries," in *History of the Language Sciences*, ed. Sylvain Auroux (Berlin: Walter de Gruyter, 2001), 1105–1108.

5. Martin Opitz, *Prosodia Germanica, Oder Buch von der Deudschen Poeterey ... jetzo aber von Enoch Hanmann an unterschiedlichen Orten vermehret* (Frankfurt am Main: Christian Klein, 1658), 113.

6. Voltaire, *Essai sur les moeurs et l'esprit des nations* (Genève: Frères Cramer, 1756), 169.

7. See, for example: Daniel Weidner, "'Menschliche, heilige Sprache': Das Hebräische bei Michaelis und Herder," in: *Monatshefte für deutschsprachige Literatur und Kultur* 95, no. 2 (2003): 171–206.

8. See: Denis Thouard, "Hamann und der Streit um die Poesie der Hebräer," in *Die Gegenwärtigkeit Johann Georg Hamanns: Acta des achten Internationalen Hamann-Kolloquiums an der Martin-Luther-Universität Halle-Wittenberg 2002*, ed. B. Gajek (Frankfurt am Main: Peter Lang, 2005): 321–334; Bernadette Malinowski, *"Das Heilige sei mein Wort": Paradigmen prophetischer Dichtung von Klopstock bis Whitman* (Würzburg: Königshausen & Neumann, 2002), 72.

9. See: Jürgen Fohrmann, *Das Project der Deutschen Literaturgeschichte* (Stuttgart: J. B. Metzler, 1989), 74–75.

10. See: Ulrich Karthaus. *Sturm und Drang: Epoche-Werke-Wirkung* (Munich: Beck, 2000).

11. See: George S. Williamson, *The Longing for Myth in Germany: Religion and Aesthetic Culture from Romanticism to Nietzsche* (Chicago: University of Chicago Press, 2004), 35–41. See also: Karl Menges, "Particular Universals: Herder on National Literature, Popular Literature, and World Literature," in *A Companion to the Works of Johann Gottfried Herder*, ed. Hans Adler and Wulf Köpke (Rochester, NY: Camden House, 2009), 189–215.

12. Johann Georg Hamann, "Aesthetica in nuce," in *Kreuzzüge der Philologen*, vol. 2 of *Sämmtliche Werke* (Wien: Herder, 1950), 211.

13. Daniel Weidner, "Ursprung und Wesen der Ebräischen Poesie" in *Urpoesie und Morgenland*, ed. Daniel Weidner (Berlin: Kadmos, 2008), 113–151.

14. For a comprehensive study of German biblical drama in the eighteenth century, see: Johannes Schmidt, "Studien zum Bibeldrama der Empfindsamkeit," PhD diss., University of Breslau, 1933.

15. See: Anna Cullhed, "Original Poetry: Robert Lowth and Eighteenth-Century Poetics," in *Sacred Conjectures: The Context and Legacy of Robert Lowth and Jean Astruc*, ed. John Jarick (New York: Clark, 2007), 25–47; Rudolf Smend, "Lowth in Deutschland," in *Epochen der Bibelkritik* (Munich: Kaiser, 1991), 43–62.

16. Jonathan Sheehan, *The Enlightenment Bible: Translation, Scholarship, Culture*, (Princeton, NJ: Princeton University Press, 2005), 153.

17. Herder, *Vom Geist der Ebräischen Poesie*, (Dessau: Buchhandlung der Gelehrten, 1782–1783), 1–6.

18. Herder, *Vom Geist der Ebräischen Poesie*, 11–12.

19. Johann Gottfried Herder, *The Spirit of Hebrew Poetry*, trans. James Marsh. (Burlington: Smith, 1833), 30.

20. The monograph was written in 1749 and published three decades later. Carl Friedrich Cramer, *Klopstock: Er, und über ihn. 1724–1747*, (Hamburg: Schniebes, 1780), 41–42.

21. Cramer, *Klopstock*, 41–42.
22. Cramer, *Klopstock*, 41–42.
23. Cramer, Klopstock, 42.
24. Malinowsky, *"Das Heilige sei mein Wort,"* 95.
25. See especially: Gerhard Kaiser, *Pietismus und Patriotismus in Literarischen Deutschland* (Frankfurt am Main: Athenäum, 1973).
26. Friedrich Gottlob Klopstock, "Von der heiligen Poesie" [1755], in *Ausgewählte Werke*, ed. K. A. Schleiden (Munich: K. Hanser, 1962), 2:1000.
27. Kaiser, *Pietismus und Patriotismus*, 151.
28. See: Ulf-Michael Schneider, *Propheten der Goethezeit: Sprache, Literatur und Wirkung der Inspirierten* (Göttingen: Vandenhoeck & Ruprecht, 1995).
29. Kaiser, *Pietismus und Patriotismus*, 137–138.
30. Katrin M. Kohl, *Rhetoric, the Bible, and the Origins of Free Verse: The Early Hymns of Friedrich Gottlieb Klopstock* (New York: Walter de Gruyter, 1990).
31. Johann Georg Hamann, *Writings on Philosophy and Language*, trans. Kenneth Haynes (Cambridge, UK: Cambridge University Press, 2007), 92.
32. Herder, *Vom Geist der Ebräischen Poesie*, 1214.
33. See the dissertation: Moustafa Mäher, *Das Motiv der orientalischen Landschaft in der deutschen Dichtung von Klopstocks Messias bis zu Goethes Divan* (Stuttgart: Heinz, 1979), 79–82.
34. In German: "Töne mir, Harfe des Palmenhains / Der Lieder Gespielin, die David sang!" Friedrich Gottlieb Klopstock, "Siona" [1764], in *Oden*, ed. von Horst Gronemeyer and Klaus Hurlebusch (Berlin: Walter de Gruyter, 2011), 240–241.
35. Klopstock, "Siona," in *Oden*, 240–241.
36. His text is "Wer ist der, so vom Kidron herauf in blutigen Schweiss kommt? / Hosiana! Auf Salems Gebirg mit Wunden bedeck wird, Schoen mit Wunden?" Klopstock, "Der Messias," sec. 4 in *Werke und Briefe*, ed. von Elisabeth Höpker-Herberg (Berlin: Walter de Gruyter, 1974), 218.
37. Friedrich Gottlob Klopstock, "Hermann und Thusnelda" [1764], in *Oden*, 124–125. See also: Kaiser, *Pietismus und Patriotismus*, 255–257, 267.
38. Friedrich Gottlob Klopstock, "Aganippe und Phiala," in *Oden*, 226.
39. See on this topic: Benjamin W. Redekop, *Enlightenment and Community: Lessing, Abbt, Herder and the Quest for a German Public* (Montreal: McGill-Queen's University Press, 2000), 44–45.
40. Hans-Martin Blitz, *Aus Liebe zum Vaterland: die deutsche Nation im 18. Jahrhundert* (Hamburg: Hamburger Edition, 2000), 52–54.
41. For example: Johann Heinrich Voß, "Trinklied," in *Sämtliche Gedichte* (Königsberg: Nicolovius, 1802), 37.
42. Johann Wilhelm Ludewig Gleim, "Schlachtgesang bey Eröffnung des Feldzuges 1757," in: *Ausgewählte Werke*, ed. von Walter Hettchr (Göttingen: Wallstein, 2003), 82–83.
43. Inka Bach and Helmut Galle, *Deutsche Psalmdichtung vom 16. bis 20. Jahrhundert.* (Berlin: Walter de Gruyter, 1989), 298–299.
44. Hartmut Lehmann, "In the Service of Two Kings: Protestant Prussian Military Chaplains, 1713–1918," in *Transformationen der Religion in der Neuzeit* (Göttingen: Vandenhoeck & Ruprecht, 2007), S. 224–227.
45. Blitz, *Aus Liebe zum Vaterland*, 138–139.

46. Alexander Altmann, *Moses Mendelssohn: A Biographical Study* (Tuscaloosa: University of Alabama Press, 1973), 68.
47. Moses Mendelssohn, "Dankpredigt über den Sieg bei Leuthen." In *Schriften: Jubiläumsausgabe*, 10 (no.1):279-288. Stuttgart: Friedrich Frommann, 1974.
48. See for example: Menges, "Particular Universals," 189-215.
49. Johann Gottfried Herder, "Tyrtäus und der Grenadier" [1767], in *Sämmtliche Werke*, ed. von Bernhard Suphan (Hildesheim: Olms, 1967), 1:335-337.
50. Herder, *Vom Geist der Ebräischen Poesie*, 1246.
51. The original text is "Von Sion wo dein Geist in Davids fromme Harfe/ des Lobes Silbertöne goß,/ begeistre du mich selbst von dir, Jehovah,/ und merke auf mein Flehn," Herder, *Vom Geist der Ebräischen Poesie*, 1246.
52. Herder, *Vom Geist der Ebräischen Poesie*, 1284.
53. Herder, *Vom Geist der Ebräischen Poesie*, 1051.
54. Johann Gottfried Herder, *Briefe zur Beförderung der Humanität*, vol. 7 in *Werke in zehn Bänden*, ed. von Hans Dietrich Irmscher (Frankfurt am Main: Bibliothek deutscher Klassiker, 1991), 534. https://books.google.com/books?id=7X_B7xTEnuQC&pg=PA225&lpg=PA225&dq=Werke+7,+ed.+von+Hans+Dietrich+Irmscher&source=bl&ots=sXFHYOL9od&sig=MtDvoWRzS01gp6EQfzmXX22ubrg&hl=en&sa=X&ved=0ahUKEwijsvqAmuvWAhVE2IMKHQREAF4Q6AEIKDAA#v=onepage&q=Werke%207%2C%20ed.%20von%20Hans%20Dietrich%20Irmscher&f=false.
55. Friedrich Schiller, "Die Schaubühne als eine moralische Anstalt betrachtet" [1784], in *Sämtliche Werke*, ed. von Gerhard Fricke and Herbert G. Göpfert (Munich: Hanser, 1960), 5:818-831.
56. Herder, *Vom Geist der Ebräischen Poesie*, 1245.
57. Herder, *Vom Geist der Ebräischen Poesie*, 372.
58. Maike Oergel, *The Return of King Arthur and the Nibelungen: National Myth in Nineteenth-Century English and German Literature* (Berlin: Walter de Gruyter, 1998), 24-25.
59. See, for instance: Herder, "Über die Wirkung der Dichtkunst auf die Sitten der Völker in alten und neuen Zeiten." In *Sämmtliche Werke: zur schönen Literatur und Kunst* (Tübingen: Cotta, 1807), 378-379.
60. Herder, *Vom Geist der Ebräischen Poesie*, 360.
61. On this topic see: Williamson, *The Longing for Myth in Germany*, 34.
62. See: Jonathan Israel, *Democratic Enlightenment: Philosophy, Revolution, and Human Rights, 1750-1790* (Oxford: Oxford University Press, 2011), 810-811.
63. Herder, *Vom Geist der Ebräischen Poesie*, 173.
64. Herder, *Vom Geist der Ebräischen Poesie*, 120-121.
65. Herder, *Vom Geist der Ebräischen Poesie*, 120-121.
66. JohannGottfried Herder, *Ideen zur Philosophie der Geschichte der Menschheit* (Riga: Hartknoch, 1784), 100-101.
67. Herder, *Vom Geist der Ebräischen Poesie*, 170-171.
68. See: Herder, *Vom Geist der Ebräischen Poesie*, 174; Thomas Willi, *Herders Beitrag zum Verstehen des Alten Testaments* (Tübingen: Mohr Siebeck, 1971), 81-83.
69. On this, see: Hans Kippenberg, *Discovering Religious History in the Modern Age* (Princeton, NJ: Princeton University Press, 2002), 14-18.

70. Frederick M. Barnard, *Herder on Nationality, Humanity, and History*. Montreal: McGill-Queen's Press, 2003 17–20; Dominic Eggel, Andre Leibich, and Deborah Mancini-Griffoli. "Was Herder a Nationalist?" *The Review of Politics* 69, no. 1 (Winter 2007): 58–61.

71. Gotthold Ephraim Lessing, "Die Begriffe, die es von seinem höchsten einigen Gott hatte, nicht eben die rechten Begriffe waren, die wir von Gott haben müssen," in *Die Erziehung des Menschengeschlechts*, (Berlin, Christian Friedrich Voss, 1780), sec. 34. For other similar renditions of Semler's claims regarding the Hebrews' national god, see for example: Anders Gerdmar, *Roots of Theological Anti-Semitism: German Biblical Interpretation and the Jews, from Herder and Semler to Kittel and Bultmann* (Leiden: Brill, 2009), 39–41.

72. Carl Leonhard Reinhold, *Die Hebräischen Mysterien oder die älteste religiöse Freymaurere*. (Leipzig: Göschen, 1788); on Reinhold and the origins of his essays, see: Jan Assmann, *Moses the Egyptian: The Memory of Egypt in Western Monotheism* (Cambridge, MA: Harvard University Press, 1997), 115–125.

73. Reinhold, *Die Hebräischen Mysterien*, 56.
74. Assmann, *Moses the Egyptian*, 126.
75. Schiller, "Die Sendung Moses," In *Kleinere prosaische Schriften*, (Leipzig: Cursius, 1802), 2.
76. Schiller, "Die Sendung Moses," 41.
77. Herder, "Eine Skizze über Moses," In *Sämmtliche Werke*, 22:211. Berlin: Weidmann, 1899, 32:211.
78. Johann Gottfried Herder, "Älteste Urkunde des Menschengeschlechts," in *Sämmtlische Werke zur Religion und Theologie* (Tübingen: Cottaschen Buchhandlung, 1802), 6:58.
79. Herder, *Vom Geist der Ebräischen Poesie*, 171.
80. Herder, *Vom Geist der Ebräischen Poesie*, 326.
81. Johann Gottried Herder, "Conformation ihro hochfürst. Durchlaucht Caroline Louise Prinzessinn von Sachsen-Weimar und Eisenach, den 15 April 1802," in *Sämmtlische Werke zur Religion und Theologie* (Tübingen: Cottaschen Buchhandlung, 1802), 4:260.
82. Herder, *Vom Geist der Ebräischen Poesie*, 122.
83. Herder, *Vom Geist der Ebräischen Poesie*, 163.
84. Herder, *Vom Geist der Ebräischen Poesie*, 164.
85. Sheehan, *Enlightenment Bible*, 178–179.
86. See, for example: Nikolaus von Amsdorf, "Ein trost an die zu Magdeburg / Und an alle fromme Christen, 10. Juni 1551," in Thomas Kaufmann, *Das Ende der Reformation*, (Tübingen: Mohr Siebeck, 2003), 432–433.
87. Pasi Ihalainen, *Protestant Nations Redefined: Changing Perceptions of National Identity in the Rhetoric of the English, Dutch and Swedish Public Churches, 1685–1772* (Leiden: Brill, 2005), 109.
88. Ihalainen, *Protestant Nations Redefined*, 139–140.
89. Philip S. Gorski, "Calvinism and State-Formation in Early-Modern Europe," in *State/Culture: State-Formation after the Cultural Turn*, ed. George Steinmetz (Ithaca, NY: Cornell University Press, 1999), 148–149.
90. Herder, *Vom Geist der Ebräischen Poesie*, 169.
91. Adam Ferguson, *Grundsätze der Moralphilosophie*, trans. Christian Garve (Leipzig: Dyck, 1772); and see also: Fania Oz-Salzberger, *Translating the Enlightenment: Scottish Civic Discourse in Eighteenth-Century Germany* (Oxford: Oxford University Press, 1995), 207.

92. Johann Christoph Doederlein, *Christlicher Religionsunterricht nach den Beduerfnissen unserer Zeit* (Leipzig, 1791), 199.

93. Josep R. Llobera, *The God of Modernity: The Development of Nationalism in Western Europe* (Oxford: Berg, 1994), 149–177.

94. Athena S. Leoussi, "Nation: A Survey of the Term in European Languages," in *Encyclopedia of Nationalism* (New Brunswick, NJ: Transaction Publishers, 2001), 304–313.

95. Johann Gottfried Herder, *Auch eine Philosophie der Geschichte* (1774), 484.

96. Burton Feldman and Robert D Richardson, *The Rise of Modern Mythology, 1680–1860* (Bloomington: Indiana University Press, 2000), 224–227.

97. On Heyne's theory of myth, see: Marianne Heidenreich, *Christian Gottlob Heyne und die Altes Geschichte* (Leipzig: K. G. Saur, 2006), 166–169; Christian Hartlich and Walter Sachs, *Der Ursprung des Mythosbegriffes in der modernen Bibelwissenschaft* (Tübingen: Mohr Siebeck, 1952), 11–19. On conceptions of myth in the Enlightenment, see also: Joseph Mali, *The Rehabilitation of Myth: Vico's "New Science."* (Cambridge, UK: Cambridge University Press, 2002), 124–126.

98. See for example: Sonia Sikka, *Herder on Humanity and Cultural Difference: Enlightened Relativism* (Cambridge, UK: Cambridge University Press, 2011), 234–236; George S. Williamson, *The Longing for Myth in Germany: Religion and Aesthetic Culture from Romanticism to Nietzsche* (Chicago: University of Chicago Press, 2004), 33.

99. Menges, "Particular Universals," 191–192.

100. "Ein Dichter ist Schöpfer eines Volkes um sich; er gibt ihnen eine Welt zu sehen, und hat ihre Seelen in seiner Hand, sie dahin zu führen." Herder, "Über die Wirkung der Dichtkunst auf die Sitten der Völker in alten und neuen Zeiten.", 488.

5 "Lovers of Hebrew Poetry": The Battle over the Bible's Relevance at the Turn of the Nineteenth Century

In 1795, Johann Gottfried Eichhorn (1753–1827) wrote a review of Johann Babor's recently published *Antiquities of the Hebrews* [*Alterthümer der Hebräer*].[1] Having succeeded Michaelis at Göttingen, Eichhorn was the reigning German Bible exegete of the time. The thriving scene of German orientalism had witnessed a flurry of publications on Hebrew history, prompting Eichhorn to offer an overview of the state of the discipline:

> How different is the spirit that animates our new investigations into the antiquities of the Hebrews, compared with essays of only several decades back! It would seem as though the Hebrews had been transformed into a whole new nation, so different is the impression one gets of their ways of thought, their customs and laws. The antiquarian investigation of the Hebrews is trifling no more ... it has now become as it should be when philosophical minds take an interest in it ... a history of the Hebrews' culture, a historical description of the gradual transformation and amelioration of their social condition.[2]

Eichhorn expresses here a conviction he shared with most scholars from Michaelis onward, that the biblical interpretation of their times was an entirely new science that had, in a matter of several decades, torn itself free from the shackles and conventions of traditional interpretation. Indeed, this new science had transformed its object of investigation, giving rise to a revised image of the Hebrews as a new nation with its own unique culture [*Cultur*]. While scholars of earlier generations had grappled with the Mosaic tradition through its texts, orientalist Bible scholars from Michaelis onward sought to reconstruct the Hebrew people so as to recreate the context in which that text was written. The Hebrew people were now configured, assessed, defined, and qualified by means of the new tools that the Enlightenment's human and social sciences provided. And classical political categories were buttressed by a further social dimension: the periodization of the Israelites' ways of life.

Eichhorn succinctly defines the essential difference between the former and new modes of research. As we see in his description, this novelty lay not in the mere publication of texts on the Hebrew antiquities—a genre that in fact went back well into the seventeenth century—but rather in the form of the new investigation of Hebrew history as well as in the questions that scholars were currently addressing. According to Eichhorn, traditional Hebraist antiquarianism consisted of content-free documentation and taxonomy [*Mikrologie*] that made no claim to innovation. In keeping with the historicist ideology that took root in German universities at the turn of the eighteenth century, however, the new research now pronounced its allegiance to philosophical logic in general and to historical logic in particular. Bible interpretation was in the process of being rewritten as a history of Hebrew culture, law, and politics.

This chapter deals with the ongoing discussion of the Hebrews during the two decades that followed the publication of Michaelis's and Herder's major works. Debate on the Bible at the turn of the eighteenth century was characterized by a bifurcated motion: an attempt to displace Hebrew myth from German culture and a simultaneous effort to build that same culture in its image. Critical Bible investigation led to the debunking of the concept of the Hebrews as agents of universal reason. Referring to the Old Testament as a text written in a particular and national vein became an almost universally accepted convention. Yet, while rationalist philosophy and theology derided the particular character of the Hebrew tradition, writers who criticized the Enlightenment adopted that very particularity as a role model, hoping to "save" besieged Christianity through the national element in Hebrew poetry. The nation-spirit identified in the Old Testament imbued this text with new meaning, facilitating an alternative reading that aligned it with new political aims.

The Dissemination of the Hebrew History Genre

Indeed, in the latter years of the eighteenth century, the academic discipline of Hebrew history reached the height of its popularity. One tractate after another concerning ancient Hebrew history and biblical history appeared in rapid succession, written by Bible scholars and orientalists, among them several of Michaelis's disciples, who were scattered throughout the different German universities. In 1788, Theodor Jacob Ditmar published *A History of the Israelites* [*Geschichte der Israeliten*] in Berlin; the next three years saw the publication of Göttingen-based Thomas Christian Tychsen's *Sketch for an Archaeology of the Hebrews* [*Grundriss einer Archaeologie der Hebräer*], Frankfurt-based Friedrich Arnold Hasenkamp's *The Israelites* [*Die Israeliten*], and Leipzig-based Christian Gottlieb Kühnöl's *History of the Jewish People* [*Geschichte des jüdischen Volks*]. Babor's aforementioned *Alterthümer der Hebräer* followed in 1794, and three years thereafter Johan Jahn of Vienna published *Biblical Archaeology* [*Biblische Archäologie*] and Lorenz Bauer of Altdorf produced his *Hebrew Antiquity* [*Hebraïschen Alterthümer*].

The extraordinary flowering of essays of this kind stemmed, above all, from the numerous departments of oriental languages established in the German universities of the time, which produced many scholars trained in the new methods of biblical interpretation. Indeed, Scottish Bible scholar Alexander Geddes (1737–1802) famously remarked that in Germany, "almost every scholar is an Orientalist."[3] The shift from Latin to German as the main vehicle for publishing academic philological texts made the disciplines accessible to ever-wider audiences, expanding the ranks of what Bauer defined as "friends of Israelite history" [*Freunde der israelitischen Geschichte*].[4]

The majority of these new texts on Hebrew history rarely offered substance of any true novelty, based as they generally were on the academic innovations of leading scholars. Criticism was frequently leveled at these Bible scholars for being nothing but "slavish copiers" of their predecessors. The objective of these texts, according to their authors, was mainly to assuage "stupid superstitions against the Bible."[5]

But Hebrew history simultaneously piqued the interest of writers from totally different fields. A good example is Friedrich August Carus (1770–1808), one of the pioneers of psychology as an empirical science, who published *The Psychology of the Hebrews* [*Psychologie der Hebräer*] during the first decade of the nineteenth century.[6] A graduate of Göttingen University, Carus approached the study of the psyche from a historical–anthropological perspective; he sought to outline a history of humanity centered on the development of the conception of the psyche and of psychological concepts. Herder's influence on the book is clearly evident in Carus's detailed historical account of the development of the Hebrews' "national character" and "national temperament," which are explained as a function of the circumstances with which the people had to contend. Like other writers since the mid-eighteenth century, Carus divides Hebrew history into different periods signifying different stages of the people's refinement (*Bildung*). But contrary to earlier authors, Carus attempts to characterize biblical heroes and the Hebrew people psychologically, analyzing Hebrew terms such as *psyche*, *spirit*, and *heart*. The psychological maturation of the Hebrew nation serves as a model for the spiritual history of humanity in general. Orientalist Anton Theodor Hartmann (1774–1838) compiled an even stranger monograph, which addressed Hebrew women's taste in clothing.[7] This three-volume treatise offers "a survey of Hebrew women's most important inventions in the field of fashion [*Moden*], from its savage origins to the heights of opulence." Among other trends, Hartmann describes in great detail the strong influence the Egyptian art of makeup had on Hebrew women, who used heavy eye shadow.

Goethe, Kant, and Criticism of the Old Testament

But while Hebraist research reached an apex in the German universities, biblical themes were relegated to the sidelines of the period's German literature and criticism. Michaelis's disciples did not enjoy the same degree of cultural influence that their master had wielded, and no Hebraist writer of Klopstock's stature could replace him in the field of literature. Goethe and Schiller herded German culture into a lengthy phase of adulation of the Greeks; and Kant's critical philosophy posited the ideal of a Christian religion anchored in the edicts of rationality, in which scripture in general and the Old Testament in particular played a minor role.

In the 1780s and 1790s, the works of Michaelis, Herder, and Eichhorn gained influence among wide circles, even outside the universities. Echoes of these exegetical discussions can be found as far afield as, for example, in Goethe's *The Sorrows of Young Werther*. In one of the novel's journal extracts, Werther recounts how the wife of the village's pastor oscillated between "Kennicott, Semler and Michaelis," comparing their different methods.[8] Werther himself falls to musing about the Bible's innocent atmosphere: sitting by a well close to his lodgings, a vivid apparition of "the patriarchal ideal" reveals itself to him, and he imagines a pastoral biblical scene where "all of the ancient Fathers are associating by the well."[9] However, Goethe exhibited no great enthusiasm for the Hebrew ideal and, in fact, devoted no major piece to a biblical theme. He generally treats the Hebrew legacy with equanimity, as something reserved for children, women, and common people. By the same token, he regarded an affinity to the Bible as a form of childhood disease that had afflicted German literature. Despite Herder's influence on his work, Goethe clearly preferred the classical to the Hebrew ideal. As Karin Schutjer demonstrated, this stance may well have had a profound effect on the ensuing development of German literature.[10]

While Goethe treated the Bible with a sympathetic reserve, Immanuel Kant expressed genuine animosity toward the Old Testament, actively seeking to write the Hebrew influence out of his contemporary culture. Kant's stand on the Bible was linked to his personal animosity toward Herder; he expressed a real abhorrence of the older writer's biblical texts in private correspondence, going so far as to accuse him of *Schwärmerei* (sentimentality).[11] He expressed equal disdain toward the Bible itself. In his 1780s lectures on anthropology, he ironically remarks that God should rather have spared us that "oriental rubbish" [*orientalischer Kram*], namely the Bible.[12] Kant, in effect, adopted the deists' negative stance toward the Bible, specifically that of Hermann Samuel Reimarus, who wrote the *Wolfenbüttel Fragments*, published anonymously by Lessing during the 1770s and which caused a real stir in the ranks of the German Enlightenment.[13] The fragments attempted to systematically undermine all sections of the Old Testament one by one, from Genesis to the last prophet.[14]

Kant's objection to Herder and his Hebrew subjects of adulation was not merely philosophical, but also aesthetic. In fact, he claimed that Herder "corrupts minds" [*verdirbt die Köpfe*] with his sensual ideas.[15] He expressed misgivings about Klopstock and the sentimental-ecstatic style he had introduced to German literature for similar reasons.[16] Kant, then, clearly sought to invalidate the aesthetics and philosophy of *Sturm und Drang*, including the aesthetic models and ideals that it celebrated. Until the 1790s, however, his objections were mainly articulated in private correspondence and lectures.

Kant's most scathing attack on the biblical legacy appeared in his theological book *Religion Within the Boundaries of Mere Reason* [*Die Religion innerhalb der Grenzen der bloßen Vernunft*], published in 1793. The theological ideal he sets out here is that of a rational "religion of reason" [*Vernunftreligion*], to be built on the progression of historical religion. Offering a more systematic elaboration of the principles set out by Lessing in his *Education of the Human Race*, this work, however, excludes Judaism from the "ladder" of progression (although Lessing included it in his developmental scheme). Kant describes "the Jewish faith" as the constitution of a "specific clan" [*besonderer Stamm*]: "The Jewish faith, as originally established, was only a collection of merely statutory laws supporting a political state; for whatever moral additions were *appended* to it, whether originally or only later, do not in any way belong to Judaism as such. Strictly speaking Judaism is not a religion at all but simply the union of a number of individuals who, since they belonged to a particular stock, established themselves into a community under political laws, hence not into a church."[17]

Kant cites Old Testament religion as the paradigm for the historical appearance of a particular people's "political religion," as opposed to the "general church" [*allgemeine Kirche*] ideal which he posits in the essay. He adopts the deists' stance regarding the "Hebrew theocracy," describing it as an aristocracy of priests who invoked God's name to further their own power. In the context of this constitution, the divinity serves only as a "secular ruler" [*weltlicher Regent*] who makes almost no demands on conscience; this constitution thus lacks a religious element.[18] As Yirmiyahu Yovel has shown, Kant employs Mendelssohn's concepts relating to the description of Judaism as a *constitution*—and reconfigures them into a distinctly anti-Jewish stance meant to exclude the Jewish element in Christianity.[19]

Other writers of the Enlightenment circle similarly proposed new political readings of the Bible to distinguish clearly between scripture and German culture. Thus, certain elements within the rationalist theology movement adopted the idea of "national hymns," but interpreted it in a totally different way than had Herder. Rationalist theologian Wilhelm Friedrich Hufnagel (1754–1830) devoted an entire book to proving the argument that the Old Testament should be understood from a "national point of view" [*Nationalgesichtpunkt*] rather than a religious one. According to Hufnagel, Bible interpretation's original sin was to overlook its national element, thereby committing terrible mistakes. "All local! A wholly national meaning!" is his verdict on the psalms; therefore, an innocent reading of the poetry is not only dangerous but positively *harmful* to Christian communities.[20]

This cleansing of the Jewish elements from Christianity was not limited to the realms of literature and philosophy, but manifested itself in the actual changes taking place at the time within the ecclesiastical and educational framework of the German principalities. In the 1780s, some north German principalities began to reform the role of the clergy.[21] Their rulers actively sought to assimilate, centralize and rationalize the church within the state apparatus in the spirit of the Enlightenment and absolutism. Some reformers who enjoyed institutional backing, headed by Karl Friedrich Bahrdt (1741–1792) and Joachim Heinrich Campe (1746–1818), both disciples of rationalist Enlightenment theology [*Aufklärungstheologie*], endeavored to limit preachers' power and independence, assigning them the more limited role of *Volkslehrer*—a public moral pedagogue who fulfilled administrative and ideological functions for the state.

Since education in the German principalities remained largely in the hands of the church, these reforms affected not only the clergy itself but impacted the very nature of education. Until the final decades of the eighteenth century, the north German education system was administered according to the Lutheran principle of church-based education, structured to teach the populace to read scripture. In 1779, the Prussian authorities began to establish public schools [*Volksschule*], thereby weakening the church's hold on education. Bahrdt's and Campe's reform plans were aligned with this trend and were thus identified with utilitarianism, centralism, and nationalism—in the sense that their stated goal was to strengthen the state, not religion.

One of the important elements of this reform plan was an alteration to preachers' training courses. In the plan he authored in 1785 for Friedrich II's education minister, Karl von Zedlitz (1731–1793), Bahrdt proposed that university training programs incorporate such applied fields as medicine, agronomy, and pedagogy, as well as history and Greek mythology, but remove the oriental languages (Hebrew and Aramaic) and Bible interpretation. The Old Testament, he claimed, dealt with "local affairs" of the Jews and studying it offered no tangible utility to the state.[22] Bahrdt, who started out in the field of biblical philology, published—alongside the reform plan—a provocative essay on scripture, attacking the "barbaric" content of the psalms, declaring that Abraham had indulged in human sacrifice, and even going so far as to claim that Moses had fabricated the lightning seen on Mount Sinai by using special effects.[23] Campe, who regarded Bahrdt as a role model, also advocated removing the study of Hebrew and "all oriental languages" from the *Volklehrer*'s training courses.[24] But unlike Bahrdt's plan, which made little impact, Campe's reform plan was adopted by the prince of Braunschweig-Wolfenbüttel and influenced reformer Karl August von Hardenberg (1750–1822) of Prussia.

Bahrdt's and Campe's reform plans were never fully implemented, partly because they aroused stiff opposition among clerical circles. Although

Enlightenment theology was a dominant force in several of the universities until the end of the 1780s, many opponents of rationalism remained in the country, and they clung to a more conservative theology.[25] As a rule, the lower rungs of the clergy sought to defend the principalities' and territories' autonomy in religious and other affairs. As John Stroup has shown, the rapid spread of Enlightenment and utilitarian ideals led preachers to fear that the church was losing power and disintegrating. Preachers in northern Germany thus tended to voice desperate allegiance to scripture in general and to the beleaguered Old Testament in particular.

University faculties of theology and oriental languages recorded an equal measure of disgruntlement. As Anthony La Vopa has shown in his research on the transformation of Protestant clergy training courses, reformers' calls to annul philological and theological training threatened the professors' professional ethos and endangered their very existence. The universities therefore stood at the forefront of opposition to the reforms.[26] Following the death of Friedrich II and the succession of conservative Wilhelm II to the throne in 1786, the opponents of reform gained the upper hand.[27] Even Michaelis and Semler, who always trod an intermediate path between radical Enlightenment and ecclesiastical conservatism, tended in their old age toward the right wing of the theological spectrum.[28] This trend was to become even more pronounced after the French Revolution.

Clergymen displayed different forms of objection to processes of centralization and secularization in an attempt to salvage the clergy's religious role. Opposition to Campe's reform was headed by Johann Kaspar Velthusen, a theologian from Helmstedt.[29] Velthusen studied with Michaelis in Göttingen, and served as tutor to the master's son. Little wonder, then, that an emphasis on the study of oriental languages formed the basis of Velthusen's opposition to the Campe reforms.[30] His response to the challenge of reform was to advocate even more rigorous training of provincial preachers. He asserted that knowledge of Hebrew and Greek was essential to comprehension of the scriptures' "religious truths," and that not only the preacher but indeed his entire community was therefore obliged to study these languages.[31] These ideas influenced an entire generation of young theologians trained during the last decade of the eighteenth century, who expressed themselves to a large extent in their stances regarding the Bible.

Translators and Readers at the Turn of the Century

A movement away from the Old Testament, then, was not the only trajectory of German culture at the time. Alongside scientific research, this period also witnessed a flowering of translations of Hebrew poetry. Many oriental language department alumni tried their hand at translating biblical hymns, publishing them in the form of modest pamphlets. These collections tended to include several psalms, excerpts from the Song of Songs or a version of the Song of Deborah, the Song of the Sea, and so forth.

Many of the translations were greeted with lively interest by contemporary critics, who savored the burgeoning competition among the new translators. Leading literary magazines such as Friedrich Nicolai's (1733–1811) *Neue allgemeine deutsche Bibliothek* and Christof Martin Wieland's (1733–1813) *Allgemeine Literatur-Zeitung* regularly carried surveys of the phenomenon. The yardstick of a translator's success was an ability to convey the spirit and world of ideas of ancient times.[32] These critiques were mostly addressed to the crowd of "lovers of Hebrew poetry" [*Liebhaber der Hebräischen Poesie*]—a phrase used by Herder for the subtitle of his book; or to "friends of Hebrew and fine literature" [*Freunde der hebräischen und schönen Literatur*], rather than the traditional "friends of religion" [*Freunde der Religion*].[33] These definitions are highly revealing of the fact that biblical translation was now read in an aesthetic context. Its authors wished to bring biblical poetry to the ever-expanding audience of German readers and to introduce a new way of reading scripture as literature, seeking "to maintain the pure pleasure of the beautiful original."[34]

At the same time, Christian authors began publishing collections of "Hebrew national hymns." It is hard to tell whether the first translations of this kind bear the direct influence of Herder or Mendelssohn, but at any rate, from its very inception, this genre conveyed an attempt to popularize ideas originating in the era's philological research.[35]

One of the most inspired and prolific members of this new generation of translators was poet and theologian Karl Wilhelm Justi (1767–1846) of Marburg. He had studied at Göttingen and Jena and, from an early age, exhibited an interest in the poetry of Ossian and the Hebrews.[36] Having returned to Marburg, he grew close to Achim von Arnim (1781–1831) and the city's circle of romantic poets. Indeed, his writing, which revolves continually around biblical poetry, exhibits a distinct romantic influence. In the introduction to one of the biblical poetry collections he published, Justi declares that some biblical passages "tower above the best Greek and Roman hymns."[37] He therefore apparently felt compelled to explain why so few readers were willing to even glance at these works as sources of aesthetic pleasure. The first reason he cites is the poor quality of German translations, which failed to convey the qualities of the oriental expressions. The better translations in his eyes—such as those of Herder and Mendelssohn—were insufficiently accessible to the wider public and were known mainly to the theological circle alone. But the main reason was that the German reading public was constricted by opinions impressed on it from childhood, equating the text with austere, dogmatic moral imperatives. They thus missed the pleasure that the Hebrew masterpieces, those "holy monuments of old" promise.[38] For this reason, Justi took it on himself to make these poems accessible to a wider audience in metric translation. Unsurprisingly, the principal model he drew on was Herder. In his later book, *Sionitische Harfenklänge* as well as in his autobiography, he cites the influence of Klopstock, Mendelssohn's translation of the psalms, and Herder's essay on the Hebrews.[39]

The concept of national hymns [*Nationalgesänge*], the main novelty of Herder's Bible interpretation, was also one of the most influential ideas to grow out of it. In 1803, Justi published *Nationalgesänge der Hebräer*, which includes annotated translations of several poems such as the Song of the Sea and David's lament for Saul. He chose this title since the biblical hymns were written "in the spirit of the Hebrew nation," but were in fact also "meant to be sung by the nation."[40]

Franz Thomas von Schönfeld's (1753-1794) *Davids Kriegsgesäng*, published in 1788 in Vienna and Leipzig, offers a unique rendition of biblical war hymns.[41] The book includes psalm translations dedicated to King Joseph II as well as verse composed in Klopstick's biblical style. Born in Bohemia as Moses Dobruška, Schönfeld was a Jew and the nephew of Jacob Frank—the leader of a notorious messianic sect in Poland. Following in his teacher's footsteps, Dobruška converted to Catholicism in 1775, and three years later, joined a Freemason group called *Asiatische Brüder*, which sought to unify Judaism and Christianity. Dobruška's life and exploits have provided fodder for extensive research—especially his final years, when, following the revolution, he joined the Jacobins, changed his name once again (to Junius Brutus Frey) and was executed, in 1794, together with Danton.[42] However, few scholars have dwelled on the link between this figure and the German Hebraist stream. *Davids Kriegsgesäng* is one of several Hebraist essays that Schönfeld penned; they are all clearly influenced by Klopstock, whom the author visited in 1792.[43] In fact, Schönfeld acclaims the venerated older writer, dedicating to him poems comparing Zion and his homeland, Germany:

> Ich soll, ich soll den hohen geflügelten
> Gesang des Isaiden im Erbe Teuts,
> Mein Vaterland! Dir würdig singen,
> Sprach sie, und weihte mich also segnend.[44]

Like Klopstock's odes, Schönfeld's poems are studded with Hebrew words [*negioth, kinor*] and return time and again to Klopstock's motif of the *Palmenhain* [palm grove]. Indeed, he even addresses them to the same muse, Siona.[45] Besides Klopstock, Schönfeld also dedicated Hebraist poems to poet Matthias Claudius (1740–1815) and to Moses Mendelssohn.[46] While Josef Karniel characterizes this poem (as well as another dealing with the Jewish people) as a "national Jewish" creation, Kabbalah scholar Klaus Davidwoicz maintains that *Davids Kriegsgesäng* bears the mark of Jacob Franks' "militarist tendencies."[47] However, in this case, the influence of Klopstock, and perhaps of Herder and other contemporary writers who were inspired by Hebrew war hymns, seems more pronounced. Against the backdrop of the works mentioned thus far, I believe these texts by Schönfeld should be read as an extraordinary manifestation of a national-political Hebraism. His poems having been published in many contemporary anthologies—they even garnered positive reviews in the press—I believe he can be regarded as one of the leading disseminators of Hebraist poetics during the period of the revolution.[48]

"The Hebrews' Patriotic Poets": Prophets as Political Model

Texts that addressed the national hymns brought "the national Hebrew poets"— that is, the prophets—into sharp focus. This interest in the prophets was not a new phenomenon. As described above, Klopstock and the writers who followed him extolled the virtues of the prophets as inspired religious poets. However, alongside the growing politicization of the German intellectual scene in the last two decades of the eighteenth century, new characteristics were attributed to them; rather than poets writing under the influence of the Holy Spirit, they were now described as political men.

In his book *Litteraturgeschichte*, Eichhorn claimed that the Hebrews' prophetic poetry, a manifestation of the political rationality of a group of patriotic sages, "has inspired our own times to the highest degree."[49] This depiction of the prophets was rapidly replicated in numerous writings devoted to the subject around the turn of the century; essays, pedagogical books, and translations of Prophets highlighted their "patriotism." In his 1790 book, Johann Christof Döderlein (1746–1792), a theologian at the University of Jena, described the prophets as "patriots whose blood boils at the sight of tyrants and oppressors,"[50] adding: "Who would fail to sense ... the patriotic spirit protecting religion, aspiring to the good of the Nation, working for virtue and fuelled by Truth, Justice and national Happiness?"[51]

Johann Christian Augusti (1772–1841), an orientalist and theologian of Jewish extraction and lecturer at the University of Jena, described the prophets as patriotic heroes leading their people with "love of the fatherland" [*Vaterlandsliebe*] and "holy enthusiasm."[52] He praises Jeremiah and other prophets as "noble patriots."[53] They are often referred to as "patriotic demagogues" or "educators and demagogues"—both in the positive sense of the term.[54] Similar descriptions appear in the many interpretive essays published on this subject during that time.

The political ideal of the biblical prophet was fashioned, by and large, during the course of the debate on two burning issues that headed the public agenda in this period: that of the clergy's social function and that of the origins of political authority. In the context of the controversy over preachers' social status, the prophets were described as the quintessence of the politically engaged man of religion.

Prophetic politics were lauded as a form of patriotism inextricably linked to "religious fervor."[55] The biblical prophet served as a towering model: as preachers were expected, according to the reform plans debated during this time, to become *Volkslehrer* serving the needs of the nation, the prophets exemplified men of religion who had fulfilled this role in combination with their spiritual calling.

This affinity between the religious and the political touches on the second context within which the figure of the prophet was invoked in relation to burning questions of the day, namely the issue of the origin of political authority. As Frederick Beiser has shown in his book on the evolution of modern German political thought, the fundamental problem that occupied German thinkers of the final decade of the eighteenth century was that of the validity and authority of reason within the political sphere.[56] Although it had been debated exhaustively beforehand, this question now demanded a clearer answer following events in France, which were interpreted as a brutal attempt to subjugate politics to rationality. The image of the prophet as a man who receives his political imperatives from God himself became highly contentious in this constellation. Writers of a rationalist bent warned of "the new Prophets"—all manner of visionaries and millenarians who sprang up in the crisis-laden atmosphere of the great political upheavals.[57] For their part, conservative writers as well as those of a romanticist bent applauded prophetic politics.

In 1789, Lindhein (Hessen) evangelical preacher Georg Konrad Horst (1767–1738) published a pamphlet titled *Die Visionen Habakuks*, which included a translation and interpretation of the book of Habakuk based mostly on the work of Herder and Eichhorn. The translation was accompanied by a philosophical essay entitled *Über den Prophetismus der Alten Welt*.[58] An admirer of Herder (to whom he in fact dedicated the book), Horst was a pioneer of early nineteenth-century romantic theology, calling, in some of his essays, for a sentimental relation to Christianity, which he describes as a "feeling," "poetry," and even a "fantasy."

Both in ambition and subject matter, Horst's treatise on prophecy exceeds the standard introductions that generally accompanied biblical translations. The author describes the books of "those great Hebrews that we know as Prophets" as an exemplary cultural ideal for the entire human race.[59] According to Horst, the appearance of the prophets made a marked impact on the people's moral, religious, and political spirit and thus indirectly constituted a decisive event in the history of mankind in general. Prophecy books were not merely culturally or aesthetically exemplary—they also had political validity. He terms the prophets' political message "prophetism" [*Prophetismus*], meaning those general laws that can be formulated from the content of divine inspiration. Following Lessing, he claims that the prophets' edicts embody divine revelation while simultaneously fitting rational principles. The prophets should be regarded as "statesmen"

[*Staatsmänner*] and true patriots dedicated to truth, justice, and religion. In summation, he recommends that statecraft should be based on their moral-political principles.

Following publication of Horst's essay, Eichhorn reviewed it in a magazine he edited, *Allgemeine Bibliothek der biblischen Literatur,* sarcastically dampening Horst's enthusiasm regarding the prophets' political relevance and stating that the author "goes too far" in finding in it the germs of both "critical philosophy" and "general laws." Horst, Eichhorn claims, confused edicts intended to further "the wholeness and happiness of humankind in its entirety" with those meant solely for the Jewish people: "Sometimes it seems he confuses the world and humanity with the Jewish people . . . the author of this essay has so far found in the words of the Prophets not this august principle but mainly a rather narrow *national viewpoint.* How poorly Images of the battle in the Valley of Jehoshaphat and their ilk fit the pure moral ideas and the cosmopolitan stances that Mister Horst has found in the words of the Old Testament Prophets!"[60]

We should assume that Eichhorn deliberately chose the term *the Jewish People,* which, as far as his readership was concerned, placed prophecy in far less grand a context than did the term Horst had originally employed. Like Kant, Reimarus, Hufnagel, and many others, Eichhorn here debunks the idea of the prophets' cosmopolitan message and refutes the role attributed to the Jewish people in the education of mankind. However, his derisive dismissal of the "national viewpoint" was less obvious to his readers than it is now.

Although briefly formulated and never fully elaborated, Horst's expounding on the politics of "prophetism" was an interesting attempt to address the question of the Old Testament's political relevance vis-à-vis the Enlightenment's critiques. Philosophers such as Kant and reformers like Campe and Bahrdt believed that if Christianity were to be "saved" and adapted to the principles of reason and natural religion, then the Old Testament had to be "sacrificed." They claimed that if Christianity were to be subjugated to the overall aim of furthering humanity, then those elements it contained that did not serve the social order, namely the Old Testament (which Kant regarded as the constitution of an oriental theocracy and as such, a valueless historical relic), should be abandoned. Horst, on the contrary, sought to save Christianity *through* the Old Testament. The prophets' patriotic sermons, according to this reading, formed the basis for a religious-political tradition that, so he claimed, had gained renewed validity in the present.

Historian Jonathan Sheehan has argued that the main thrust of biblical scholarship within the Enlightenment entailed a functional division between the Old and New Testaments: while the Old Testament offered beauty and transcendence, the New Testament was attributed truth and morality.[61] But the political reading described above positions the text in a different context. In many instances, this reading moves the poetic parts of scripture to center stage while placing them in a national context. This reading is linked to central characteristics of nascent German nationalism, stressing the connection between religion, culture, and nationalism.

Hebrew Mythology as a Cultural-Pedagogical Project: Scherer and His Circle

One of the ways in which writers at the turn of the eighteenth century sought to "save" the Bible was to transform it into mythology. As we have seen, Herder's poetic reading of scripture encouraged this process, even if the author himself preferred other formulations. Indeed, Bible scholars and theologians of Herder's period went so far as to define the Bible as "Hebrew mythology." The most prominent among them were Eichhorn and his disciple-colleague Johann Philip Gabler (1753–1826).[62] These ideas were propounded in Eichhorn's 1790 essay "Urgeshcichte," which featured Gabler's notes, as well as in his influential book *Einleitung in das Alte Testament*, published in 1780–1783. Contrary to earlier rationalist interpreters, Eichhorn and Gabler did not attempt to extract historical elements from the stories of the Creation, the Flood and the Tower of Babel, but rather interpreted them as mythic creations, the outcome of a "childish phase" in the education [*Bildung*] of mankind.[63] They claimed that only when interpreted in this fashion did these "documents" disclose their full truth.

Mythical interpretation of the stories of Genesis appeared some years later in an early essay by Wilhelm Schelling (1775–1854) titled *On the Myths of the Ancient World* [*Über die Mythen der ältesten Welt*],[64] and in other writings. The most extreme example of this method was Georg Lorenz Bauer's (1755–1806) *Hebrew Mythology* [*Hebraïsche Mythologie*], which includes, among other topics, comparisons between biblical motifs and Greek, Persian, and other myths.[65]

While Eichhorn and his disciples used the concept of "myth" as a philological-interpretive category, another no less influential group of Bible scholars embarked on a cultural project to endow biblical mythology with aesthetic and political significance. One member of this group of young theologians was Horst; like him, most were preachers employed in north Germany's provincial towns, and in particular, in Hessen.

The group's leading figure was Bible scholar, orientalist, translator, and prolific writer Wilhelm Scherer (1777–1825), who also edited the magazine *Schriftforscher zur Belebung eines gründlichen Bibelstudiums*. Although some of his essays raised a certain stir in the German "republic of letters," Scherer failed to gain significant recognition on the German literary scene of his time. Most of his writings have been forgotten, have left no noticeable imprint, and have attracted no scholarly interest, even though his prolific output is a wonderful example of the connection between biblical scholarship, theology, and politics during the shift from Enlightenment to romanticism. While other scholars of the ancient Hebrews who were active during his time confined themselves to the academic or theological fields, Scherer merged novel ways of reading the Bible with a larger pedagogical-cultural project. Indeed, his work can be viewed as the most ambitious attempt at carrying forward Herder's Hebraistic cultural project. Some of his ideas even precede a number of de Wette's innovations, published several years later.

Scherer was born in Nidda, near Darmstadt, to a high-ranking state official.[66] From a young age he exhibited a penchant for theology, and with his father's encouragement, studied with a private Hebrew tutor. He claimed to have read the Bible fluently in Hebrew by the age of fifteen, and already at that tender age, became concerned by biblical contradictions. In early 1793, his mother, father, aunt, and brother—to whom he was especially close—died in quick succession, apparently succumbing to a plague that ravaged this area of the Rhine Valley that year. This disaster, which left Scherer and his sisters orphaned, may explain his volatile character and the strange contradictions in his intellectual biography. At any rate, the Graf of Hessen came to the aid of the disaster-stricken family, and Scherer won a scholarship that allowed him to attend the University of Giessen, where he studied under orientalist Johann Wilhelm Friedrich Hezel (1754–1824).

Two years thereafter, Scherer's interest in theology had cooled and he left the university, returning to take up philosophy studies. He began to publish his first articles and to socialize with other scholars in Mainz. In 1795, his home was plundered during the French invasion, and, having completed his doctorate in philosophy, he began preaching in several Hessen hamlets—first in Dauernheim and then in Echzell. In 1798, at the age of twenty-one, he completed his first book, *Neue Religionsgeschichte für die Jugend*, published in Leipzig.[67] As contemporary critics noted, this was a biblical history [*biblische Geschichte*] of the Hebrews and the ancient world rather than a work of religious history.[68] In it, Scherer explains the complexities of teaching the Bible to young people directly from Luther's translation. It appears that his claims are based on his experiences while teaching at the Sunday school he founded in Echzell to acquaint the youth of the area with modern learning. In another textbook, published several years later, he explains that scripture was taught by antiquated methods in both public and private classes—by continuous, uncritical reading from Genesis straight through to the Epistle of James at the very end of the New Testament, without knowing or even wondering "who wrote them and to what end."[69] This mode of instruction struck Scherer as illogical and positively harmful. He argued that such antiquated teaching of the Bible played into the hands of reformers who wished to remove the book from school curricula. He therefore sought to modernize biblical teaching and biblical culture by utilizing the critical research of Hezel and Michaelis, as well as that of Faber, Warnekros Babor, Jahn, and others.[70]

On what type of material would the new, critical form of Bible study, which was to replace the church's traditional teaching over many generations, center? An answer to this question can be gleaned from Scherer's *Bible Commentary* [*Bibelcommentar*], published in 1799.[71] The introduction to this work was penned by a familiar figure—Horst—who was a preacher in a neighboring town and apparently knew Scherer from a young age. As in his aforementioned essay on the prophets (which he published around the same time), here too, Horst sings the Hebrews' praises, stressing their writings' cultural relevance. He asserts that throughout the cultural history of mankind, no single other group of people have commanded our attention like the Hebrews. More than a religious creation, he regards the Old Testament as "the oldest relic [*Ueberbleibsel*] we have of world human history," predating the earliest of the Greek writings by hundreds of years.[72] The books of the Bible embody the way the human race discarded "raw sensuality," climbing the rungs of morality until it attained the moral stature of the prophets, who are hence of interest to the thinking man of any age. Thus, at the core of the biblical project is a reading of the Bible as a valuable cultural document. Despite its origins in the orient, Biblical poetry still kindles the contemporary reader's heart.[73]

This characterization of biblical poetry as a majestic creation affecting readers' emotions is familiar to us from the writings of Klopstock and Herder, published several decades earlier. To a greater extent than the *Sturm und Drang* writers, Horst and Scherer emphasize Hebrew poetry's *patriotic* quality. Writing while France's revolutionary army was conquering the Rhine Valley, the authors hail the ways in which the prophets express their people's political upheavals, disasters, and triumphs.

In 1803, Scherer produced another essay on the Bible, a history of the Israelites aimed at the general public and adapted to "the needs of our time."[74] Here, too, he declares his intention of presenting "the advancements made by Bible interpretation scholars" over recent decades. Going farther than his predecessors, he does not hesitate to sidestep the tradition that identifies Moses as the author of the Torah; he calls the author of Genesis "a Semitic wise man" [*ein Semitischer Weise*] or simply "the Semite" [*der Semite*]. By doing so, he embraces the conceptual novelties of 1790s ethnography and philology.[75]

Scherer's book differs from those of the other Bible scholars he follows by virtue of his decision to present Hebrew history in poetic form, broken up into short, metered lines. It was this element that drew the lion's share of criticism of the book.[76] Scherer rewrote the biblical narrative into poetic epopoeia, adding several informative interjections, and claimed that since poetry was the ancient mode of writing, if contemporary readers were to understand the orientals, this was the way the text should be presented. As Polaschegg notes, this desire to present oriental texts by following the original form and alliteration was shared by many translators of the early nineteenth century; a simple translation was considered insufficient to convey the spirit of the "Hebrew myth" [*die Hebraïsche Mythe*] to the German reading public and assimilate it into German poetry.[77] Scherer repeatedly compares the heroes of the patriarchal period to those of Homer and seeks to relate Moses's life story itself as an "epopoeia." At a time when the German cultural elite was becoming ever more alienated from the Old Testament, he endeavored to renew interest in it by transforming it into a colorful romantic myth. Indeed, he goes so far as to refer to the language of Genesis as "Romantic poetry language."

Contemporary critics attacked Scherer's book as being simultaneously too trivial for a scholarly essay and too complicated for lay readers.[78] And compared to the earlier writings in the Hebrew history genre, Scherer's stance toward the Bible is indeed distinctly unusual. On the one hand, he displays radical misgivings about the consistency, cohesiveness, and historical credibility of the biblical narrative; on these issues, his stance is not dissimilar to those of the most rationalist Bible critics such as Edelmann, Reimarus, and Campe. On the other hand, Scherer is not a rationalist, and does not seek to undermine religion as such. He poeticizes and mythologizes the Bible; more than any other Bible translation published in his time, Scherer's German text is full of Hebrew grammatical structures, described as "orientalisms" and "Hebraisms." In a critique of the book in *Allgemeine Literatur-Zeitung*, the reviewer states that: "[the author] translated the passages faithfully according to the original . . . and tried to imitate Hebrew structures. But a translation should be written in actual German, be legible and comprehensible in our times."[79]

The archaic-Hebraist style Scherer chose was deliberate, although he was unsuccessful in his aim. Distancing the text from ordinary language and modern experience was meant to make it accessible as myth. Contrary to Michaelis, Scherer does not seek to argue with the antireligionists in the historical arena, but rather to complete the mission of transforming the Bible into fiction. Its undermined authenticity is restored by reading it as an exotic epic, an archaic myth of the ancient Semites.

Despite his book's cool reception by the critical establishment, Scherer developed his project of biblical mythicization in a series of further books and in two journals he founded, *Archiv zur Vervollkommnung des Bibelstudiums* (1801), published in Mainz, and *Der Schriftforscher* (1803), published in Weimar.[80] During these years, a group of young theologians and Bible scholars congregated around the Echzell preacher. Though the men of this circle were influenced by a number of contemporary intellectual fashions, they shared a deep disdain for the conservative methods practiced by the theology faculties at the time, and decried the inordinate influence Kant's transcendental philosophy was exerting on theologians. The aforementioned Horst, Justi, Hufnagel, and Hezel (as well as

Hebrew fashion scholar Hartmann) all contributed to the journals. None of these was clearly aligned with a theological camp, but the ideas they furthered revolved around Horst's call to transform religion into "poetry, fantasy and mythology."[81]

Some of the articles written by Scherer's circle were truly provocative. A piece entitled *Ueber den Priester-und Prophetenclub der Hebräer*, contributed by an author named Ottmar (actually Scherer himself) sparked the greatest controversy.[82] The article describes a clique or secret club of priests and prophets who had directed the major events of Hebrew history and had undermined the nation's independence to further its agendas. The article claims, for example, that the voice of God speaking to Samuel the child (1 Samuel 3) was actually that of one of the Levites, working for a secret organization of priests that connived to overthrow the family of Eli. Similarly, the prophet Elijah is presented as a saboteur plotting to dethrone Ahab by unseemly means. Scherer made similar claims in another book he published dealing with the visions of the prophets; and he apparently was the author of a further anonymous article published in Berlin, which quotes Scherer's work extensively.[83] In all of these writings, the prophets are presented as hucksters and compared to Indian shamans or radical revolutionaries.

Scherer's theory appears to be a biblical variation on the conspiracy theories of the "Illuminati" and Freemason kind, which exploded during the French Revolution.[84] At any rate, even conspiracy theorists were not overly impressed by the article. One of the "Illuminati" theory's main propagators, Johann August von Starck (1741–1816), fiercely attacked Scherer, castigating his mythological interpretation as an especially scandalous form of deism.[85] In all, it would seem that the appearance of these articles was what contributed to Scherer's infamy: they were dismissed as speculative, ridiculous, and inappropriate, especially since they had appeared in a theological journal. One critic described Scherer as a poor imitator of Herder, while another attacked him for describing the Hebrew prophets as if they belonged to some Jacobin club [*Jakobinerklub*] and were embroiled in the kind of political intrigue that characterized the modern world.[86] Other detractors maintained that the author was straining to be as "savage" and "uncivilized" as the period he wrote about.[87] On top of all this, Scherer also became embroiled in a public journalistic standoff with theologian Johann Ludwig Wachler (1767–1838).[88] Finally, *Der Schriftforscher* folded after only two volumes.

The dramatic political events of the time also contributed to the demise of Scherer's Hebraist project. In 1806, Hessen was annexed to the pro-Napoleonic Rhine Confederacy, thereby significantly expanding the area under the control of Ludwig, Graf Hessen-Darmstadt (Scherer's patron), who was in fact retitled *Grossherzog*. Scherer voiced great enthusiasm for the new order, as evidenced by a sermon he delivered at a thanksgiving celebration held in 1806, following

Prussia's defeat and the annulment of the German Reich. Similar celebrations, ordered by the occupying power, were held after the fall of the Reich in all the major cities of the Rhineland. Scherer's response was particularly ebullient; the title of his sermon was "The Homeland in Peril, God is Her Savior! To Him Honor and Thanks!" and Scherer used it to extol the part played by providence in removing the threat of war from Hessen and enhancing the Graf's powers.[89]

He likewise celebrates the victorious Napoleon, depicting him as God's emissary. Unsurprisingly, he invokes heroic biblical images to this end; he compares Napoleon to Moses, David, and Judas Maccabeus (as well as to Frederick the Great). While pro-Napoleonic sermons were commonplace in the Rhine Confederacy, Scherer's sycophantic adulation of the French potentate evoked criticism.[90] In any event, it is interesting to note that many sermons of a similar biblical character were delivered, several years thereafter, following Napoleon's famous defeat at the Battle of Leipzig—only this time it was the King of Prussia who was described as Moses and David.

In the following years, Scherer delivered further political sermons in response to current events and the needs of his various patrons, such as those he produced in the context of the peace accords following France's triumph over Austria in 1809.[91] Following Napoleon's downfall, he appears to have shied away from political issues. He continued to write about "oriental poetry" and translated passages of it, but also turned his attention to other subjects, primarily the appropriate treatment of animals.[92] From this point onward, it seems his literary output gained little attention outside his close circle of readers. His colleague Horst turned to encyclopedic research into the history of magic and the occult, the field for which he remained renowned throughout the nineteenth century.

From History to Mythology: de Wette's Interpretive Revolution

Scherer's aim was to transform scripture into mythology and thus introduce Hebrew myth to the German Bourgeoisie's *Bildung*, alongside the Greek classics. But this project was received coolly. No significant figure in the literary field adopted Scherer's approach, and the theological establishment regarded him with no less a degree of suspicion. Scripture was still too laden with religious significance, and critics and readers alike found it hard to reconcile Scherer's enthusiastic advocacy of the Bible and its heroes with his iconoclastic attack on the text's—and implicitly, its heroes'—authenticity. Even though they were culturally close to romanticism, the romantic poets distanced themselves from Scherer and his circle in their refusal to adopt Herder's Hebraistic poetics and thematic elements, as elaborated below.

Yet while Scherer's biblical mythicization project is now all but forgotten, another Bible scholar of his time initiated a true ground shift in German Bible scholarship, signifying the beginning of a distinctly new era in this field. He was

Wilhelm Lebrecht de Wette (1780–1849).[93] As a young man, de Wette studied with Herder in Weimar and continued his studies in Jena, where he was deeply influenced by the philosophy of Kant and Schelling (1755–1854). These influences led him to adopt an interpretive-theological position, sidestepping the rationalism-orthodoxy divide that so polarized eighteenth-century Bible exegesis. De Wette spearheaded a new critical methodology that fundamentally undermined scripture's historical interpretation, anchoring the Christian religion in new meanings of sentiment and nationalism.

Contrary to the other Bible scholars discussed in this book, de Wette's texts have remained largely relevant, and are familiar to contemporary Bible scholars. His principal intellectual innovation is considered a foundation of modern Bible scholarship: his assertion that the book of Deuteronomy was in fact "the Book of the Law" that High Priest Hilkiah found in the Temple in Jerusalem during the reign of King Josiah of Judah (2 Kings 22). In his book *A Contribution to an Introduction to the Old Testament* [*Beiträge zur Einleitung in das Alte Testament*], published in 1806, de Wette sought to prove that Deuteronomy was in fact written not long prior to its "discovery," and may actually have been written by Hilkiah himself.[94] Since the Bible itself offers no proof of the existence of the Torah before Josiah's time, de Wette concludes that all the books of the Bible were collected and edited during the reign of this king.

The identity of the Torah's author had occupied scholars since the seventeenth century and even earlier. But de Wette used his origin theory to formulate an almost totally new way of reading scripture. According to this reading, since the books of the Bible were written hundreds of years after the events they depict, they are in fact worthless as historical documents. The author of the Bible, transformed in this reading into a "storyteller" [*Erzähler*], had little interest in describing the past and rather fashioned the text according to the political demands of the late kingdom period. Therefore, the Bible can't be used to investigate Hebrew history. Already in his 1805 book, de Wette asserts that the Bible is a holy book and has *religious* value—but no historical, political, or juridical merit.[95]

With this assertion, half a century of German Bible interpretation under the aegis of historical criticism came to an end. The interpretive project of Michaelis and his generation rested on affirming Moses's interlocking functions as both *author* of the Torah and *legislator*. Michaelis's investigations revolved around "great men"—with Moses as chief among them—and sought to recreate the historical context of biblical events. He had little to say about the text's origins and how it had evolved. In the eighteenth century, both admirers and critics of the Bible shared the assumption that the events described therein—from the conquest of Canaan to David's exploits—were real. But in the context of the new interpretive approach that de Wette founded, no assumption is made regarding the possibility of drawing valid scientific conclusions regarding Hebrew history, politics, or law from reading the Bible. If the work of Michaelis and Herder was epitomized by the reconstruction of the Hebrew people and its culture by comparing the Bible with ethnographic studies, de Wette believed that biblical narrative presented an obstacle to historical knowledge. From now on, he maintained, scripture could only be analyzed as text; employing ethnographic methods to reconstruct the figures of biblical heroes therefore made no sense. Abraham, for example, appears in Genesis as the mythical figure of a nation-founder, thus it would be meaningless to portray him as an Arab sheikh, as Michaelis and his disciples did.

De Wette compares the Bible to classical epics such as Virgil's *Aeneid*. Just like this Latin epos, written during the reign of Emperor Augustus, the Bible was intended to offer the subjects of the Kingdom of Judah answers to their questions about their communal existence: how did we come into being? How was our state founded under the reign of Jehovah? And how were our laws legislated?[96] As we have seen in earlier chapters, similar questions occupied members of the historical school of biblical scholarship throughout the eighteenth century; however, according to de Wette, it is precisely because the Bible was written with the express intention of delivering a mythological response to these questions that it cannot provide material for contemporary researchers of Hebrew history.

In fact, de Wette's interpretation treads the path outlined by Herder, Eichhorn, and Gabler in their writings about Hebrew poetry and Hebrew myth. However, he makes no attempt to distinguish between the poetic and historical elements in the Bible. Eichhorn employed the method of mythic interpretation apologetically, to bridge the gulf between the Hebrews' ancient concepts and those of contemporary German culture. De Wette, on the contrary, assigns myth a distinctly positive significance.

The Bible's mythic role supersedes its historical content; it is this element in de Wette's system that signifies its rupture with rationalist interpretation and ties it to romanticism and nationality. De Wette does not negate the historicity of scripture to undermine its importance, but on the contrary, to imbue it with new meaning. According to his method, this literary work must be understood through its religious and artistic content. While Herder alternated between treating the Bible as a universal creation and stressing its national elements, de Wette describes it first and foremost as a "Hebrew national epos" [*hebraïsches Nationalepos*], written and edited according to the national interests of a Hebrew theocracy at a specific point in time: "Treated as poetry and myth, [the Old Testament] appears as a rich, significant subject... It is an outcome of the Israelite people's religious homeland, where its spirit, manner of thinking, patriotism and religious philosophy play out, and therefore it is one of the most primary sources of cultural and religious history."[97]

In the history of Bible interpretation, de Wette's approach is generally associated with Kant's philosophy.[98] Indeed, in a way similar to the Copernican revolution Kant formulated in his *Critique of Pure Reason*—pointing metaphysical investigation away from the object and toward the structure of consciousness itself—de Wette diverts Bible interpretation from the events portrayed in it and points it toward the structure of the text itself. However, a further context that informs this revolution should not be overlooked, namely poets' and philologists' growing interest in founding a national literature and national mythology by gathering and editing medieval works and popular stories. The creation of the Hebrew national epos, as described by de Wette, strikingly resembles the romantics' creation of a "German mythology," exhibited, for example, in a growing interest in the *Nibelungenlied* and in German folk tales.

Unsurprisingly, de Wette was one of the main proponents of the creation of a German Protestant mythology. Having settled in Berlin University in 1810, he developed a fervently nationalist worldview. In his essay *Über Religion und Theologie*, published in 1815, he sets out a vision for a new popular liturgy—a religious epos to be founded on a series of mythological signs drawn from nature and history.[99] He credits Herder with laying the groundwork for such a mythology through his receptiveness to and love of the popular poetry of all peoples—the Hebrews and the Greeks, northern and southern nations. His project had since expanded, with Germany becoming a nursery for "the most beautiful flowers of antiquity," proving the Germans to be the most religious of all nations. We clearly see the impact of romanticism on this vision: this religion would come to fruition only with the assimilation of a natural philosophy into epic poetry, culminating in a new "epos of cosmogony" [*Epos der Kosmogonie*].

German romanticism's appeal to nature and to folk tales is transformed here into a new Christian religion. But as Williamson has noted, while similar to the ancient Hebrews' or the Catholic Church's rituals, this religion in fact sought to replace these with a German Protestant mythology.[100] Although both de Wette and other admirers of myth based themselves on Herder, they differed from him markedly; while he showed a universal interest in the poetry of all ancient peoples, they increasingly focused on a search for the ethnic roots of the German people.

German poets of the nineteenth century looked further east, to India, for the authentic roots of their people's mythology. Like Klopstock and Herder, Friedrich Schlegel (1772–1829) and Novalis also yearned for an ancient, mythic-poetic oriental culture that would offer an alternative to the Greek cultural-political model. However, they now discovered such a culture among the Indian Brahmins, rather than among the Hebrew prophets.[101] Hebrew poetry was removed from the pedestal Herder had built for it—the universal source of all culture—and reconstituted as a foreign oriental document. Yet, as it was being deserted by mainstream

German culture, the Hebrews' poetic and cultural tradition was embraced by another group of Enlightenment men: Jewish *Maskilim*. Gradually, the Hebrew poetic ideal migrated from Christian to Jewish writers.

German Hebraism and the Origins of Modern Hebrew Literature

The idea of writing an epos centering on Moses occupied several major German Enlightenment writers. Even Michaelis, who was not especially inclined to poetry writing, penned a poem in 1753 entitled *Moses: Ein heldengedischt* (*Moses: A Hero's Poem*).[102] Herder, too, began to write a similar piece in his youth, but subsequently abandoned the idea, commenting that such a poem should rightfully be written by a poet of the Hebrew nation itself. In his book *Adrastea*, he again draws a comparison between the Homeric epos and the biblical narrative of the Hebrew nation [*Ebräische Nation*] and its "Guardian God" [*Schutzgott*], concluding with the question: "Is all this not wonderfully epic, perhaps even more so than Vulcan's shield or the gods' war on Troy's shore? Is there no Hebrew to create a whole from these disparate materials, bringing the holy word of his nature closer to the heart?"[103]

It is unclear whether Herder meant this as a general remark or was referring to a specific piece published several years beforehand, *Songs of Glory* (Shirei Tiferet) by Naphtali Hirz Wessely (1725–1805), considered the inaugural work of modern Hebrew literature. Some scholars regard this epic poem, dealing with Jewish history, as a response to Herder's call in *Vom Geist der Ebräischen Poesie*.[104] Wessely himself, however, never mentions Herder's name, and some cast doubt on Herder's influence, regarding this as the invention of later Jewish Enlightenment figures [*Maskilim*].[105] Whatever the case may be, no less interesting than the motivation for its writing is the circumstance of its translation into German: Wessely had originally published the first ode of the collection in the journal *Hame'asef*, as an elegy to the Duke of Braunschweig-Wolfenbüttel, who died when the Oder River flooded in 1785. Hufnagel, professor of theology in Erlangen at the time, then translated it into German for *Zeitschrift für Christenthum*. Apparently while writing *Songs of Glory*, Wessely had sent an impassioned plea to Hufnagel to translate the complete work into German.[106] Hufnagel ultimately translated only its first part (the second was translated by theologian Johann Joachim Spalding, 1714–1804). The German version was entitled *Mosaide*, a clear parallel to Klopstock's *Messias*.[107]

One of the axioms of the Herderian ideal of Hebraistic nationality was the distinction between *Hebrews* and *Jews*.[108] Several scholars, including Lilliane Weissberg, maintain that Herder's praise of the Hebrews was intended to further distinguish them from the Jews of his time.[109] However, in much of German Hebraist writing, the Jew makes an occasional appearance to haunt the biblical text. The connection between ancient Hebrews and present-day Jews is to be found in some of the texts, and is formulated in different ways. In fact, some contemporary writers chose to title their essays on the Bible "A History of the Jews" or "A History of the Jewish People."[110] The distinction between Hebrews and contemporary Jews is, for the most part, unclear and sometimes self-contradictory.

Furthermore, despite its Christian character, Hebraist discourse was relatively accessible to Jews, facilitating various kinds of relations, albeit limited, between Christian and Jewish writers. In several cases, Herderian and Klopstockian Hebraism offered a way for Jewish intellectuals to establish a place for themselves within German culture; in others, this discourse allowed Jewish writers to constitute a culture distinct from the German one—and even embryonic forms of nationality.

The target audience for the German-biblical genre, defined as *"Liebhaber der hebräischen Sprache"* (lovers of the Hebrew language) was not religiously designated. It comes as little surprise, then, that the group of *Maskilim* that published *Hame'asef* in 1782 named itself *Hevrat Doreshei Leshon Ever* [The Society of Friends of the Hebrew Language].[111] Isaac Euchel (1756–1804), the group's founder, studied in Königsberg under biblical scholar Johann Bernhard Köhler (1742–1802) and regarded Herder as a major source of influence on modern Hebrew literature. In a 1790 critique, he commended Wessely for responding to Herder's appeal by dedicating a Hebrew piece to the life of Moses.[112] Moses Philippsohn (1775–1814), a teacher at the Jewish School in Dessau who published the German-Hebrew reader *Mudah Livnei Binah* in 1808, gave it the subtitle "A Book of Learning and Reading for Jewish Nation Youths and All Lovers of the Hebrew Language."[113]

Three years later, evangelical preacher Justi published a translation of an excerpt from *The Song of Moses* (Deuteronomy 32) in the *Haskalah* periodical *Sulamith*, edited by David Fränkel (1865–1779) also of Dessau. In his short introduction to the translation, he asks the readers of the periodical, "Who among patriotic Israelites fails to feel a jolt of happiness when reading this, Moses' swansong?"[114] While in introducing his translations, targeted at a German-speaking audience, Justi declared that the Hebrews' national poems "were meant to be sung by the nation," he now turns to "the Israelite patriots" directly, calling on them to display enthusiasm for this poetry.

As David Sorkin has noted, *Sulamith* was the first Jewish periodical to blur the distinction between educational writing aimed at the Jewish community (mostly in Hebrew) and apologetic writing addressed to Christians (in German). The periodical carried articles on ethics and religion and translations of biblical and other Jewish sources, as well as articles on general topics (such as science and ethnography), and sought to establish a new readership comprising people of both religions to facilitate the furthering of the emancipation. Like other *Maskilim*, the writers of *Sulamith* tended to excoriate the Jews for the pitiful state of their culture, calling on them to update their customs and to educate themselves in the spirit of the *Bildung* ideal of German culture. The classical model played a pivotal role in this cultural project. The first volume of *Sulamith* included an extensive essay by classicist Johann Andreas Lebrecht Richter (1772–1844), a paean to the ancient Greeks' superiority to "our culture." However, in many of the periodical's articles, and in many other contemporary *Haskalah* publications, it is the Hebrews that are posited as the classical cultural ideal. In this context, Lowth and Herder are presented as leaders in the rebirth of ancient Hebrew poetry.

Reliance on the German Hebraist ideal is a pronounced feature of the work of poet Salomon Ya'akov Cohen (1771–1845), Wessely's disciple. His 1807 *Oriental Groves of Northern Shores* [*Morgenländische Pflanzen auf nördlichem Boden*] is a bilingual text comprising Hebrew plays and hymns on biblical themes accompanied by German translations. In his introduction to the compendium, Cohen eulogizes two august figures who worked during the eighteenth century. "The Hebrew muse," he wrote, grieves the departure of "great British Hebrew Robert Lowth," followed by "the genius Herder."[115] According to Cohen, Herder was one of the Hebrews' greatest admirers, who knew how to "listen to their most delicate ways." To these two luminaries he added Wessely, who had died two years prior to the compendium's publication: "With the death of Herder and Wessely, these two fast friends of our oriental art of poetry, it seems it has lost its lustrous fame and the appreciation of its merits—even if not the art itself . . . Wessely is dead, and with him the hope of a rebirth of Hebrew literature."[116]

Cohen outlines a canon for a reawakening Hebrew, placing Jewish and Christian scholars side by side. As mentioned above, this conception was articulated by Euchel as early as the last decade of the eighteenth century. The concern in Cohen's words should be noted; it seems he recognized the fact that with Herder's death, the Hebrew model's influence in the German "republic of letters" was waning. Thus the *Maskil*, who seeks to assimilate with the new German Hebraist creation, finds himself frustrated.

Summary: The Rise and Demise of the Hebrew Model

The Hebraist culture of the late eighteenth century was in large part a reaction to the anticlerical mindset of rationalism and deism. Voltaire, the English deists and even several German rationalist writers regarded an attack on scripture as a central element in their campaign against the institution of religion as such. Simultaneously, governmental reforms enacted in Prussia and other principalities threw the church and its supporters into a defensive position, causing preachers to feel that they were a dying breed. And since Bible critics tended to attack the Old Testament more fiercely than the New, defense of the Hebrew Bible became a religious-cultural rallying call. Sympathy for Hebrew poetry expressed opposition to the deists' and French philosophers' unsettling attack. An almost personal insult sustained by Voltaire's and the deists' attacks on the Bible can be discerned in the writing of many of the period's German authors. Facing the enemies of the Bible, Herder dedicates his book to "lovers of Hebrew poetry" [*Liebhaber der hebräischen Poesie*].

Even though Herder's political outlook was in part radical, this preacher-philosopher's texts inspired antireformist preachers and theologians. In many of his writings, Herder defended the clergy's special religious functions and its beleaguered status vis-à-vis the absolutist civil leadership. His stance, formed largely in response to the contemporary battle over the clergy's role in a centralized state, was inextricably linked to his poetic, political, and theological ideas. The ancient peoples from which Herder drew inspiration—and chiefly the Hebrews—provided him a model for a religious leadership of poet-priests during his own time.[117]

In this respect, Hebraism is a form of Christian awakening and defense against the liberal political ideas that sprang up during this period. The motivations of the German Hebraist stream of the eighteenth and nineteenth centuries cannot be appreciated without placing them against the backdrop of these fierce attacks on scripture and especially on the Old Testament. However, it would be imprecise to describe the resurrection of the Bible as purely a conservative reaction to rationalist theology. The attempt to lay the foundations for a Hebrew-Christian mythology such as that which Scherer and his colleagues promoted may be considered a radically modern form of Protestant theology seeking to assimilate Christianity into the national discourse through use of primordial material originating in the Old Testament.

Patriotic German intellectuals used Hebraist aesthetic ideology to formulate their own cultural identity; but the power of this cultural trend did not endure. Even though Herder's concept of history and culture would become one of the most important influences on turn-of-the-century romanticism, the Hebraist element of his thought was not well received in this school. Contrary to the *Sturm und Drang* poets of a generation earlier, the disciples of this movement moved away from biblical influences in their writing. Like Herder and Klopstock, the romantics also glorified nature and authenticity, but their natural ideal was distinctly different: they were attracted by nature's dark and gloomy side. Their taste for ironic or fantastic writing styles and their preoccupation with the individual's psyche led them to seek inspiration in fairy tales, fictional medieval accounts, and pagan mythologies, and they left biblical poetry by the wayside.

In principle, the Hebrew political model was destined for successful immersion in the political imagination of large swaths of the German public, since the psalms and Luther's translations of the Bible constituted the principal body of reading material available to a large majority of the population (besides the highly educated elite).[118] German Protestant culture—like that of the Dutch and the English—had, since the sixteenth century, sustained a tradition of political Hebraism, namely the invocation of biblical language for purposes of community formation or when confronting enemies. However, this tradition was inextricably tied to religious and ecclesiastical identity, while the liberal discourse that grew out of the Enlightenment at the end of the eighteenth century—and the political community it addressed—leaned heavily on an attempt to build alternatives to the religious community. For this reason, intellectuals like Schiller, Kant, and Hegel usually shied away from biblical language; and in this sense, the trajectory of Herderian Hebraism flew in the face of the dominant moods of the period. The framing of the biblical tradition as the national culture of an oriental people acted to highlight, for many writers, the mental remove between themselves and the people of the Bible, as well as the total foreignness of "the national Hebrew myth" to their own culture.

Notes

1. Johann Gottfried Eichhorn, *Allgemeine Bibliothek der biblischen Litteratur*, (Leipzig: Weidmann, 1795), 4:528–531.
2. Eichhorn, *Allgemeine Bibliothek der biblischen Litteratur*, 4:528–529.
3. Alexander Geddes, *Prospectus of a New Translation of the Holy Bible* (Glasgow, 1786), 140.
4. See: Ursula Wokoeck, *German Orientalism: The Study of the Middle East and Islam from 1800 to 1945* (London: Routledge, 2009), 99–100; Georg Lorenz Bauer, *Handbuch der Geschichte der hebräischen Nation von ihrer Entstehung bis zur Zerstörung ihres Staats* (Altdorf: Monath & Kussler, 1800), iv.
5. For instance: Christian Gottlieb Kühnöl, *Geschichte des jüdischen Volks von Abraham an bis auf Jerusalems Zerstörung* (Leipzig: J. F. Junius, 1791), viii.
6. Friedrich August Carus. *Psychologie der Hebräer* (Leipzig: Barth & Kummer, 1809). The book was published after Carus's death, but was apparently written about a decade beforehand.
7. Anton Theodor Hartmann, *Die Hebräerin am Putztische und als Braut* (Amsterdam, 1809).
8. Johann Wolfgang von Goethe, *Die Leiden des jungen Werthers* (Leipzig: Göschen, 1774), 199. Benjamin Kennicott (1718–1783) was an English Bible critic who dealt mostly in textual criticism.
9. Goethe, *Leiden des jungen Werthers*, 11.
10. Karin Schutjer, *Goethe and Judaism: The Troubled Inheritance of Modern Literature* (Evanston, IL: Northwestern University Press, 2015).
11. He was alluding to the book *Älteste Urkunde des Menschengeschlechts*. See: John H. Zammito, *The Genesis of Kant's Critique of Judgment* (Chicago: University of Chicago Press, 1992), 38–39.

12. Immanuel Kant, *Reflexionen zur Anthropologie*, vol. 15 of *Kants Gesammelte Schriften* (Berlin: Walter de Gruyter, 1928), 345.

13. On Semler's influence on Kant, see: Nathan Rotenstreich, *The Recurring Pattern: Studies in Anti-Judaism in Modern Thought* (London: Horizon Press, 1963), 44-45.

14. On the *Fragments*' argument and its importance to the development of German Enlightenment, see: Jonathan Israel, *Democratic Enlightenment: Philosophy, Revolution, and Human Rights 1750–1790* (Oxford: Oxford University Press, 2011), 315–325.

15. Kant, *Reflexionen zur Anthropologie*, 399.

16. Kant, *Reflexionen zur Anthropologie*, 393. And see: Zammito, *The Genesis of Kant's Critique of Judgment*, 43.

17. Immanuel Kant, *Religion within the Boundaries of Mere Reason*, trans. George di Giovanni (Cambridge, UK: Cambridge University Press, 1996) 130.

18. Kant, *Religion within the Boundaries of Mere Reason*, 130.

19. Yirmiyahu Yovel, *Dark Riddle: Hegel, Nietzsche and the Jew* (Cambridge, UK: Polity Press, 1998). See also: Miriam Leonard, *Socrates and the Jews: Hellenism and Hebraism from Moses Mendelssohn to Sigmund Freud* (Chicago: University of Chicago Press, 2012), 56–58.

20. Wilhelm Friedrich Hufnagel, *Die Schriften des alten Testaments* (Erlangen: Jacob Palm, 1784), 160.

21. For a detailed discussion of these reforms and the responses to them, see: John Stroup, *The Struggle for Identity in the Clerical Estate: Northwest German Protestant Opposition to Absolutist Policy in the Eighteenth Century* (Leiden: Brill, 1984).

22. Günter Muhlpfordt, "Karl Friedrich Bahrdt und die radikale Aufklarung," *Jahrbuch des Instituts fur deutsche Geschichte* 5 (1976): 49–100.

23. Carl Friedrich Bahrdt, *Ausführung des Plans und Zwecks Jesu: In Briefen an Wahrheit suchende Leser* (Berlin: Mylius, 1784), 1:100–104.

24. Stroup, *The Struggle for Identity in the Clerical Estate*, 113.

25. See: Edward Dixon Junkin, "Religion versus Revolution: The Interpretation of the French Revolution by German Protestant Churchmen, 1789–1799" (Austin, TX: Best, 1974), 774–775.

26. Anthony J. La Vopa, *Grace, Talent, and Merit: Poor Students, Clerical Careers, and Professional Ideology in Eighteenth-Century Germany* (Cambridge, UK: Cambridge University Press, 2002), 343–344.

27. Stroup, *The Struggle for Identity in the Clerical Estate*, 188–191.

28. Suzanne L. Marchand, *German Orientalism in the Age of Empire: Religion, Race, and Scholarship* (Cambridge, UK: Cambridge University Press, 2009), 36.

29. Marchand, *German Orientalism in the Age of Empire*, 133–136.

30. Velthusen, *Über die nächste Bestimmung des Landpredigerstandes: Ein durch hernn Campe's Fragmente veranlasster Beitrag zur Pastoraltheologie* (Helmstedt, 1787), 144.

31. La Vopa, *Grace, Talent, and Merit*, 344–345.

32. "Gottesgelahrtheit", *Allgemeine Literatur-Zeitung*, November 20, 1799, 457.

33. See for instance: *Allgemeine Literatur-Zeitung*, October 2, 1789, 15–16.

34. *Geist der Zeit*, 1809, 254.

35. Another early work that belongs to this genre is Leonard Johann Karl Justi's *Weissagungs-Gesang Mosis an die Israeliten, aus der Urschrift von Neuem übersetzt und mit einer Erläuterung begleitet* (Göttingen, 1774). Justi (1753–1780) was a Magdeburg preacher who had studied with Michaelis. There is apparently no connection to the later Wilhelm Justi.

36. Wolf Gerhard Schmidt, *"Homer des Nordens" und "Mutter der Romantik": James Macphersons Ossian und seine Rezeption in der deutschsprachigen Literatur* (Berlin: Walter de Gruyter, 2003), 393–401.
37. Karl Wilhelm Justi, *Blumen althebräischer Dichtkunst* (Giessen: G. F. Heyer, 1809), v.
38. Karl Wilhelm Justi, *Blumen althebräischer Dichtkunst*, vi.
39. Karl Wilhelm Justi, *Sionitishche Harfenklänge* (Leipzig, 1829); Karl Wilhelm Justi, *Selbstbiographie* (Marburg, 1818), 11. He also mentions Herder's influence in the introduction to *Sionitishche Harfenklänge*.
40. Karl Wilhelm Justi, *National-Gesänge der Hebräer* (Marburg, 1803), viii.
41. Franz Thomas von Schönfeld, *Davids Kriegsgesänge: Deutsch (aus dem Grundtexte): dem Heere Josephs* (Vienna: R. Gräffer, 1788).
42. See especially Gershom Scholem, *A Career of a Frankist: The Metamorphoses of Moses Dobruska* (Jerusalem: Mossad Bialik, 1974), in Hebrew.
43. Horst Gronemeyer & Adolf Beck (Hg.), *Klopstock: Werke und Briefe: historisch-kritische Ausgabe* (Berlin: Walter de Gruyter, 1999), 2:910.
44. Franz Thomas von Schönfeld, "Bey Uebersendung meiner Davidischen Kriegsgesänge: An Klopstock," in *Blumenlese der Musen* (Vienna: Jakob Kaiserer, 1790), 96–98.
45. See: Rainer Stichel, *Beiträge zur frühen Geschichte des Psalters und zur Wirkungsgeschichte der Psalmen* (Düsseldorf: Schöningh, 2007), 687–688.
46. The poem "Mendelssohn" includes the lines: "Es müsse meiner Rechte vergessen seyn / Jerusalem vergäß ich dein / Willkommen willkommen im Palmenhain." Schönfeld, *Blumenlese der Musen*, 43.
47. Words of the poem dealing with the Jewish people are "Das Kindlein geboren aus Davids Geschlecht / wird wieder erneuern Judäas Recht," Franz Thomas von Schönfeld, "Das unschuldige Kindlein," in *Blumenlese der Musen*, 43; See: Josef Karniel, "Jüdischer Pseudomessianismus und deutsche Kultur, der Weg der frankistischen Familie Dobruschka-Schönfeld im Zeitalter der Aufklärung," in *Jahrbuch des Instituts für Deutsche Geschichte* 4 (1983): 43. And *see also*: Manfred Voigts, "Das Ende der David-Tradition: Jakob Frank und die Französische Revolution," in *König David: biblische Schlüsselfigur und europäische Leitgestalt* (Fribourg, Switzerland: Universitätsverlag Freiburg, 2003), 262–263; Klaus S. Davidowicz, *Die Kabbala: Eine Einführung in die Welt der jüdischen Mystik und Magie* (Vienna: Böhlau, 2009), 140–143.
48. *Allgemeine deutsche Bibliothek* 100 (1791):113–114.
49. Johann Gottfried Eichhorn, *Litteraturgeschichte* (Göttingen: J. G. Rosenbusch, 1799), 1:14.
50. Johann Christoph Doederlein, *Christlicher Religionsunterricht nach den Bedürfnissen unserer Zeit* (Altdorf: Monath und Kußler, 1790), 198. On Doederlein, see: Albrecht Beutel, *Kirchengeschichte im Zeitalter der Aufklärung: Ein Kompendium* (Göttingen: Vandenhoeck & Ruprecht, 2009), 141–142.
51. Doederlein, *Christlicher Religionsunterricht nach den Bedürfnissen unserer Zeit*, 198.
52. Johann Christian Wilhelm Augusti, *Grundriss einer historisch-kritischen Einleitung in's Alte Testament* (Leipzig, 1806), 180–181.
53. Augusti, *Grundriss*, 305–306.
54. Augusti, *Grundriss*, 20; J. Jak Hottinger, ed., *Bibliothek der neuesten theologischen, philosophischen, und schonen Litteratur* (Zürich: Orell, 1784), 1:304.
55. See, for example: Christoph G. Herrmann, *Versuch einer philosophischen und critischen Einleitung in die Christliche Theologie* (Göttingen: Vandenhoeck & Ruprecht, 1792), 150.

56. Frederick C. Beiser, *Enlightenment, Revolution and Romanticism: The Genesis of Modern German Political Thought, 1790-1800* (Cambridge, MA: Harvard University Press, 1992), 1-13.

57. See for instance: Johann Friedrich Köhler, *Gallerie der neuen Propheten, apokaliptischen Träumen, Geisteslehre und Revolutionsprediger: ein Beitrag z. Geschichte der menschlichter Narrheit* (Leipzig: Wiegand, 1799).

58. Georg Conrad Horst, *Die Visionen Habakuks, neu übersetzt, Nebst einer Abhandlung über den Prophetismus der alten Welt, und insbesondere der biblischen Propheten* (Gotha, 1798).

59. Horst, *Die Visionen Habakuks*, vi.

60. *Allgemeine Bibliothek der biblischen Litteratur* 9 (1799):278-279.

61. Jonathan Sheehan, *The Enlightenment Bible: Translation, Scholarship, Culture* (Princeton, NJ: Princeton University Press, 2005), 178-179.

62. On the mutual influence between Eichhorn and Herder, see, for example: Ebehard Sehmsdorf, *Die Prophetenauslegung bei J. G. Eichhorn* (Göttingen: Vandenhoeck & Ruprecht, 1971).

63. See, for instance: Peter G. Bietenholz, *Historia and Fabula: Myths and Legends in Historical Thought from Antiquity to the Modern Age* (Leiden: Brill, 1994), 256-258; Maike Oergel, *The Return of King Arthur and the Nibelungen: National Myth in Nineteenth-Century English and German Literature* (Berlin: Walter de Gruyter, 1998), 15-16; Ian Balfour, *The Rhetoric of Romantic Prophecy* (Stanford, CA: Stanford University Press, 2002), 120-121.

64. Friedrich Wilhelm Schelling, "Über die Mythen der ältesten Welt" *Paulus Memorabilien* (1793): 5.

65. Georg Lorenz Bauer, *Hebräische Mythologie* (Leipzig: Weygand, 1802).

66. These details of Scherer's biography are drawn from an entry on him, which he himself wrote at the age of twenty, in Friedrich Wilhelm Strieder, *Grundlage zu einer Hessischen Gelehrten und Schriftsteller Geschichte: seit der Reformation bis auf gegenwärtige Zeiten* (Cassel: Griesbach, 1797), 11:314.

67. Johann Ludwig Wilhelm Scherer, *Neue Religionsgeschichte für die Jugend: zum Gebrauch für Aeltern, Prediger und Lehrer* (Leipzig, 1798).

68. See: *Neue allgemeine deutsche Bibliothek* 44 (1799): 528.

69. Scherer, *Historische Einleitung zum richtigen Verstehen der Bibel: mit Rücksticht auf den zerrennerschen Auszug: für Gymnasien und Schulen nach den geläuterten Erklärungsgrundsätzen unserer Zeit* (Halle: Johann Jacob Gebauer, 1802).

70. Scherer, *Historische Einleitung zum richtigen Verstehen der Bibel*.

71. Scherer, *Bibelcommentar, zum Handgebrauch für Prediger, Schullehrer und Layen*. (Altenburg: Richter, 1799).

72. Scherer, *Bibelcommentar*, 1.

73. Scherer, *Bibelcommentar*, 8.

74. Scherer, *Die Geschichte der Israeliten vor Jesus nach ihren heiligen Bücher, für die Bedürfnisse unserer Zeit bearbeitet* (Zerbst: Andreas Füchsel, 1803).

75. On the roots of the term "Semite," see, for example: Martin F. J. Baasten, "A Note on the History of 'Semitic,'" in *Hamlet on a Hill: Semitic and Greek Studies Presented to Professor T. Muraoka*, ed. M. F. J. Baasten and W. Th. van Peursen (Leuven: Peeters, 2003), 57-73.

76. See, for instance: *Neue allgemeine deutsche Bibliothek* 84 (1803): 51-53.

77. Andrea Polaschegg, "Die Regeln der Imagination: Faszinationsgeschichte des deutschen Orientalismus zwischen 1770 und 1850," in *Der Deutschen Morgenland*. ed. Charis Goer and Michael Hofmann (Munich: Fink, 2008), 13-36.

78. *Neue allgemeine deutsche Bibliothek*, 52.

79. *Allgemeine Literatur-Zeitung*, May 26, 1806:381–382.

80. The books included: Johann Ludwig Wilhelm Scherer, *Die Geschichte des Alten Testaments* (Giesen: Krieger, 1803) and Johann Ludwig Wilhelm Scherer, *Biblische Völkergeschichte* (Leipzig: Weygand, 1804); *Der Schriftforscher*'s full title is: *Der Schriftforscher zur Belebung eines gründlischen Bibelstudiums und Verbreitung der reinen, verschonernden Religion*.

81. Georg Conrad Horst, "Ideen über Religion, Mythologie und Christenthum, in Beziehung auf den Zeitgeist," *Der Schriftforscher* 1 (1803): 88.

82. The author's identity was revealed soon enough in the press, see: *Neue theologische Annalen* 39 (1801): 725.

83. Johann Ludwig Wilhelm Scherer, *Ausführliche Erklärung der Weissagungen aller Propheten des alten und neuen Testaments* (Leipzig: Weygand, 1801); [Johann Ludwig Wilhelm Schererz?], *Ausführliche Erklärung der sämmtlichen Wundergeschichten des alten Testaments: aus natürlichen Ursachen, durchaus begleitet mit philologischen, kritischen und historischen Anmerkungen, nebst einer Abhundlung über Wunder und Offenbarung* (Berlin, 1800), 92–93. Critics alluded to the book's author as being "a renowned preacher known for copious writing . . . as well as being fickle and one-sided. See: *Allgemeine Literatur-Zeitung*, July 3, 1807, 17.

84. On this subject see for instance: Junkin, "Religion versus Revolution," 721.

85. Johann August von Starck, *Der Triumph der Philosophie im Achtzehnten Jahrhunderte oder Geschichte der Verschwörung des Rationalismus gegen Religion und Kirche* (Germantown: Rosenblatt, 1803), 2:582–584.

86. See: *Jenaische Allgemeine Literatur-Zeitung* 96 (1814): 381–382; *Allgemeine Literatur-Zeitung*, January 13, 1802, 99–100.

87. Ibid. *Allgemeine Literatur-Zeitung*, January 13, 1802, 99–100.

88. See, for instance, his impassioned self-defense article: *Allgemeiner Anzeiger und Nationalzeitung der Deutschen*, February 1, 1805, 385.

89. Johann Ludwig Wilhelm Scherer, *"Das Vaterland in Gefahr! Gott sein Retter Ihm Lob und Dank!" Dargestellt in einer heil. Rede am allgemeinen Dankfeste in den Grosherzogl. Hess. Staaten, in glücklich abgewendeter Kriegsgefahr* (Frankfurt am Main, 1806).

90. On pro-Napoleonic sermons, see: Michael Rowe, *From Reich to State: The Rhineland in the Revolutionary Age, 1780–1830* (Cambridge, UK: Cambridge University Press, 2003), 123–125; For criticism of Scherer's adulation, see: *Neue theologische Annalen* 3 (1807): 42.

91. Johann Ludwig Wilhelm Scherer, *Friede, Stimme Gottes vom Himmel! Friede, Segen der Menschheit! dargestellt in einer heiligen Rede am allgemeinen Dankfeste in den Großherzoglich Hessischen Staaten wegen des zwischen Frankreich, dem Rheinbunde und Oesterreich am 14ten Oktob. 1809 zu Wien geschlossenen Friedens* (Darmstadt: Leske, 1809).

92. Johann Ludwig Wilhelm Scherer, *Die schönsten Geistes-Blüthen des ältesten Orients: für Freunde des Grossen und Schönen* (Karlsruhe: Macklot, 1809); Johann Ludwig Wilhelm Scherer *Biblische Lieder, Parabeln und andere Dichtungen* (Karlsruhe, 1818).

93. On de Wette's innovations, see for example: Thomas Albert Howard, *Religion and the Rise of Historicism: W. M. L de Wette, Jacob Burckhardt, and the Theological Origins of Nineteenth-Century Historical Consciousness* (Oxford: Oxford University Press, 2006), 43–56; Daniel Weidner, "Politik und Ästhetik: Lektüre der Bibel bei Michaelis, Herder und de Wette," in *Hebräsiche Poesie und jüdischer Volksgeist: Die Wirkungsgeschichte Johann Gottfried Herders im Judentum Mittel- und Osteuropas*, ed. Christoph Schulte (Hildesheim: Olms, 2003), 57–63.

94. Wilhelm Martin Lebrecht De Wette, *Beiträge zur Einleitung in das Alte Testament* (Halle: Schimmepfennig, 1806), 179.
95. Wilhelm Martin Lebrecht De Wette, *Aufforderung zum Studium der hebräischen Sprache und Literatur* (Jena: Gabler, 1805), 27.
96. De Wette, *Beiträge*, 32.
97. De Wette, *Beiträge*, 98.
98. See for example: John William Rogerson, *W. M. L. de Wette, Founder of Modern Biblical Criticism: An Intellectual Biography* (Sheffield: Continuum, 1992), 27–30.
99. Wilhelm Martin Lebrecht De Wette, *Ueber Religion und Theologie: Erläuterungen zu seinem Lehrbuche der Dogmatik* (Berlin: Reimer, 1815), 64. See also: George S. Williamson, *The Longing for Myth in Germany: Religion and Aesthetic Culture from Romanticism to Nietzsche* (Chicago: University of Chicago Press, 2004), 92–98.
100. Williamson, *The Longing for Myth in Germany*, 96.
101. Chen Tzoref-Ashkenazi, *Der romantische Mythos vom Ursprung der Deutschen: Friedrich Schlegels Suche nach der indogermanischen Verbindung* (Göttingen: Wallstein, 2009); Tuska Benes, *In Babel's Shadow: Language, Philology, and the Nation in Nineteenth-Century Germany*. (Detroit, MI: Wayne State University Press, 2008).
102. Johann David Michaelis, "Moses: Ein Heldengedicht (Epos)," *Hamburgische Beyträge* 58 (1752), 545.
103. Johann Gottfried Herder, *Adrastea*, in *Sämmtliche werke: zur schönen Literatur und Kunst* (Vienna: Franz Hass, 1801), 336.
104. For example: Yosef Hayim Yerushalmi, *Freud's Moses: Judaism Terminable and Interminable* (New Haven, CT: Yale University Press, 1991), 9.
105. Moshe Pelli, *Haskalah and Beyond: The Reception of the Hebrew Enlightenment and the Emergence of Haskalah Judaism* (Lanham, MD: University Press of America, 2012), 114–116. See also: Selma Stern, *Der preussische Staat und die Juden: Die Zeit Friedrichs des Großen* (Tübingen: Mohr Siebeck, 1971), 406.
106. This was according to Weisel's introduction to the German translation.
107. See: Hartwig Wessely, *Die Moseide: in 18 Gesängen. Uebersetzt nach dem hebräischen Originale von dem Herrn Senior Hufnagel, dem Herrn Professor Spalding* (Berlin: Vieweg, 1795), v.
108. Wolf-Daniel Hartwich, *Romantischer Antisemitismus: von Klopstock bis Richard Wagner* (Göttingen: Vandenhoeck & Ruprecht, 2005), 69–83.
109. Liliane Weissberg, "Juden oder Hebräer? Religiöse und politische Bekehrung bei Herder," in Martin Bollacher (ed.), *Johann Gottfried Herder: Geschichte und Kultur* (Würzburg: Königshausen & Neumann, 1994), 191–211. For similar references, see also: Hartwich, *Romantischer Antisemitismus*.
110. For instance: Christian Gottlieb Kühnöl, *Geschichte des jüdischen Volks von Abraham an bis auf Jerusalems Zerstörung* (Leipzig: J. F. Junius, 1791), viii.
111. Michalis published a critique of *Hame'asef* and described its founders as a "Gesellschaft Liebhaber der Hebräischen Sprache," in *Orientalische und exegetische Bibliothek* 23, (1785), 75.
112. Itzik Eichel, "Bikorei Shirei Tiferet," *Hame'asef* 6 (1790): 211, in Hebrew.
113. Moses Phillipsohn, *Kinderfreund, Lehr-und Lesebuch für die Kinder jüdischer Nation* (Dessau, 1811). A similar subtitle was given to the periodical *Jedidja*, published in 1816: *Eine Quartalschrift in hebräischer und deutscher Sprache zunächst für Israeliten und für Freunde der hebräischen und biblischen Literatur*.

114. Karl Wilhelm Justi, "Zwei Uebersetzungen," *Sulamith: eine Zeitschrift zur Beförderung der Cultur und Humanität unter den Israeliten* (1811), 108.

115. Shalom Cohen, *Mata'ei Kedem al Admat Tzafon* (Rödelheim: Heidenheim, 1807), iii.

116. Cohen, *Mata'ei Kedem al Admat Tzafon*, iii.

117. Stroup, *The Struggle for Identity in the Clerical Estate*, 126.

118. See: Franklin Kopitzsch, "Die Sozialgeschichte der deutschen Aufklärung als Forschungsaufgabe," in *Aufklärung, Absolutismus und Burgertum in Deutschland*, ed. Franklin Kopitzsch (Munich: Nymphenburg, 1976), 77.

Conclusion

EIGHTEENTH-CENTURY BIBLICAL SCHOLARSHIP was informed by two intellectual trends that characterized the Enlightenment in the German cultural space. On the one hand, scholars in German universities were striving to reform methods of interpretation, especially through the historicization of Bible study; on the other, they sought to protect the Bible and reassert their authority in response to the attacks of a radical Enlightenment.

The growing political authority of the state in the German principalities (at the expense of ecclesiastical authority) resulted in a transformation in the structure of the universities. The power of theology faculties waned, and fields earlier included under their jurisdiction were taken up by other faculties. From auxiliary subjects in support of theology, history and philology became independent fields of knowledge. Subsequently, even questions pertaining to the Bible were increasingly addressed through the use of historical and juridical tools, whereby biblical events were explained in circumstantial-natural terms.

Early eighteenth-century developments in research into oriental languages—especially the analysis of kinship between Hebrew and Arabic—prompted disavowal of the thesis that posited that the biblical language was the mother of all human languages. The history of the ancient Hebrews was subsequently dethroned from its privileged status as *historia sacra*. Michaelis and his disciples distanced themselves from dynastic explanations tying the customs, beliefs, and languages of different peoples to their ancient Hebraic sources. They strove to prove that the Hebrews' customs and laws were not unique but had rather developed in a natural manner, in a fashion similar to those of other nomadic peoples. This relativistic approach toward Hebrew customs rested on the ethnographic and orientalist discourses of the period, fed by new data gathered on "natural peoples" in the Orient and in the New World.

Attacks on the Bible launched by deists and radical Enlightenment philosophers transformed the prevalent image of the biblical past because of the very opposition they engendered within the German "republic of letters." These attacks challenged and transformed the debate over Hebrew history within all the fields in which it took place—ethnography, jurisprudence, and poetry. Representations of the Hebrews as a savage oriental people were countered by an idealization of their *natural*, nomadic lifestyle; criticism of the Hebrew regime's particularity was answered with a recontextualization of this legislative regime as popular custom entrenched in national tradition; and disparaging accounts of the Hebrew language and of Hebrew poetry prompted poets and other writers to posit it as a model of sentimental and patriotic poetry.

The historical image of the Hebrew nation that emerged during the eighteenth century was the product of a reconstruction project that began in response to religious skepticism and secularization. In the context of this project, the Hebrew people's history, society, culture, and political structures were put under the spotlight. Initially, attempts to portray the Hebrews as a historical entity were nothing more than *ancillia theologia* employed for exegetical ends; through this project, however, the Hebrew people, as a historical entity, became an object of study—and even a national model—in its own right.

German intellectuals found several central elements in the Hebrew model that allowed them to imagine an alternative political paradigm to that of the Enlightenment: a Christian source of legitimacy for a particular national existence; a political system integrated with religion; a conservative constitution based on the people's organic traditions; a *Kulturnation* built around an epic or myth, and led by poets; and a federative regime maintaining the liberty of its constituent tribes.

This use of the Hebrew national model at the end of the eighteenth century may be seen as a response to the political ideas of the Enlightenment. Rather than a continuation of traditional trends in political Christian Hebraism, it is a variation on the modern national idea with the Bible as its source of inspiration. It references the Old Testament—or at least parts of it—as a myth read collectively by its national subjects.

Under the influence of critical Bible research, the conception of the Hebrews as the educators of the human race was eroded; and the Old Testament gradually came to be treated as a product of a particular, national spirit. However, while rationalist philosophy and theology ridiculed the particular character of the Hebrew tradition, writers critical of the Enlightenment saw this very particularity as an inspiration, hoping indeed to save beleaguered Christianity through the national element of Hebrew poetry. The national spirit [*Nationalgeist*] they identified in the Old Testament imbued the text with new meaning, facilitating new readings that enlisted it in new political causes.

Herder and other Protestant writers of his generation alternate between conserving the Christian-universalist apologetic framework of scripture on the one hand, and conferring new meaning on "the national Hebrew poetry" on the other as an expression of particular nationality linked to a national religion, which thus expresses the traditions of this peculiar people. In the final account, the national reading of scripture opens the door to a theological development no less—and perhaps more—radical than the skeptical criticism of Spinoza, Voltaire, and the deists. As scholars of the Enlightenment have noted, rationalist criticism of the Old Testament in many ways constitutes a continuation of radical movements within Christianity itself, such as socinianism.[1] It was ultimately the anticlerical philosophers of the seventeenth and eighteenth centuries who developed several of the theological ideas that formed the basis for Christian critique of Mosaic law and Judaism's particularity. In this sense, the Enlightenment's universalism is a continuation of the Pauline movement that strove to distance Christianity from Mosaic law, while the idea of a particularistic Christianity based on the Old Testament and the development of ideas such as the national God and local providence, signify a fundamental break with the Pauline tradition.

*

In a letter that Friedrich Schlegel (1772–1829)—who had recently founded the Romantic School of Jena with his brother—wrote to his friend Novalis (1772–1801) in October 1798, he reviewed his literary situation, his mood, and his upcoming plans. "I have lately had several revelations, and now can better understand you, as I understand Religion ... As far as I am concerned, the aim of my literary efforts is to write a new Bible, following in Muhammad's and Luther's footsteps."[2]

Unsurprised by his colleague's ambitious plans, Novalis merely commented in his response on the fact that Schlegel seemed to have read his own mind. The Bible, he said, was "the ideal of any future book," and "every man's story must become a Bible." His own biblical project was apparently to have been embodied in his book *Heinrich von Ofterdingen*, which he never actually completed. Writing a Bible became a sort of friendly jousting affair among the members of this circle. In a letter to Friedrich Schleiermacher (1768–1834), Schlegel wrote that he hoped to stir Novalis's jealousy in such a way as to goad the latter into writing "a Bible or a novel" [*eine Bibel oder einen Roman*]. In another letter he wrote in parallel to Novalis, Schlegel clearly stated that by "writing a Bible" he did not mean just writing a literary prototype but that his words should be understood literally: "Now I have a Bible in mind, not anything resembling it in any known sense but quite literally a Bible for all intents and purposes, the first Artwork of this kind, since all those that came before it were nothing but products of Nature ... But my biblical project is not a literary one, but—biblical, absolutely religious."[3]

The new Bible was to stand at the center of a modern religion which Schlegel was working on at that time. This romantic religion would, under the influence of Friedrich Wilhelm Schelling (1775–1854), become a poetic "new mythology" made up of fairy tales [*Märchen*].[4] Schlegel regarded this development as the fruition of Lessing's vision in his *Education of the Human Race* of "the new, eternal gospel" that would complement the Old and New Testaments. According to Schlegel, this gospel was to materialize in the form of a Bible, which, like the original Bible, would include a complete set of books.[5] Aside from Luther and Muhammad, Schlegel drew inspiration for his new Bible from the writing of Baruch Spinoza and Winckelmann—two thinkers responsible for a philosophical and cultural alternative to scripture.[6]

This idea of "the new Bible" embodies the romantics' relation to scripture. On the one hand, the biblical ideal expresses the book's centrality to the cultural background of these German writers, most of whom received a strict Protestant upbringing. To no less an extent, though, it also constituted an explicit revolt against the Bible, drawing its inspiration from historically unorthodox forms of Christianity. As Abraham Albert Avni has asserted, early romanticism clearly moved away from scripture in general, and from the Old Testament in particular.[7] Romanticism's literary project was intended to replace the Bible and make it redundant. Several scholars have argued that the idea of positing literature as a substitute for the Bible also informed Herder's biblical project, although he himself would probably not have accepted this claim.[8] Positioning the Bible in a historical context—as Michaelis, Herder, and others did—played a key role in erasing the boundaries between holy and secular text. Conversion of the idea of revelation into that of creative inspiration allowed romantic poets to view their own work as a kind of new revelation; and relabeling the psalms as "national hymns" paved the way for a new national poetry to replace them. With the transformation of scripture into literature, secular poetry and literature became a form of new scripture.

Throughout the eighteenth century, the strongest attacks made against the scriptures' authority emanated from deism and rationalism. During the Age of Reason, the main bone of contention was the question of the Bible's morality and credibility. From Pierre Bayle to Immanuel Kant, philosophers and critics labeled the Hebrews cruel, sensual, crass, and particular. They depicted the biblical fathers as unrefined nomads, and the Hebrew state as a corrupt oriental theocracy. In response to this attack, critics of universalism and liberalism adopted the Hebrew model as an alternative aesthetic and political ideal. But the dawn of the nineteenth century witnessed the emergence of a new configuration of concepts and rivalries in German culture and thinking, which also affected intellectuals' relation to the Bible, posing new challenges to its adherents. The rise of nationalism as the dominant ideology in the early nineteenth century generated different forms of suspicion of the Bible, unleashing a new strain of criticism of Hebrew influence on German culture. Now, the major question that occupied thinkers did not concern the Bible's rationality, but rather revolved around whether it belonged to or was alien to German culture. German intellectuals were now revisiting myth, seeking to find an exclusivist national mythology.

Notes

1. See, for example: Alan Charles Kors, *Atheism in France, 1650–1729: The Orthodox Sources of Disbelief* (Princeton, NJ: Princeton University Press, 1990); Diego Lucci, *Scripture and Deism: The Biblical Criticism of the Eighteenth-Century British Deists* (New York: P. Lang, 2008), 58–60.
2. Letter from Friedrich Schlegel to Novalis, October 20, 1798, in *Kritische Friedrich-Schlegel-Ausgabe*, ed. Ernst Behler (Paderborn: F. Schöningh, 1991), 24: 183.
3. Schlegel to Novalis, 204.
4. Heinz Gockel, *Mythos und Poesie: Zum Mythosbegriff in Aufklärung und Frühromantik* (Frankfurt am Main: Klostermann, 1981), 270–275.
5. In Schlegels words: "Als Bibel wird das neue ewige Evangelium erscheinen, von dem Lessing geweissagt hat: aber nicht als einzelnes Buch im gewöhnlichen Sinne. Selbst was wir Bibel nennen ist ja ein System von Büchern." Friedrich Schlegel, "Ideen," *Athenaeum* 3 (1800): 20 (sec. 95).
6. Bernd Auerochs, *Die Entstehung der Kunstreligion* (Göttingen: Vandenhoeck & Ruprecht, 2006), 402–404.
7. Abraham Albert Avni, *The Bible and Romanticism: The Old Testament in German and French Romantic Poetry* (Paris: Mouton, 1969), 22–26. See also: Stephen Prickett, *Origins of Narrative: The Romantic Appropriation of the Bible* (Cambridge, UK: Cambridge University Press, 1996), 182–186.
8. Jonathan Sheehan, *The Enlightenment Bible: Translation, Scholarship, Culture* (Princeton, NJ: Princeton University Press, 2005), 172–176; Maike Oergel, *The Return of King Arthur and the Nibelungen: National Myth in Nineteenth-Century English and German Literature* (Berlin: Walter de Gruyter, 1998), 32–33; Auerochs, *Die Entstehung der Kunstreligion*, 363–365.

Bibliography

Primary Sources

Abel, Casper. *Deutsche und Sächsische Alterthümer*. Braunschweig: Schröder, 1729.
———. *Hebräische Alterthümer*. Leipzig: Campe, 1736.
Alexander, William. *An Encouragement to Colonies*. London: W. Stansby, 1624.
Augusti, Johann Christian Wilhelm. *Grundriss einer historisch-kritischen Einleitung in's Alte Testament*. Leipzig, 1806.
Babor, Johann. *Alterthümer der Hebräer*. Vienna: V. Kurzbeck, 1794.
Bahrdt, Carl Friedrich. *Ausführung des Plans und Zwecks Jesu: In Briefen an Wahrheit suchende Leser*. Berlin. Mylius, 1784.
Bauer, Georg Lorenz. *Handbuch der Geschichte der hebräischen Nation von ihrer Entstehung bis zur Zerstörung ihres Staats*. Altdorf: Monath & Kussler, 1800.
———. *Hebräische Mythologie*. Leipzig: Weygand, 1802.
Beyschlag, August Adolf. *Betrachtung über das Schreiben des Herrn Moses Mendelssohn an den Diaconus Lavater zu Zürich*. Leipzig, 1770.
Blair, Hugh. *A Critical Dissertation on the Poems of Ossian, the Son of Fingal*. London: T. Becket, 1763.
———. *The Works of Ossian, the Son of Fingal*. London: T. Becket, 1765.
Bochart, Samuel. *Geographia Sacra, seu Phaleg et Canaan*. Caen, 1646.
Bolingbroke, Henry St. John. *Philosophical Works*. London: J. Whiston, 1754.
Bradford, William. *History of Plymouth Plantation, 1620–1647*. Boston: Massachusetts Historical Society, 1912.
Brandes, Simon Wolf. *Die geheime Weissagung Des Königlichen Propheten / Welcher in seinem XXI. Psalm verkundiget/ Daß Der ... Fürst und Herr Friderich der Dritte / Churfürst zu Brandenburg / Den 18. Januarii im Jahr 1701. Zu Königsberg in Preussen / Zum König In Preussen gekrönet werden solle*. Cölln an der Spree: Liebpert, 1701.
Carus, Friedrich August. *Psychologie der Hebräer*. Leipzig: Barth & Kummer, 1809.
Chubb, Thomas. "The Author's Farewell to His Readers." In *The Posthumous Works of Mr. Thomas Chubb*. London: R. Baldwin, 1748.
Cramer, Carl Friedrich. *Klopstock: Er, und über ihn. 1724–1747*. Hamburg: Schniebes, 1780.
De Wette, Wilhelm Martin Leberecht. *Aufforderung zum Studium der hebräischen Sprache und Literatur*. Jena: Gabler, 1805.
———. *Beiträge zur Einleitung in das Alte Testament*. Halle: Schimmepfennig, 1806.
———. *Lehrbuch der hebräisch-jüdischen Archäologie nebst einem Grundrisse der hebräisch-jüdischen Geschichte*. Leipzig: Vogel, 1830.
———. *Ueber Religion und Theologi: Erläuterungen zu seinem Lehrbuche der Dogmatik*. Berlin: Reimer, 1815.
Die hochteutsche Rechtsgelahrte Società̈t. "Ob und wie weit die Reichs Fürsten und dero Unterthanen an die in Scriptura sacra befindliche Gesetze gebunden." In *Allgemeines juristisches Oraculum*, 298–299. Leipzig: Heinsius, 1746.

Ditmar, Theodor Jakob. *Geschichte der Israeliten bis auf den Cyrus*. Berlin: Maurer, 1788.
Doederlein, Johann Christoph. *Christlicher Religionsunterricht nach den Bedürfnissen unserer Zeit*. Altdorf: Monath und Kußler, 1790.
Dohm, Christian Wilhelm. *Über die bürgerliche Verbesserung der Juden*. Berlin: Nicolai, 1781.
Edelmann, Johann Christian. "Moses mit aufgedeckten Angesichte." in *Sämmtliche Schriften*. Edited by Walter Grossmann. Stuttgart: F. Frommann, 1972.
Eichhorn, Johann Gottfried. *Allgemeine Bibliothek der biblischen Literatur*. Leipzig: Weidmann, 1787–1803.
———. *Geschichte der Literatur von ihrem Anfang bis auf die neuesten Zeiten*. Göttingen: Vandenhoek & Ruprecht, 1810.
Eisenmenger, Johann Andreas. *Entdecktes Judenthum*. Koenigsberg, 1700.
Epiphanius. *Panarion*. Translated by Frank Williams. Leiden: Brill, 2009.
Faber, Johann Ernst. *Archäologie der Hebräer*. Halle: Curt, 1773.
———. *Beobachtungen über den Orient als Reisebeschreibungen, zur Aufklärung der heiligen Schrift*. Hamburg: Bohn, 1772–1774.
———. *Diss. De animalibus, quorum sit mentio Zephan. 2, 14*. Göttingen: Barmeier, 1769.
———. *Historia Mannae inter Hebraeos*. Jenna: Fickelscherr, 1773.
Ferguson, Adam. *Grundsätze der Moralphilosophie*. Translated by Christian Garve. Leipzig: Dyck, 1772.
Fleury, Claude. *Unterweisung / Den Statt zu regieren/ und die Sitten zu verbessern*. Translated by Johannes Enckhusen. Hannover: Förster, 1709.
Freudentheil, Wilhelm Nicolaus. "Ueber den Einfluß des Alten Testaments auf Klopstocks Messias." In *Siona: Darstellungen das Alte Testament betreffend*, 95–111. Hamburg: Hoffmann, 1809.
———. "Ueber die Siegslieder der Hebräer." In *Nachträge zu Sulzers allgemeiner Theorie der schönen Künste*, 4:253–270. Leipzig: Weidmann, 1795.
Geddes, Alexander. *Prospectus of a New Translation of the Holy Bible*. Glasgow, 1786.
Gleim, Johann Wilhelm Ludwig. "Schlachtgesang." In *Sämmtliche Werke*, 7. Carlsruhe, 1820.
Goethe, Johann Wolfgang von. *Aus meinem Leben: Dichtung und Wahrheit*. Tübingen: Cotta, 1811.
———. *Leiden des jungen Werthers*. Leipzig: Göschen, 1774.
———. "Noten und Abhandlungen zu besserem Verstandniß dea West-östlichen Divans." In *Werke*, 6:156–157, Tübingen: Cotta, 1827.
———. *West-oestlicher Divan*. Stuttgart: Cotta, 1819.
Gottsched, Johann Christoph. *Erste Gründe der gesamten Weltweisheit*. Leipzig: Breitkopf, 1777 [originally published in 1733].
Gray, Robert. *A Good Speed to Virginia*. London: Wiliam Welbie, 1609.
Grotius, Hugo. *De Jure Belli Ac Pacis*. Paris: Buon, 1625.
Hamann, Johann Georg. "Aesthetica in nuce." In *Kreuzzüge der Philologen*. Vol. 2 of *Sämtliche Werke*, 195–217. Vienna, 1950.
Hartmann, Anton Theodor. *Die Hebräerin am Putztische und als Braut*. Amsterdam, 1809.
Hasenkamp, Friedrich Arnold. *Die Israeliten, die aufgeklärteste Nation, unter den ältesten Völkern in der Erkenntniss der Heiligkeit und Gerechtigkeit Gottes*. Duisberg: Königl. Stadt-Buchdruckerei, 1790.
Hegel, Georg Wilhelm Friedrich. "The Positivity of Christian Religion," in *Early Theological Writing*, trans. T. M. Knox (Chicago: University of Chicago Press, 1948), 146–147.

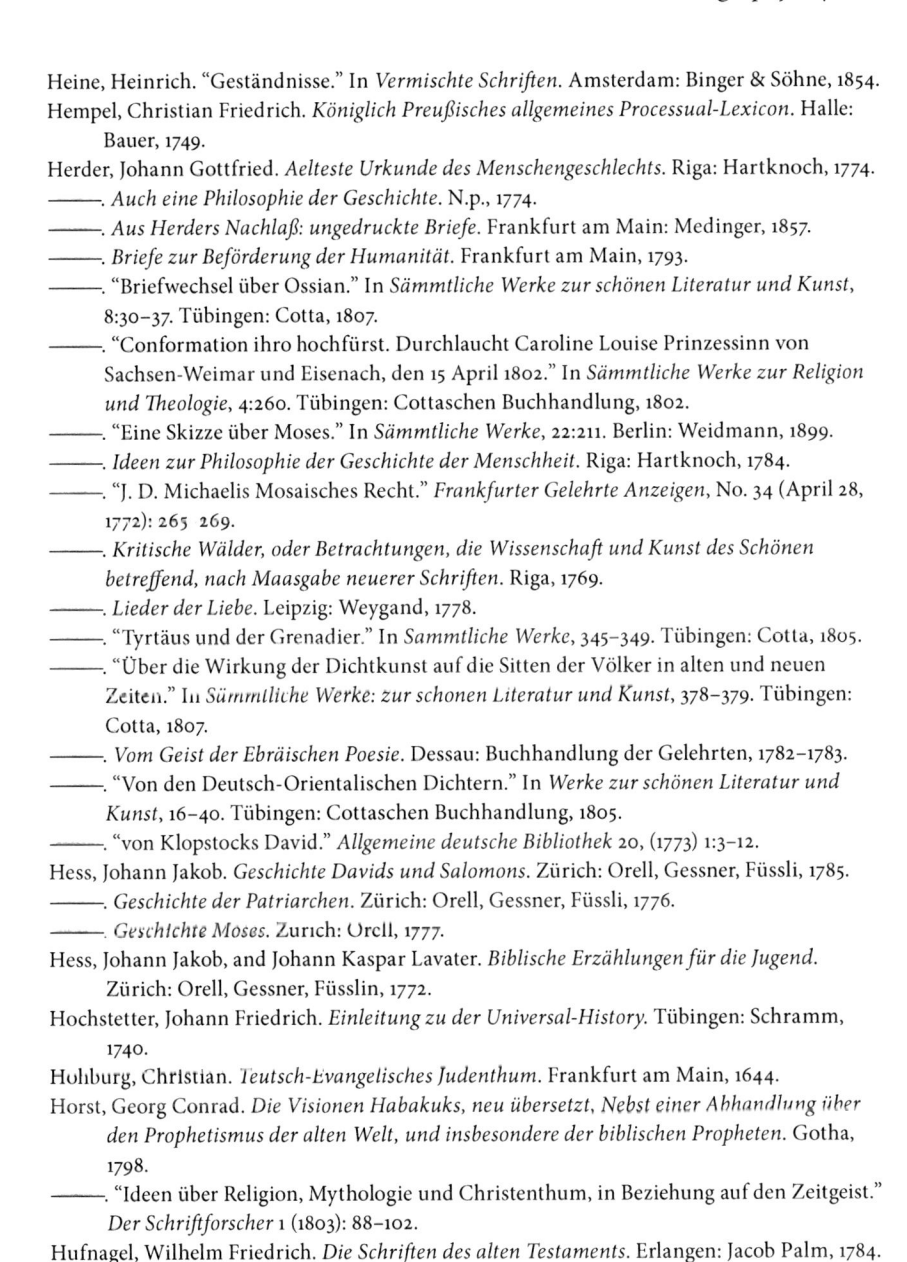

Heine, Heinrich. "Geständnisse." In *Vermischte Schriften*. Amsterdam: Binger & Söhne, 1854.
Hempel, Christian Friedrich. *Königlich Preußisches allgemeines Processual-Lexicon*. Halle: Bauer, 1749.
Herder, Johann Gottfried. *Aelteste Urkunde des Menschengeschlechts*. Riga: Hartknoch, 1774.
———. *Auch eine Philosophie der Geschichte*. N.p., 1774.
———. *Aus Herders Nachlaß: ungedruckte Briefe*. Frankfurt am Main: Medinger, 1857.
———. *Briefe zur Beförderung der Humanität*. Frankfurt am Main, 1793.
———. "Briefwechsel über Ossian." In *Sämmtliche Werke zur schönen Literatur und Kunst*, 8:30–37. Tübingen: Cotta, 1807.
———. "Conformation ihro hochfürst. Durchlaucht Caroline Louise Prinzessinn von Sachsen-Weimar und Eisenach, den 15 April 1802." In *Sämmtliche Werke zur Religion und Theologie*, 4:260. Tübingen: Cottaschen Buchhandlung, 1802.
———. "Eine Skizze über Moses." In *Sämmtliche Werke*, 22:211. Berlin: Weidmann, 1899.
———. *Ideen zur Philosophie der Geschichte der Menschheit*. Riga: Hartknoch, 1784.
———. "J. D. Michaelis Mosaisches Recht." *Frankfurter Gelehrte Anzeigen*, No. 34 (April 28, 1772): 265–269.
———. *Kritische Wälder, oder Betrachtungen, die Wissenschaft und Kunst des Schönen betreffend, nach Maasgabe neuerer Schriften*. Riga, 1769.
———. *Lieder der Liebe*. Leipzig: Weygand, 1778.
———. "Tyrtäus und der Grenadier." In *Sammtliche Werke*, 345–349. Tübingen: Cotta, 1805.
———. "Über die Wirkung der Dichtkunst auf die Sitten der Völker in alten und neuen Zeiten." In *Sämmtliche Werke: zur schonen Literatur und Kunst*, 378–379. Tübingen: Cotta, 1807.
———. *Vom Geist der Ebräischen Poesie*. Dessau: Buchhandlung der Gelehrten, 1782–1783.
———. "Von den Deutsch-Orientalischen Dichtern." In *Werke zur schönen Literatur und Kunst*, 16–40. Tübingen: Cottaschen Buchhandlung, 1805.
———. "von Klopstocks David." *Allgemeine deutsche Bibliothek* 20, (1773) 1:3–12.
Hess, Johann Jakob. *Geschichte Davids und Salomons*. Zürich: Orell, Gessner, Füssli, 1785.
———. *Geschichte der Patriarchen*. Zürich: Orell, Gessner, Füssli, 1776.
———. *Geschichte Moses*. Zürich: Orell, 1777.
Hess, Johann Jakob, and Johann Kaspar Lavater. *Biblische Erzählungen für die Jugend*. Zürich: Orell, Gessner, Füsslin, 1772.
Hochstetter, Johann Friedrich. *Einleitung zu der Universal-History*. Tübingen: Schramm, 1740.
Hohburg, Christian. *Teutsch-Evangelisches Judenthum*. Frankfurt am Main, 1644.
Horst, Georg Conrad. *Die Visionen Habakuks, neu übersetzt, Nebst einer Abhandlung über den Prophetismus der alten Welt, und insbesondere der biblischen Propheten*. Gotha, 1798.
———. "Ideen über Religion, Mythologie und Christenthum, in Beziehung auf den Zeitgeist." *Der Schriftforscher* 1 (1803): 88–102.
Hufnagel, Wilhelm Friedrich. *Die Schriften des alten Testaments*. Erlangen: Jacob Palm, 1784.
Hume, David. "On National Character." In *Essays and Treatises on Several Subjects*, 1:223–241. London: Millar, 1753.
Jahn, Johann. *Biblische Archaeologie*. Vienna: Christian Friedrich Wappler, 1802.
Jerusalem, Johann Friedrich Wilhelm. *Beantwortung der Frage Ob die Ehe mit der Schwester Tochter, nach den göttlichen Gesetzen zuläßig sey*. N.p., 1754.

Jones, William. "On the Origin and Families of Nations." In *Works*, 3:189–190. London: Walker, 1807.
Justi, Karl Wilhelm. *Blumen althebräischer Dichtkunst*. Giessen: G. F. Heyer, 1809.
———. *Nationalgesänge der Hebräer*. Marburg: Neue Akadem, 1803.
———. *Selbstbiographie*. Marburg, 1818.
Justi, Leonard Johann Karl. *Weissagungs-Gesang Mosis an die Israeliten, aus der Urschrift von Neuem übersetzt und mit einer Erläuterung begleitet*. Göttingen, 1774.
Kant, Immanuel. *Die Religion innerhalb der Grenzen der blossen Vernunft*. Königsberg: Friedrich Nicolovius, 1794.
———. *Reflexionen zur Anthropologie*. Vol. 15 of *Kants Gesammelte Schriften*. Berlin: Walter de Gruyter, 1928.
Klopstock, Friedrich Gottlieb. *Sämtliche Werke*. Leipzig: G. J. Göschen, 1823.
Köhler, Johann Friedrich. *Gallerie der neuen Propheten, apokalyptischen Träumen, Geisteslehre und Revolutionsprediger: ein Beitrag z. Geschichte der menschlichter Narrheit*. Leipzig: Wiegand, 1799.
Kolbe, Peter. *Caput Bonae Spei Hodiernum*. Nürnberg: P. C. Monath, 1719.
Kühnöl, Christian Gottlieb. *Geschichte des jüdischen Volks von Abraham an bis auf Jerusalems Zerstörung*. Leipzig: J. F. Junius, 1791.
Leland, John. *An Answer to a Late Book Intituled: Christianity as Old as the Creation*. Dublin: Bradley, 1733.
Lessing, Gotthold Ephraim. *Die Erziehung des Menschengeschlechts*. Berlin, Christian Friedrich Voss, 1780.
Linnaeus, Carolus. *Systema Naturae*. Stockholm, 1758.
Locke, John. *A Letter Concerning Toleration*. London: Churchill, 1690.
———. *Second Treatise on Government*. London, 1690.
Lowth, Robert. *De sacra poesi Hebraeorum: notas et epimetra adjecit Ioannes David Michaelis*. Göttingen: Pockwiz u. Barmeier, 1758
———. *De sacra poesi Hebraeorum: praelectiones academicae Oxonii habitae, subjicitur metricae Harianae brevis confutatio et oratio Crewiana*. Oxford, 1753.
Luther, Martin, "Außlegung der Epistel St. Pauli an die Galater." [1531], in *Werke*, (Weimarer Ausgabe) 40, no. 1, 480–490. Weimar: Böhlau, 1883.
———. "Commentary on the First Twenty-Two Psalms," in Selected Works, trans. Henry Cole (London: Bensley, 1826), 493.
———. "Eyn Unterrichtung, wie sich die Christen yn Moses sollen schicken." [1525]. In *Werke* (Weimarer Ausgabe) 40, no. 1, 363–393. Weimar: Böhlau, 1883.
Maimonides, Moses, *The Guide for the Perplexed*. Trans. Chaim Rabin (Indianoplois, IN: Hackett, 1996).
Mendelssohn, Moses. "Dankpredigt über den Sieg bei Leuthen." In *Schriften: Jubiläumsausgabe*, 10 (no. 1):279–288. Stuttgart: Friedrich Frommann, 1974.
———. *Jerusalem oder über religioese Macht und Judentum*. Berlin: Maurer, 1783.
———. "Robert Lowth, De sacra poesi Hebraeorum." In *Gesammelte Schriften*, 4:20–22. Stuttgart: Friedrich Frommann, 1977.
———. "Robert Lowth's akademische Vorlesungen von der heiligen Dichtkunst der Hebräer." In *Bibliothek der schönen Wissenschaften und der freyen Künste*, 1757.
———. *Schriften zur Philosophie und Aesthetik*. Leipzig: Voss, 1880.
Meslier, Jean. *Le bon sens du curé J. Meslier, suivi de son testament*. Paris: Guillaumin, 1830.

Michaelis, Christian Benedikt. *Disputatio academica de Muhammedismi laxitate morali.* Halle: Henckel, 1708.

———. *Dissertatio philologica de antiquitatibus oeconomiae patriarchalis.* Halle: Henckel, 1728.

Michaelis, Johann David. *Abhandlung von den Ehegesetzen Mosis welche die Heyrathen in die nahe Freundschaft untersagen.* Göttingen: Vandenhoeck, 1755.

———. "Abhandlung von der herumziehenden Schafzucht der Morgenländer." In *Johann David Michaelis vermischte Schriften,* Frankfurt am Main: Garbe, 1766.

———. "Adair's History of the American Indians." *Orientalische und Exegetische Bibliothek* 10–11 (1776): 12.

———. *Beurhteilung der Mittel, welche man anwendet, die ausgestorbene hebräische Sprache zu verstehen.* Göttingen, 1757.

———. *Commentatio de nomadibus Palaestinae.* Göttingen, 1759.

———. *De nomadibus Palaestinae.* Göttingen: Vandenhoeck, 1759.

———. *De Troglodytis Seiritis.* Göttingen: Vandenhoeck, 1759.

———. *Deutsche Uebersetzung des Alten Testaments.* Göttingen: Dieterich, 1773.

———. "Forster's Observations." *Orientalische und Exegetische Bibliothek* 14–16 (1779): 48.

———. *Lebensbeschreibung von ihm selbst abgefasst.* Leipzig: Barth, 1793.

———. *Literarischer Briefwechsel.* Edited by Johann Gottlieb Buhle. Leipzig: Weidmann, 1796.

———. *Mosaisches Recht.* Frankfurt am Main: J. Gottlieb Garbe, 1775.

———. "Moses: Ein Heldengedicht (Epos)." *Hamburgische Beyträge* 58 (1752), 545.

Micraelius, Johannes. *Antiquitates Pomeraniae: oder die sechs Bücher vom alten Pommerlande.* Leipzig: Kunckels, 1723.

Montaigne, Michel de. "De cannibales." In *Les Essais: Oeuvres complètes.* Edited by Maurice Rat and Albert Thibaudet. Paris: Gallimard, 1962.

Montesquieu, Charles de Secondat. *De l'Esprit des lois.* Geneva: Barillot & Fils, 1749.

Morgan, Thomas. *The Moral Philosopher: In a Dialogue between Philalethes a Christian Deist, and Theophanes a Christian Jew.* London, 1738.

Mosheim, Johann Lorenz. *Sitten-Lehre der Heiligen Schrift.* Leipzig: Weygand, 1765.

Müller, Philipp. *Der Fang des edlen Lebens durch frembde Glaubens-Ehe.* N.p., 1689.

Opitz, Martin. *Prosodia Germanica, Oder Buch von der Deudschen Poeterey ... jetzo aber von Enoch Hanmann an unterschiedlichen Orten vermehret.* Frankfurt am Main: Christian Klein, 1658.

Penn, William. *Account of the Leni Lenape.* Somerset: Middle Atlantic Press, 1970.

Phillipsohn, Moses. *Kinderfreund, Lehr- und Lesebuch für die Kinder jüdischer Nation.* Dessau, 1811.

Pyra, Jacob Immanuel. *Der Tempel der Wahren Dichtkunst: Ein Gedicht in reimfreyen Versen.* Halle im Magdeburgischen: Fritsch, 1737.

Reimarus, Hermann Samuel. *Apologie: oder, Schutzschrift für die vernünftigen Verehrer Gottes.* Edited by Gerhard Alexander. Frankfurt am Main: Insel, 1972.

Reinhold, Carl Leonhard. *Die Hebräischen Mysterien oder die älteste religiöse Freymaurerey.* Leipzig: Göschen, 1788.

Rückert, Friedrich. "Geharnischten Sonette." In *Gesammelte Gedichte,* 2:165. Erlangen: Heyder, 1839.

Sack, August Wilhelm. *Der gerettete David in einer am 23: Sonntage nach Trinitatis 1757. über Psalm 18, v. 18, 19, 20. in der Ober-Pfarr- und Dohm-Kirche gehaltenen Predigt vorgestellet.* Berlin: Christian Ludewig Kunst, 1757.

Schelling, Friedrich Wilhelm. "Über die Mythen der ältesten Welt." *Paulus Memorabilien* 1793: 1–68.
[Scherer, Johann Ludwig Wilhelm?]. *Ausführliche Erklärung der sämmtlichen Wundergeschichten des alten Testaments: aus natürlichen Ursachen, durchaus begleitet mit philologischen, kritischen und historischen Anmerkungen, nebst einer Abhundlung über Wunder und Offenbarung.* Berlin, 1800.
Scherer, Johann Ludwig Wilhelm. *Ausführliche Erklärung der Weissagungen aller Propheten des alten und neuen Testaments.* Leipzig: Weygand, 1801.
———. *Bibelcommentar, zum Handgebrauch für Prediger, Schullehrer und Leyen.* Altenburg: Richter, 1799.
———. *Biblische Völkergeschichte.* Leipzig: Weygand, 1804.
———. *"Das Vaterland in Gefahr! Gott sein Retter Ihm Lob und Dank!" Dargestellt in einer heil. Rede am allgemeinen Dankfeste in den Grosherzogl. Hess. Staaten, in glücklich abgewendeter Kriegsgefahr.* Frankfurt am Main, 1806.
———. *Die Geschichte der Israeliten vor Jesus nach ihren heiligen Büchern, für die Bedürfnisse unserer Zeit bearbeitet.* Zerbst: Andreas Füchsel, 1803.
———. *Die Geschichte des Alten Testaments.* Giesen: Krieger, 1803.
———. *Die schönsten Geistes-Blüthen des ältesten Orients: für Freunde des Grossen und Schönen.* Karlsruhe: Macklot, 1809.
———. *Friede, Stimme Gottes vom Himmel! Friede, Segen der Menschheit! dargestellt in einer heiligen Rede am allgemeinen Dankfeste in den Großherzoglich Hessischen Staaten wegen des zwischen Frankreich, dem Rheinbunde und Oesterreich am 14ten Oktob. 1809 zu Wien geschlossenen Friedens.* Darmstadt: Leske, 1809.
———. *Historische Einleitung zum richtigen Verstehen der Bibel: mit Rücksicht auf den Zerrennerschen Auszug: für Gymnasien und Schulen nach den geläuterten Erklärungsgrundsätzen unserer Zeit.* Halle: Johann Jacob Gebauer, 1802.
———. *Neue Religionsgeschichte für die Jugend: zum Gebrauch für Aeltern, Prediger und Lehrer.* Leipzig, 1798.
Schiller, Friedrich. "Die Schaubühne als eine moralische Anstalt betrachtet." In *Kleine prosaische Schriften*, 4:23–29. Leipzig: Crusius, 1802.
———. "Die Sendung Moses." In *Kleinere prosaische Schriften*, 2–22. Leipzig: Cursius, 1802.
Schlegel, August Wilhelm. *Kritische Schriften und Briefe.* Stuttgart: Kohlhammer, 1962.
Schlegel, Friedrich. "Ideen." *Athenaeum* 3 (1800): 4–33.
———. *Kritische Ausgabe.* Paderborn: F. Schöningh, 1958–1991.
———. "Über den Anfang unserer Geschicht ... von J.G. Rhode." *Jahrbüchern der Literatur* 8 (1819): 459–470.
———. *Über die Sprache und Weisheit der Indier.* Heidelberg: Mohr und Zimmer, 1808.
Schlözer, August Ludwig von. *Fortsetzung der Allgemeinen Welthistorie.* Halle: Gebauer, 1771.
Schönfeld, Franz Thomas von. "Bey Uebersendung meiner Davidischen Kriegsgesänge: An Klopstock." In *Blumenlese der Musen*, 96–98. Vienna: Jakob Kaiserer, 1790.
———. *Davids Kriegsgesänge: Deutsch (aus dem Grundtexte): dem Heere Josephs.* Vienna: R. Gräffer, 1788.
Scott, Thomas. *An Answer to Paine's "Age of Reason."* London: L. B. Seeley, 1796.
Spencer, John. *De legibus hebraeorum ritualibus et earum.* Cambridge: Chiswel, 1685.
Spinoza, Benedict. *Tractatus Theologico-Politicus.* Translated by S. Shirley. Leiden: Brill, 1989.

Strieder, Friedrich Wilhelm. *Grundlage zu einer Hessischen Gelehrten und Schriftsteller Geschichte: seit der Reformation bis auf gegenwärtige Zeiten.* Cassel: Griesbach, 1797.

Strodtmann, Johann Christoph. *Übereinstimmung der deutschen Alterthümer mit den biblischen, sonderlich hebräischen.* Wolfenbüttel, 1755.

Tertullian. *Adversus Marcionem.* Oxford: Clarendon, 1972.

Thomasius, Christian. *Eröterung von der Lutherischen und Reformirten Fürstlichen Personen Heyrath.* Leipzig: Renger, 1689.

Thorowgood, Thomas. *Jews in America: or Probabilities That the Americans Are of That Race.* London: Brome, 1650.

Tindal, Matthew. *Christianity as Old as the Creation.* London: W. Innys, 1730.

Velthusen, Johann Caspar. *Der Amethyst: Beytrag historisch kritischer Untersuchungen über das Hohe Lied.* Braunschweig: Waisenhaus Buchhandlung, 1786.

———. *Einfluss frommer Juden und ihrer Harfe auf den Geist roher Nationen, insonderheit auf Ossians Bardenlieder.* Leipzig: S. L. Crusius, 1807.

———. *Über die nächste Bestimmung des Landpredigerstandes: Ein durch hernn Campe's Fragmente veranlasster Beitrag zur Pastoraltheologie.* Helmstedt, 1787.

Voltaire. *Dictionnaire philosophique.* Geneva: Bruyset, 1756.

———. *Essai sur les moeurs et l'esprit des nations.* Genève: frères Cramer, 1756.

———. *La philosophie de l'histoire.* Geneva, 1765.

Voß, Johann Heinrich. "Trinklied." In *Sämtliche Gedichte*, 37. Königsberg: Nicolovius, 1802.

———. *Vermischte Gedichte und prosaische Aufsätze.* Leipzig, 1784.

Walther, Friedrich Andreas. *Geschichte der Weltweisheit der alten Hebräer.* Göttingen: Victorinus Boßiegel, 1750.

Warnekros, Heinrich Ehrenfried. *Entwurf der hebräischen Alterthümer.* Weimar: Hofmann, 1782.

Watson, Richard. *An Apology for the Bible, in a Series of Letters, Addressed to T. Paine.* Cambridge: Evans, 1796.

Webb, Francis. *A Defence of Revelation in General, and the Gospel in Particular.* London: W. Sandby, 1766.

Wessely, Hartwig. *Die Moseide: in 18 Gesängen. Uebersetzt nach dem hebräischen Originale von dem Herrn Senior Hufnagel, dem Herrn Professor Spalding.* Hamburg, 1806.

Williams, Robert A., Jr. *The American Indian in Western Legal Thought: The Discourses of Conquest.* New York: Oxford University Press, 1990.

Winckelmann, Johann Joachim. "Gedancken über die Nachahmung der Griechischen Wercke in der Mahlerey und Bildhauer-Kunst." In *Kleine Schriften.* Berlin: Walter der Gruyter, 1968.

Secondary Sources

Adergeg, Johannes, and Edith Anaa Kunz, eds. *Goethe und die Bibel.* Stuttgart: Deutsche Bibelgesellschaft, 2005.

Ahnert, Thomas. *Religion and the Origins of the German Enlightenment: Faith and the Reform of Learning in the Thought of Christian Thomasius.* Rochester, NY: University of Rochester Press, 2006.

Almond, Philip C. *Adam and Eve in Seventeenth-Century Thought.* Cambridge, UK: Cambridge University Press, 1999.

Altgeld, Wolfgang. *Katholizismus, Protestantismus, Judentum: Über religiös begründete Gegensätze und national-religiöse Ideen in der Geschichte des deutschen Nationalismus.* Mainz: Matthias-Grünewald, 1992.
Altmann, Alexander. *Moses Mendelssohn: A Biographical Study.* Tuscaloosa: University of Alabama Press, 1973.
Aravamudan, Srinivas. "Hobbes and America." In *The Postcolonial Enlightenment: Eighteenth-Century Colonialism and Postcolonial Theory,* edited by Daniel Carey and Lynn Festa, 37–70. New York: Oxford, 2009.
Arendt, Hanna. "The Enlightenment and the Jewish Question." In *Jewish Writings,* 3–19. New York: Shocken, 2007.
Arneil, Barbara. *John Locke and America: The Defence of English Colonialism.* Oxford: Oxford University Press, 1996.
Asad, Talal. *Formations of the Secular: Christianity, Islam, Modernity.* Stanford, CA: Stanford University Press, 2003.
Assmann, Jan. *Moses the Egyptian: The Memory of Egypt in Western Monotheism.* Cambridge, MA: Harvard University Press, 1997.
Auerbach, Erich. "Figura." In *Scenes from the Drama of European Literature,* trans. Ralph Manheim. Gloucester: Peter Smith, 1985.
Auerochs, Bernd. *Die Entstehung der Kunstreligion.* Göttingen: Vandenhoeck & Ruprecht, 2006.
———. "Poesie als Urkunde. Zu Herders Poesiebegriff." In *Johann Gottfried Herder–Aspekte seines Lebenswerkes,* ed. Martin Keßler and Volker Leppin, 93–114. Berlin: Walter de Gruyter, 2005.
Baasten, Martin F. J. "A Note on the History of 'Semitic.'" In *Hamlet on a Hill: Semitic and Greek Studies Presented to Professor T. Muraoka,* ed. Martin F. J. Baasten and W. Th. van Peursen, 57–73. Leuven: Peeters, 2003.
Bach, Inka, and Helmut Galle. *Deutsche Psalmdichtung vom 16. bis 20. Jahrhundert.* Berlin: Walter de Gruyter, 1989.
Baecker, Dirk. "Moderne Kultur und ihre Genealogie." In *Über Kultur: Theorie und Praxis der Kulturreflexion,* ed. Dirk Baecker and Matthias Kettner. Bielefeld: transcript, 2008.
Baildam, John D. *Paradisal Love: Johann Gottfried Herder and the Song of Songs.* Sheffield: Sheffield Academic Press, 1999.
Balfour, Ian. *The Rhetoric of Romantic Prophecy.* Stanford, CA: Stanford University Press, 2002.
Bar, Ludwig von. *A History of Continental Criminal Law.* Boston: Little Brown, 1916.
Barnard, Frederick M. "The Hebrews and Herder's Political Creed." *The Modern Language Review* 54, no. 4 (1959): 533–546.
———. *Herder on Nationality, Humanity, and History.* Montreal: McGill-Queen's Press, 2003.
———. *Self-Direction and Political Legitimacy: Rousseau and Herder.* Oxford: Clarendon Press, 1988.
Barnett, S. J. *The Enlightenment and Religion: The Myths of Modernity.* Oxford: Oxford University Press, 2004.
Baron, Salo Wittmayer. *Modern Nationalism and Religion.* New York: Harper, 1947.
Barth, Ulrich. *Aufgeklärter Protestantismus.* Tübingen, 2004.
Beck, *Adolf,* and Horst Gronemeyer, eds. *Klopstock: Werke und Briefe: historisch-kritische Ausgabe.* Berlin: Walter de Gruyter, 1999.

Beiner, Ronald. *Civil Religion: A Dialogue in the History of Political Philosophy.* Cambridge, UK: Cambridge University Press, 2010.
Beiser, Frederick C. *Enlightenment, Revolution and Romanticism: The Genesis of Modern German Political Thought, 1790-1800.* Cambridge, MA: Harvard University Press, 1992.
Belaval, Yvon, and Dominique Bourel, eds. *Le siècle des Lumières et la Bible.* Paris: Beauchesne, 1986.
Bell, David. *Spinoza in Germany from 1670 to the Age of Goethe.* London: University of London, 1984.
Benes, Tuska. "From Indo-Germans to Aryans: Philology and the Racialization of Salvationist National Rhetoric, 1806-30." In *The German Invention of Race,* ed. Sara Eigen and Mark Larrimore, 167-184. Albany: State University of New York, 2006.
———. *In Babel's Shadow: Language, Philology, and the Nation in Nineteenth-Century Germany.* Detroit, MI: Wayne State University Press, 2008.
Ben-Tov, Asaph. *Lutheran Humanists and Greek Antiquity: Melanchthonian Scholarship between Universal History and Pedagogy.* Leiden: Brill, 2009.
Berghahn, Cord-Friedrich. "'Mythologische Nationalgesänge vom Ursprunge': biblische Poesie, Judentum und europäische Gegenwart bei Johann Gottfried Herder und Moses Mendelssohn." *Germanisch-Romanische Monatsschrift* 57, no. 1 (2007): 113-133.
Berry, Christopher J. *Social Theory of the Scottish Enlightenment.* Edinburgh: Edinburgh University Press, 1997.
Beyme, Klaus von. *Geschichte der politischen Theorien in Deutschland 1300-2000.* Wiesbaden: VS, 2009.
Bhabha, Homi K. "The Other Question: Stereotype, Discrimination and the Discourse of Colonialism." In *The Location of Culture,* 66-84. New York: Routledge, 2004.
Bietenholz, Peter G. *Historia and Fabula: Myths and Legends in Historical Thought from Antiquity to the Modern Age.* Leiden: Brill, 1994.
Blitz, Hans-Martin. *Aus Liebe zum Vaterland: die deutsche Nation im 18. Jahrhundert.* Hamburg: Hamburger Edition, 2000.
———. "'Gieb, Vater, mir ein Schwert!' Identitätskonzepte und Feindbilder in der 'patriotischen' Lyrik Klopstocks und des Göttinger 'Hain.'" In *Machtphantasie Deutschland: Nationalismus, Männlichkeit und Fremdenhaß im Vaterlandsdiskurs deutscher Schriftsteller des 18. Jahrhunderts,* ed. Hans Peter Herrmann, 80-122 Frankfurt am Main: Suhrkamp, 1996.
Braude, Benjamin. "The Sons of Noah and the Construction of Ethnic and Geographical Identities in the Medieval and Early Modern Periods." *William and Mary Quarterly* 54 (January 1997): 103-142.
Breisach, Ernst. *Historiography: Ancient, Medieval, & Modern.* Chicago: University of Chicago Press, 2007.
Breuer, Edward. *The Limits of Enlightenment: Jews, Germans, and the Eighteenth-Century Study of Scripture.* Cambridge, MA: Harvard University Press, 1996.
Bultmann, Christoph. "Bewunderung oder Entzauberung? Johann Gottfried Herders Blick auf Mose." In *Johann Gottfried Herder: Aspekte seines Lebenswerkes,* ed. Martin Keßler and Volker Leppin, 15-28. Berlin: Walter de Gruyter, 2005.
———. *Die biblische Urgeschichte in der Aufklärung: Johann Gottfried Herders Interpretation der Genesis als Antwort auf die Religionskritik David Humes.* Tübingen: Mohr Siebeck, 1999.

Bultmann, Christoph and Lutz Danneberg, eds. *Hebraistik – Hermeneutik – Homiletik: Die, "Philologia Sacra" im frühneuzeitlichen Bibelstudium.* Berlin: Walter de Gruyter, 2011.
Burdach, Konrad. *Die nationale Aneignung der Bibel und die Anfänge der germanischen Philologie.* Halle: Max Niemeyer, 1924.
———. *"Faust und Moses," Sitzungsberichte der Koniglichen Preussischen Akademie der Wissenschaft* (1912), 358-403.
Burnett, Stephen G. *Christian Hebraism in the Reformation Era (1500–1660): Authors, Books, and the Transmission of Jewish Learning.* Leiden: Brill, 2012.
Butler, Eliza Marian. *The Tyranny of Greece over Germany.* Cambridge, UK: Cambridge University Press, 1935.
Campos, Edmund Valentine. "West of Eden: American Gold, Spanish Greed, and the Discourses of English Imperialism." In *Rereading the Black Legend: The Discourses of Religious and Racial Difference in the Renaissance Empires*, ed. Margaret R. Greer, Walter D. Mignolo, and Maureen Quilligan, 247–269. Chicago: University of Chicago Press, 2007.
Carhart, Michael M. *The Science of Culture in Enlightenment Germany.* Cambridge, MA: Harvard University Press, 2007.
Carl, Horst. "'Die Aufklärung unsres Jahrhunderts ist ein bloßes Nordlicht' Konfession und deutsche Nation im Zeitalter der Aufklärung." In *Nation und Religion in der deutschen Geschichte*, ed. Heinz-Gerhard Haupt and Dieter Langewische, 105–141. Frankfurt am Main: Campus, 2001.
Carrithers, David Wallace. *The Spirit of Laws: A Compendium of the First English Edition.* Berkeley: University of California Press, 1979.
Cassirer, Ernst. *The Myth of the State.* New Haven, CT: Yale University Press, 1946.
Cave, Alfred A. "Canaanites in a Promised Land: The American Indian and the Providential Theory of Empire." *American Indian Quarterly* 12 (1988): 277–297.
Coudert, Allison, and Jeffrey S. Shoulson, eds. *Hebraica Veritas? Christian Hebraists and the Study of Judaism in Early Modern Europe.* Philadelphia: University of Pennsylvania Press, 2004.
Cullhed, Anna. "Original Poetry: Robert Lowth and Eighteenth-Century Poetics." In *Sacred Conjectures: The Context and Legacy of Robert Lowth and Jean Astruc*, ed. John Jarick, 25–47. New York, T & T Clark, 2007.
Dabhoiwala, Faramerz. *The Origins of Sex: A History of the First Sexual Revolution.* Oxford: Oxford University Press, 2012.
Davidowicz, Klaus S. *Die Kabbala: Eine Einführung in die Welt der jüdischen Mystik und Magie.* Vienna: Böhlau, 2009.
Deutsch, Yaacov. *Judaism in Christian Eyes: Ethnographic Descriptions of Jews and Judaism in Early Modern Europe.* Oxford: Oxford University Press, 2012.
Deutschlander, Leo. *Goethe und das Alte Testament.* Frankfurt am Main: Sänger & Friedberg, 1923.
Docker, John. *The Origins of Violence: Religion, History and Genocide.* Sydney: University of New South Wales Press, 2008.
Döring, Heinrich. *Die gelehrten Theologen Deutschlands im achtzehnten und neunzehnten Jahrhundert: nach ihrem Leben und Wirken dargestellt.* Neustdat a. d. Orla: J. K. G. Wagner, 1831.

Dunkelgrün, Theodor. "'Neerlands Israel': Political Theology, Christian Hebraism, Biblical Antiquarianism, and Historical Myth." In *Myth in History, History in Myth*, ed. Laura Cruz and Willem Frijhoff, 201–236. Leiden: Brill, 2009.

Düwel, Klaus, and Harro Zimmermann. "Germanenbild und Patriotismus in der deutschen Literatur des 18. Jahrhunderts." In *Germanenprobleme in heutiger Sicht*, ed. Heinrich Beck, 358–395. Berlin: Walter de Gruyter, 1986.

Dyck, Joachim. *Athen und Jerusalem: Die Tradition der argumentativen Verknüpfung von Bibel und Poesie im 17. und 18. Jahrhundert*. Munich: C. H. Beck, 1977.

Echternkamp, Jörg. *Der Aufstieg des deutschen Nationalismus (1770–1840)*, Frankfurt am Main: Campus, 1998.

Eco, Umberto. *The Search for the Perfect Language*. Oxford: Blackwell, 1995.

Edelstein, Dan. *The Enlightenment: A Genealogy*. Chicago: University of Chicago Press, 2010.

Eggel, Dominic, Andre Leibich, and Deborah Mancini-Griffoli. "Was Herder a Nationalist?" *The Review of Politics* 69, no. 1 (Winter, 2007): 48–78.

Eibach, Joachim. "Preußens Salomon: Herrschaftslegitimation und Herrscherpflichten in Predigten anläßlich der Krönung Friedrichs I." In *Dreihundert Jahre preußische Königskrönung: eine Tagungsdokumentation*, ed. Johannes Kunisch, 135–157. Berlin: Duncker & Humblot, 2002.

Eilberg-Schwartz, Howard. *The Savage in Judaism: An Anthropology of Israelite Religion and Ancient Judaism*. Bloomington: Indiana University Press, 1990.

Elssner, Thomas R. *Josua und seine Kriege in jüdischer und christlicher Rezeptionsgeschichte*. Stuttgart: W. Kohlhammer, 2008.

Elukin, Jonathan. "Maimonides and the Rise and Fall of the Sabians: Explaining Mosaic Laws and the Limits of Scholarship." *Journal of the History of Ideas* 63, no. 4 (2002): 619–637.

Engelsing, Rolf, "Die Perioden der Lesergeschichte in der Neuzeit." *Archiv für Geschichte des Buchwesens* 10 (1970): 945–1002.

Escher, Heinrich. *Johann Jakob Hess, Doktor der Theologie und Antistes der zürcherischen Kirche: Skizze seines Lebens und seiner Ansichten*. Zürich: S. Hohr, 1837.

Fabian, Johannes. *Time and the Other*. New York: Columbia University Press, 1983.

Ferris, David S. *Silent Urns: Romanticism, Hellenism, Modernity*. Stanford, CA: Stanford University Press, 2000.

Figueira, Dorothy Matilda. *Aryans, Jews, and Brahmins: Theorizing Authority through Myths of Identity*. Albany: State University of New York Press, 2002.

———. *The Exotic: A Decadent Quest*. Albany: State Univesity of New York Press, 1994.

Fink, Gonthier-Louis. "Vom universalen zum nationalen Literaturmodell im deutsch-französischen Konkurrenzkampf (1760–1770)." In *Tradition, Norm, Innovation: Soziales und literarisches Traditionsverhalten*, ed. Wilfried Barner and Elisabeth Müller-Luckner, 33–67. Munich: Oldenbourg, 1989.

Fischer, Bernd, *Das Eigene und das Eigentliche: Klopstock, Herder, Fichte, Kleist*, Berlin: Schmidt, 1995.

Fohrmann, Jürgen. *Das Projekt der deutschen Literturgeschichte*. Stuttgart: Metzler, 1989.

Frank, Armin Paul. "Zum Begriff der Nationalliteratur in Herders abweichender Antwort auf Lowth." In *Urpoesie und Morgenland: Johann Gottfried Herders "Vom Geist der Ebräischen Poesie,"* ed. Daniel Weidner, 300–326. Berlin: Kadmos, 2008.

Frei, Hans W. *The Eclipse of Biblical Narrative: A Study in Eighteenth and Nineteenth Century Hermeneutics.* New Haven, CT: Yale University Press, 1974.
Freist, Dagmar. "One Body, Two Confessions: Mixed Marriages in Germany." In *Gender in Early Modern German History*, ed. Ulinka Rublack, 275–305. Cambridge, UK: Cambridge University Press, 2002.
Freudenthal, Gideon. *No Religion without Idolatry: Mendelssohn's Jewish Enlightenment.* Notre Dame, IN: University of Notre Dame Press, 2012.
Friedman, Jerome. *The Most Ancient Testimony: Sixteenth-Century Christian-Hebraica in the Age of Renaissance Nostalgia.* Athens: Ohio University Press, 1983.
Frey, Christiane. "Gramma, Hieroglyphe und jüdisch-hebräische Kultur (Herder, Dohm, Mendelssohn)." In *Die Ordnung der Kulturen: Zur Konstruktion ethnischer, nationaler und zivilisatorischer Differenzen*, ed. Hansjörg Bay and Kai Merten, 149–172. Würzburg: Königshausen & Neumann, 2006.
Friedman, Jerome. *The Most Ancient Testimony: Sixteenth-Century Christian-Hebraica in the Age of Renaissance Nostalgia.* Athens: Ohio University Press, 1983.
Funkenstein, Amos. "Jews, Christians and Muslims: Religious Polemics in the Middle Ages." In *The Jews in European History*, ed. Wolfgang Beck. Cincinnati, OH: Hebrew Union College Press, 1994.
Gardt, Andreas, ed. *Nation und Sprache: Die Diskussion ihres Verhältnisses in Geschichte und Gegenwart.* Berlin: Walter de Gruyter, 2000.
Garrison, Mary. "The Franks as the New Israel? Education for an Identity from Pippin to Charlemagne." In *The Uses of the Past in the Early Middle Ages*, ed. Yitzhak Hen and Matthew Innes, 114–161. New York: Cambridge University Press, 2000.
Gawthrop, Richard L. *Pietism and the Making of Eighteenth Century Prussia.* Cambridge, UK: Cambridge University Press, 1993.
Gerdmar, Anders. *Roots of Theological Anti-Semitism: German Biblical Interpretation and the Jews, from Herder and Semler to Kittel and Bultmann.* Leiden: Brill, 2009.
Germana, Nicholas A. *The Orient of Europe: The Mythical Image of India and Competing Images of German National Identity.* Newcastle upon Tyne: Cambridge Scholars Publishing, 2009.
———. "Self-Othering in German Orientalism: The Case of Friedrich Schlegel." *The Comparatist* 34 (May 2010): 80–94.
Gillingham, Susan E. *Psalms through the Centuries.* Oxford: Blackwell, 2008.
Gockel, Heinz. *Mythos und Poesie: Zum Mythosbegriff in Aufklärung und Frühromantik.* Frankfurt am Main: Klostermann, 1981.
Goetschel, Willi. *Spinoza's Modernity: Mendelssohn, Lessing, and Heine.* Madison: University of Wisconsin Press, 2004.
Goodman, Dena. *The Republic of Letters: A Cultural History of the French Enlightenment.* Ithaca, NY: Cornell University Press, 1994.
Gorski, Philip S. "Calvinism and State-Formation in Early Modern Europe." In *State / Culture: State-Formation after the Cultural Turn*, ed. George Steinmetz, 147–181. Ithaca, NY: Cornell University Press, 1999.
———. "The Mosaic Moment: An Early Modernist Critique of Modernist Theories of Nationalism." *The American Journal of Sociology* 105, no. 5 (March 2000): 1428–1468.
Graf, Gerhard. *Gottesbild und Politik: Eine Studie zur Frömmigkeit in Preußen während der Befreiungskriege, 1813–1815.* Göttingen: Vandenhoeck & Ruprecht, 1993.

Greenfeld, Liah. *Nationalism: Five Roads to Modernity*. Cambridge, MA: Harvard University Press, 1992.

Grosby, Steven Elliott. *Biblical Ideas of Nationality: Ancient and Modern*. Winona Lake, IN: Eisenbrauns, 2002.

Grossman, Walter. *Johann Christian Edelmann: From Orthodoxy to Enlightenment*. The Hague: Mouton, 1976.

Gusdorf, Georges. *Les sciences humaines et la pensée occidentale*. Vol. 6, *L'avènement des sciences humaines au siecle des Lumieres*. Paris: Payot, 1973.

Harrington, Joel F. *Reordering Marriage and Society in Reformation Germany*. Cambridge, UK: Cambridge University Press, 1995.

Harrison, Peter. "'The Book of Nature' and Early Modern Science." In *The Book of Nature in Early Modern and Modern History*, ed. Klaas van Berkel and Arjo Vanderjagt, 1–26. Leuven: Peeters, 2006.

Harrisville, Roy, and Walter Sundberg. *The Bible in Modern Culture*. Cambridge, UK: Erdman, 1995.

Hartlich, Christian, and Walter Sachs. *Der Ursprung des Mythosbegriffes in der modernen Bibelwissenschaft*. Tübingen: Mohr Siebeck, 1952.

Hartwich, Wolf-Daniel. *Die Sendung Moses: von der Aufklärung bis Thomas Mann*. Munich: Fink, 1997.

Hastings, Adrian. *The Construction of Nationhood: Ethnicity, Religion, and Nationalism*. Cambridge, UK: Cambridge University Press, 1997.

Hayes, Carlton. "Contributions of Herder to the Doctrine of Nationalism." *American Historical Review* 32 (July 1927): 719–736.

Haym, Rudolph. *Herder*. Berlin: Gaertner, 1880.

Heftrich, Eckhard. *Novalis: Vom Logos der Poesie*. Frankfurt am Main: Klostermann, 1969.

Heidemann, Stefan. "Zwischen Theologie und Philologie: Der Paradigmenwechsel in der Jenaer Orientalistik 1770 bis 1850." *Der Islam* 84 (2008): 140–184.

Hendy, Andrew von. *The Modern Construction of Myth*. Bloomington: Indiana University Press, 2002.

Herrick, James A. *The Radical Rhetoric of the English Deists: The Discourse of Skepticism, 1680–1750*. Columbia: University of South Carolina Press, 1997.

Herrmann, Hans-Martin, ed. *Machtphantasie Deutschland: Nationalismus, Männlichkeit und Fremdenhaß im Vaterlandsdiskurs des 18. Jahrhunderts*. Frankfurt am Main: Suhrkamp, 1996.

Heschel, Susannah. *The Aryan Jesus: Christian Theologians and the Bible in Nazi Germany*. Princeton, NJ: Princeton University Press, 2008.

Hess, Jonathan M. *Germans, Jews and the Claims of Modernity*. New Haven, CT: Yale University Press, 2002.

Horowitz, Eliott. *Reckless Rites: Purim and the Legacy of Jewish Violence*. Princeton, NJ: Princeton University Press, 2006.

Houtman, Cornelius. "Josua im Urteil einiger Freidenker." In *The Land of Israel in Bible, History, and Theology: Studies in Honour of Ed Noort*, ed. Jacques van Ruiten and J. Cornelius de Vos, 339–344. Leiden: Brill, 2009.

Howard, Thomas Albert. *Protestant Theology and the Making of Modern German University*. Oxford: Oxford University Press, 2006.

———. *Religion and the Rise of Historicism: W. M. L. de Wette, Jacob Burckhardt, and the Theological Origins of Nineteenth-Century Historical Consciousness*. Cambridge, UK: Cambridge University Press, 2000.

Hsia, R. Po-chia. "Eine religiöse Minderheit in einer konfessionellen Gesellschaft: Juden im Heiligen Römischen Reich des 17. Jahrhunderts." In *Im Zeichen der Krise. Religiosität im Europa des 17. Jahrhunderts*, ed. Hartmut Lehmann, 295–310. Göttingen: Vandenhoeck & Ruprecht, 1999.

———. *The Myth of Ritual Murder, Jews and Magic in Reformation Germany*. New Haven, CT: Yale University Press, 1988.

———. "The Usurious Jew: Economic Structure and Religious Representations in Anti-Semitic Discourse." In *In and Out of the Ghetto*, ed. R. Po-chia Hsia and Hartmut Lehmann, 161–176. Cambridge, UK: Cambridge University Press, 1995.

Hull, Isabel V. *Sexuality, State, and Civil Society in Germany, 1700–1815*. Ithaca, NY: Cornell University Press, 1996.

Hunter, Ian. *Rival Enlightenments: Civil and Metaphysical Philosophy in Early Modern Germany*. Cambridge, UK: Cambridge University Press, 2001.

Ihalainen, Pasi. *Protestant Nations Redefined: Changing Perceptions of National Identity in the Rhetoric of the English, Dutch and Swedish Public Churches, 1685–1772*. Leiden: Brill, 2005.

Israel, Jonathan. *Democratic Enlightenment: Philosophy, Revolution, and Human Rights 1750–1790*. Oxford: Oxford University Press, 2011.

———. *Enlightenment Contested: Philosophy, Modernity, and the Emancipation of Man 1670–1752*. Oxford: Oxford University Press, 2006.

———. *Radical Enlightenment: Philosophy and the Making of Modernity, 1650–1750*. Oxford: Oxford University Press, 2001.

Jarzebowski, Claudia. *Inzest: Verwandtschaft und Sexualität im 18. Jahrhundert*. Cologne: Böhlau, 2006.

Jones, William J. "Early Dialectology, Etymology and Language History in German Speaking Countries." In *History of the Language Sciences*, ed. Sylvain Auroux, 1105–1108. Berlin: Walter de Gruyter, 2001.

Junkin, Edward Dixon. *Religion versus Revolution: The Interpretation of the French Revolution by German Protestant Churchmen, 1789–1799*. Austin, TX: Best, 1974.

Kaiser, Gerhard. *Aufklärung, Empfindsamkeit, Sturm und Drang*. Munich: Francke, 1976.

———. *Klopstock: Religion und Dichtung*. Mainz: Scriptor, 1975.

———. *Pietismus und Patriotismus im literarischen Deutschland: Ein Beitrag zum Problem der Säkularisation*. Frankfurt am Main: Athenäum, 1973.

Kalmar, Ivan Davidson, and Derek J. Penslar, eds. *Orientalism and the Jews*. Waltham, MA: Brandeis University Press, 2004.

Karniel, Josef. "Jüdischer Pseudomessianismus und deutsche Kultur, der Weg der frankistischen Familie Dobruschka-Schönfeld im Zeitalter der Aufklärung." In *Jahrbuch des Instituts für Deutsche Geschichte* 4 (1983): 31–54.

Karthaus, Ulrich. *Sturm und Drang: Epoche-Werke-Wirkung*. Munich: Beck, 2000.

Katz, David S. *God's Last Words: Reading the English Bible from the Reformation to Fundamentalism*. New Haven, CT: Yale University Press, 2004.

Kaufmann, Thomas. *Das Ende der Reformation*. Tübingen: Mohr Siebeck, 2003.

Kippenberg, Hans. *Discovering Religious History in the Modern Age*. Princeton, NJ: Princeton University Press, 2002.

Kirn, Hans Martin. *Deutsche Spätaufklärung und Pietismus: ihr Verhältnis im Rahmen kirchlich-bürgerlicher Reform bei Johann Ludwig Ewald (1748–1822)*. Göttingen: Vandenhoeck & Ruprecht, 1998.

Kohl, Katrin M., *Rhetoric, the Bible, and the Origins of Free Verse: The Early Hymns of Friedrich Gottlieb Klopstock*, New York: Walter de Gruyter, 1990.

Kohn, Hans. *The Idea of Nationalism: A Study in Its Origins and Background*. New York: Macmillan, 1944.

———. *Prelude to Nation-States: The French and German Experience, 1789–1815*. Princeton, NJ: Van Nostrand, 1967.

Kontje, Todd. *German Orientalisms*. Ann Arbor: University of Michigan Press, 2004.

Kopitzsch, Franklin. "Die Sozialgeschichte der deutschen Aufklärung als Forschungsaufgabe." In *Aufklärung, Absolutismus und Burgertum in Deutschland*, ed. Franklin Kopitzsch, 11–169. Munich: Nymphenburg, 1976.

Kors, Alan Charles. *Atheism in France, 1650–1729: The Orthodox Sources of Disbelief*. Princeton, NJ: Princeton University Press, 1990.

Koselleck, Reinhart, ed. *Geschichtliche Grundbegriffe: Historisches Lexikon zur politisch-sozialen Sprache in Deutschland*. Stuttgart: Klett-Cotta, 1972.

———. *Preußen zwischen Reform und Revolution: allgemeines Landrecht, Verwaltung und soziale Bewegung von 1791 bis 1848*. Stuttgart: Klett, 1987.

———. "'Progress' and 'Decline': An Appendix to the History of Two Concepts," In *The Practice of Conceptual History: Timing Concepts, Spacing Concepts*, 219–235. Stanford, CA. Stanford University Press, 2002.

———. *Vergangene Zukunft*. Frankfurt am Main: Suhrkamp, 1979.

Kraeling, Emil G. *The Old Testament since the Reformation*. London: Lutterworth, 1955.

Krapf, Ludwig. *Germanenmythos und Reichsideologie: Fruhhumanistische Rezeptionsweisen der taciteischen "Germania."* Tubingen: Max Niemeyer, 1979.

Kraus, Hans-Joachim. *Geschichte der historisch-kritischen Erforschung des Alten Testaments von der Reformation bis zur Gegenwar*. Neukirchen-Vluyn: Neukirchener, 1969.

Kühnemann, Eugen, ed. "Herders Werke." In *Deutsche National-Litteratur*. Stuttgart: W. Spemann, 1882.

Langhals, Ralf-Carl. *"Zurück nach Lascaux": eine Höhlengeschichte*. Marburg: Tactum, 2003.

Larimore, Mark Joseph. "Race, Freedom and the Fall in Steffens and Kant." In *The German Invention of Race*, ed. Sara Eigen and Mark J. Larimore, 91–120. Albany: State University of New York Press, 2006.

La Vopa, Anthony J. *Grace, Talent, and Merit: Poor Students, Clerical Careers, and Professional Ideology in Eighteenth-Century Germany*. Cambridge, UK: Cambridge University Press, 2002.

———. "Herder's Publikum: Language, Print, and Sociability in Eighteenth-Century Germany." *Eighteenth-Century Studies* 29, no. 1 (Fall, 1995): 5–24.

Legaspi, Michael. *The Death of Scripture and the Rise of Biblical Studies*. Oxford: Oxford University Press, 2010.

Lehmann, Hartmut. "In the Service of Two Kings: Protestant Prussian Military Chaplains, 1713–1918. In *Transformationen der Religion in der Neuzeit*, 221–235. Göttingen: Vandenhoeck & Ruprecht, 2007.

Leonard, Miriam. *Socrates and the Jews: Hellenism and Hebraism from Moses Mendelssohn to Sigmund Freud*. Chicago: University of Chicago Press, 2012.

Leventhal, Roberts S. "The Emergence of Philological Discourse in the German States, 1770–1810." *Isis* 77 (1986): 243–260.
Lifschitz, Avi. *Language and Enlightenment: The Berlin Debates of the Eighteenth Century.* Oxford: Oxford University Press, 2012.
Llobera, Josep R. *The God of Modernity: The Development of Nationalism in Western Europe.* Oxford: Berg, 1994.
Lovejoy, Arthur O. *Essays in History of Ideas.* New York: Capricorn, 1960.
Löwenbrück, Anna-Ruth. "Johann David Michaelis et les débuts de la critique biblique." In *Le siecle des Lumieres et la Bible*, ed. Yvon Belaval and Dominique Bourel. Paris: Beauchesne, 1986.
———. *Judenfeindschaft im Zeitalter der Aufklärung: eine Studie zur Vorgeschichte des modernen Antisemitismus am Beispiel des Göttinger Theologen und Orientalisten Johann David Michaelis (1717–1791).* Frankfurt am Main: Lang, 1995.
Lucci, Diego. *Scripture and Deism: The Biblical Criticism of the Eighteenth-Century British Deists.* New York: P. Lang, 2008.
Lüdeke, Henry, ed. *Ludwig Tieck und die Brüder Schlegel: Briefe mit Einleitung und Anmerkungen.* Frankfurt am Main: J. Baer, 1930.
Lüder, Andreas. *Historie und Dogmatik.: Ein Beitrag zur Genese und Entfaltung von Johann Salomo Semlers Verständnis des Alten Testaments.* Berlin: Walter de Gruyter, 1995.
Mäher, Moustafa. *Das Motiv der orientalischen Landschaft in der deutschen Dichtung von Klopstocks Messias bis zu Goethes Divan.* Düsseldorf: Laskowsky, 1962.
Mali, Joseph. *Mythistory: The Making of a Modern Historiography.* Chicago: University of Chicago Press, 2003.
———. *The Rehabilitation of Myth: Vico's "New Science."* Cambridge, UK: Cambridge University Press, 2002.
Malinowski, Bernadette. *"Das Heilige sei mein Wort": Paradigmen prophetischer Dichtung von Klopstock bis Whitman.* Würzburg: Königshausen & Neumann, 2002.
Mancall, Peter C. *Envisioning America: English Plans for the Colonization of North America, 1580–1640.* Boston: St. Martin's Press, 1995.
Manuel, Frank. *The Broken Staff: Judaism through Christian Eyes.* Cambridge, MA: Harvard University Press, 1992.
———. *The Eighteenth Century Confronts the Gods.* New York: Atheneum, 1967.
Marchand, Suzanne L. *Down from Olympus: Archaeology and Philhellenism in Germany, 1750–1970.* Princeton, NJ: Princeton University Press, 1996.
———. *German Orientalism in the Age of Empire: Religion, Race, and Scholarship.* Cambridge, UK: Cambridge University Press, 2009.
Marino, Luigi. *Praeceptores Germaniae: Göttingen 1770–1820.* Göttingen: Vandenhoeck & Ruprecht, 1995.
Masalha, Nur. "Reading the Bible with the Eyes of the Canaanites: Neo-Zionism, Political Theology and the Land Traditions of the Bible (1967 to Gaza 2009)." *Holy Land Studies* 8 (2009): 55–108.
Matzger, Hans-Dieter. "David und Saul in Staats- und Widerstandslehren der Frühen Neuzeit." In *König David – biblische Schlüsselfigur und europäische Leitgestalt*, ed. Walter Dietrich and Hubert Herkommer, 437–487. Fribourg, Switzerland: Universitätsverlag Freiburg, 2003.

Meek, Ronald L. *Social Science and the Ignoble Savage*. Cambridge, UK: Cambridge University Press, 1976.
Meinecke, Friedrich. *Die Entstehung des Historismus*. Munich: Oldenbourg, 1965.
Melton, James Van Horn. "Pietism, Politics, and the Public Sphere in Germany." In *Religion and Politics in Enlightenment Europe*, ed. James E. Bradley and Dale K. Van Kley. Notre Dame, IN: University of Notre Dame Press, 2001.
Menges, Karl. "Particular Universals: Herder on National Literature, Popular Literature, and World Literature." In *A Companion to the Works of Johann Gottfried Herder*, ed. Hans Adler and Wolf Koepke, 189–214. Rochester, NY: Camden House, 2009.
Momigliano, Arnaldo. "Alte Geschichte und antiquarische Forschung." In *Wege in die Alte Welt*. Berlin: Wagenbach, 1991.
Moore, Brighton. *Moral Purity and Persecution in History*. Princeton, NJ: Princeton University Press, 2000.
Mosse, George L. *The Image of Man: The Creation of Modern Masculinity*. Oxford: Oxford University Press, 1996.
Muhlpfordt, Günter. "Karl Friedrich Bahrdt und die radikale Aufklärung." *Jahrbuch des Instituts für deutsche Geschichte* 5 (1976): 49–100.
Mulsow, Martin. "Antiquarianism and Idolatry: The Historia of Religions in the Seventeenth Century." In *Historia: Empiricism and Erudition in Early Modern Europe*, ed. Gianna Pomata and Nancy G. Siraisi. Cambridge, MA: MIT Press, 2005.
Muthu, Sankar. *Enlightenment against Empire*. Princeton, NJ: Princeton University Press, 2003.
Nelson, Eric. *The Hebrew Republic: Jewish Sources and the Transformation of European Political Thought*. Cambridge, MA: Harvard University Press, 2010.
Nipperdey Thomas. *Deutsche Geschichte 1800–1866*. Munich: C. H. Beck, 1984.
Oergel, Maike, *The Return of King Arthur and the Nibelungen: National Myth in Nineteenth-Century English and German Literature*. Berlin: Walter de Gruyter, 1998.
Otto, Rüdiger. "Johann Christian Edelmanns' Criticism of the Bible and Its Relation to Spinoza." In *Disguised and Overt Spinozism around 1700*, ed. Wiep van Bunge and W. N. A. Klever, 171–191. Leiden: Brill, 1996.
Oz-Salzberger, Fania. *Translating the Enlightenment: Scottish Civic Discourse in Eighteenth-Century Germany*. Oxford: Oxford University Press, 1995.
Padgen, Anthony. *The Fall of Natural Man: The American Indian and the Origins of Comparative Ethnology*. Cambridge, UK: Cambridge University Press, 1992.
———. *Lords of All the World. Ideologies of Empire in Spain, Britain and France c.1500–c.1800*. New Haven, CT: Yale University Press, 1995.
Pasto, James. "Islam's 'Strange Secret Sharer': Orientalism, Judaism, and the Jewish Question." *Comparative Studies in Society and History* 40, no. 2 (July 1998): 437–442.
Penn, Nigel. "Peter Kolb and the VOC Voyages to the Cape." In *Many Middle Passages: Forced Migration and the Making of the Modern World*, ed. Emma Christopher and Cassandra Pybus. Berkeley: University of California Press, 2007.
Perkins, Mary Anne. *Nation and Word, 1770–1850: Religious and Metaphysical Language in European National Consciousness*. Aldershot: Ashgate, 1999.
Pinson, Koppel Shub. *Pietism as a Factor in the Rise of German Nationalism*. New York: Columbia University Press, 1934.

Pocock, John Greville Agard. *Barbarism and Religion: Barbarians, Savages and Empires.* Cambridge, UK: Cambridge University Press, 2005.
Polaschegg, Andrea. *Der andere Orientalismus: Regeln deutsch-morgenländischer Imagination im 19. Jahrhundert.* Berlin: Walter De Gruyter, 2005.
———. "Die Regeln der Imagination: Faszinationsgeschichte des deutschen Orientalismus zwischen 1770 und 1850." In *Der Deutschen Morgenland*, ed. Charis Goer and Michael Hofmann, 13–36. Munich: Fink, 2008.
Poliakov, Leon. *The History of Anti-Semitism: From Voltaire to Wagner.* London: Routledge & Kegan Paul, 1975.
Popkin, Richard. "Bible Criticism and Social Science." In *Methodological and Historical Essays in the Natural and Social Sciences*, ed. Robert Cohen and Marx Wartofsky. Dordrecht: Reidel, 1973.
———. "The Rise and Fall of the Jewish Indian Theory." In *Menasseh Ben Israel and His World*, ed. Yosef Kaplan and Richard Popkin. Leiden: Brill, 1985.
Prickett, Stephen. *Words and The Word: Language, Poetics and Biblical Interpretation.* Cambridge, UK: Cambridge University Press, 1986.
Prignitz, Christoph. *Vaterlandsliebe und Freiheit: Deutscher Patriotismus von 1750–1850.* Wiesbaden: Steiner, 1981.
Prior, Michael. *The Bible and Colonialism: A Moral Critique.* Sheffield: Shefield Academic Press, 1997.
Proß, Wolfgang. "Kommentar zu 'Ideen zur Philosophie der Geschichte der Menschheit." In *Herders Werke*, vol. 3, no. 2. Munich: Carl Hanser, 2002.
Raeder, Siegfried. "The Exegetical and Hermeneutical Work of Martin Luther." In *Hebrew Bible / Old Testament: The History of Its Interpretation – from the Renaissance to the Enlightenment*, ed. Magne Saebo, 363–406. Göttingen: Vandenhoeck & Ruprecht, 2008.
Räisänen, Heikki. "Marcion." In *A Companion to Second-Century Christian "Heretics,"* ed. Antti Marjanen and Petri Luomanen, 100–124. Leiden: Brill, 2008.
———. *Paul and the Law.* Tübingen: Mohr Siebeck, 1987.
Rawson, Claude Julien. *God, Gulliver, and Genocide: Barbarism and the European Imagination, 1492–1945.* Oxford: Oxford University Press, 2002.
Redekop, Benjamin W. *Enlightenment and Community: Lessing, Abbt, Herder and the Quest for a German Public.* Montreal: McGill-Queen's Press, 2000.
Reed, Terence James. *The Classical Centre: Goethe and Weimar, 1775–1832.* London: Croom Helm, 1980.
Reill, Peter Hanns. *The German Enlightenment and the Rise of Historicism.* Berkeley: University of California Press, 1975.
Reusch, Johann J. K. "Germans as Noble Savages and Castaways: Alter Egos and Alterity in German Collective Consciousness during the Long Eighteenth Century." *Eighteenth-Century Studies* 42, no. 1 (2008): 91–129.
Revard, Stella P. *Pindar and the Renaissance Hymn-Ode, 1450–1700.* Tempe: Arizona Center for Medieval and Renaissance Studies, 2001.
Revenlow, Henning Graf. *Historische Kritik und biblischer Kanon in der deutschen Aufklärung.* Wiesbaden: Otto Harrassowitz, 1988.
Revenlow, Henning Graf, ed. *Epochen der Bibelauslegung* Munich: Beck, 1994.
Rivera, Luis N. *A Violent Evangelism: The Political and Religious Conquest of the Americas.* Louisville, KY: Westminster/John Knox, 1992.

Rogerson, John William. *W. M. L. de Wette, Founder of Modern Biblical Criticism: An Intellectual Biography*. Sheffield: Continuum, 1992.

Römer, Nils. "Sprachverhältnisse und Leseverhalten der Juden in Deutschland (1770–1830)." In *Dialog zwischen den Kulturen: Erziehungshistorische und religionspägogische Gesichtspunkte interkultureller Bildung*, ed. Ingrid Lohmann and Wolfram Weisse, 49–68. Münster: Waxmann, 1994.

Rossi, Paolo. *The Dark Abyss of Time*. Chicago: University of Chicago, 1984.

Rowe, Michael, *From Reich to State: The Rhineland in the Revolutionary Age, 1780–1830*. Cambridge, UK: Cambridge University Press, 2003.

Rowlett, Lori L. *Joshua and the Rhetoric of Violence: A New Historicist Analysis*. Sheffield: Sheffield Academic Press, 1996.

Saebo, Magne, ed. *Hebrew Bible / Old Testament: The History of Its Interpretation*. Göttingen: Vandenhoeck & Ruprecht, 2008.

Said, Edward W. "Michael Walzer's 'Exodus and Revolution': A Canaanite Reading." In *Blaming the Victims: Spurious Scholarship and the Palestinian Question*, 159–176. New York: Verso, 1988.

———. *Orientalism*. New York: Vintage Books, 1978.

Saine, Thomas P. *The Problem of Being Modern: Or The German Pursuit of Enlightenment from Leibniz to the French Revolution*. Detroit, MI: Wayne State University Press, 1997.

Sanders, Seth L. *The Invention of Hebrew*. Urbana: University of Illinois Press, 2009.

Sayre, Gordon Mitchell. *Les Sauvages Américains: Representations of Native Americans in French and English Colonial Literature*. Chapel Hill: University of North Carolina Press, 1997.

Schechter, Ronald. *Obstinate Hebrews: Representations of Jews in France, 1715–1815*. Berkeley: University of California Press, 2003.

Schmidt, Johannes. "Studien zum Bibeldrama der Empfindsamkeit." PhD diss., University of Breslau, 1933.

Schmidt, Wolf Gerhard. *"Homer des Nordens" und "Mutter der Romantik": James Macphersons Ossian und seine Rezeption in der deutschsprachigen Literatur*. Berlin: Walter de Gruyter, 2003.

Schneider, Ulf-Michael. *Propheten der Goethezeit: Sprache, Literatur und Wirkung der Inspirierten*. Göttingen: Vandenhoeck & Ruprecht, 1995.

Schochet, Gordon, Fania Oz-Salzberger, and Meirav Jones, eds. *Political Hebraism: Judaic Sources in Early Modern Political Thought*. Jerusalem: Shalem Press, 2008.

Schönnert, Jörg. "Gott donnerte bei Lowositz: 'Zu den 'Preußischen Kriegsliedern in den Feldzugen 1765 und 1757' des Kanonikus Gleim." In *Gedichte und Interpretationen*. Vol. 2, *Aufklärung und Sturm und Drang*, ed. Klaus Richter, 126–137. Stuttgart: Reclam, 1983.

Schramm, Brooks. *Martin Luther, the Bible, and the Jewish People: A Reader*. Minneapolis, MN: Fortress Press, 2012.

Schulte, Christoph, ed. *Hebräische Poesie und jüdischer Volksgeist: Die Wirkungsgeschichte von J. G. Herder im Judentum Mittel- und Osteuropas*. Hildesheim: Georg Olms, 2003.

Schutjer, Karin. *Goethe and Judaism: The Troubled Inheritance of Modern Literature*. Evanston, IL: Northwestern University Press, 2015.

Schwab, Raymond. *Vie d'Anquetil-Duperron*. Paris: Leroux, 1934.

Shaffer, Elinor S. *'Kubla Khan' and the Fall of Jerusalem: The Mythological School in Biblical Criticis and Secular Literature*. Cambridge, UK: Cambridge University Press, 1980.
Shalev, Eran. *American Zion: The Old Testament as a Political Text from the Revolution to the Civil War*. New Haven, CT: Yale University Press, 2013.
Shavit, Yaacov, and Mordechai Eran. *The Hebrew Bible Reborn: From Holy Scripture to the Book of Books: A History of Biblical Culture and the Battles over the Bible in Modern Judaism*. Berlin: Walter de Gruyter, 2007.
Sheehan, Jonathan. *The Enlightenment Bible: Translation, Scholarship, Culture*. Princeton, NJ: Princeton University Press, 2005.
Sikka, Sonia. *Herder on Humanity and Cultural Difference: Enlightened Relativism*. Cambridge, UK: Cambridge University Press, 2011.
Smend, Rudolf. "Aufgeklärte Bemühung um das Gesetz: Johann David Michaelis 'Mosaisches Recht.'" In *Wenn nicht jetzt, wann dann? Festschrift für Hans-Joachim Kraus zum 65. Geburtstag*, 129–139. Neukirchen-Vluyn: Neukirchener, 1983.
———. *Bibel und Wissenschaft: historische Aufsätze*. Tübingen: Mohr Siebeck, 2004.
———. *Deutsche Alttestamentler in drei Jahrhunderten*. Gottingen: Vandenhoeck & Ruprecht, 1989.
———. *Die Mitte des Alten Testaments: Exegetische Aufsätze*. Tübingen: Mohr-Siebeck, 2002.
———. "Lowth in Deutschland." In *Epochen der Bibelkritik*. Munich: Chr. Kaiser, 1991.
Smith, Anthony D. *Chosen Peoples: Sacred Sources of National Identity*. Oxford: Oxford University Press, 2003.
———. *The Nation in History: Historiographical Debates about Ethnicity and Nationalism*. Hanover, NH: University Press of New England, 2000.
Smith, Helmut Walser. *The Continuities of German History: Nation, Religion, and Race across the Long Nineteenth Century*. Cambridge, UK: Cambridge University Press, 2008.
Sorkin, David Jan. *The Religious Enlightenment: Protestants, Jews, and Catholics from London to Vienna*. Princeton, NJ: Princeton University Press, 2008.
Spalding, Paul. *Seize the Book, Jail the Author: Johann Lorenz Schmidt and Censorship in Eighteenth-Century Germany*. West Lafayette, IN: Purdue University Press, 1998.
Spinks, Bryan D. *Reformation and Modern Rituals and Theologies of Baptism*. Burlington: Ashgate, 2006.
Srbik, Heinrich von. *Geist und Geschichte vom deutschen Humanismus bis zur Gegenwart*. Salzburg: O. Müller, 1950.
Stahl, Ernst Ludwig, and William Eduard Yuill. *German Literature of the Eighteenth and Nineteenth Centuries*. London: Cresset Press, 1970.
Starkey, Armstrong. *War in the Age of Enlightenment, 1700–1789*. Westport, CT: Praeger, 2003.
Starobinsky, Jean, *Blessings in Disguise: Or The Morality of Evil*, Cambridge, MA: Harvard University Press, 1993.
Stephenson, Gunther. "Geschichte und Religionswissenschaft im ausgehenden 18. Jahrhundert." *Numen* 13 (1966): 43–79.
Stern, Selma. *Der preussische Staat und die Juden*: Vol. 3, *Die Zeit Friedrichs des Großen*. Tübingen: Mohr Siebeck, 1971.
Stevens, Laura M. *The Poor Indians: British Missionaries, Native Americans, and Colonial Sensibility*. Philadelphia: University of Pennsylvania Press, 2004.
Stevens, Paul. "'Leviticus Thinking' and the Rhetoric of Early Modern Colonialism." *Criticism* 35 (1993): 441–461.

Stichel, Rainer. *Beiträge zur frühen Geschichte des Psalters und zur Wirkungsgeschichte der Psalmen*. Düsseldorf: Schöningh, 2007.

Stroumsa, Guy G. *A New Science: The Discovery of Religion in the Age of Reason*. Cambridge, MA: Harvard University Press, 2010.

Stroup, John. *The Struggle for Identity in the Clerical Estate: Northwest German Protestant Opposition to Absolutist Policy in the Eighteenth Century*. Leiden: Brill, 1984.

Sutcliffe, Adam. *Judaism and Enlightenment*. Cambridge, UK: Cambridge University Press, 2003.

Sutcliffe, Adam, and Jonathan Karp. "A Brief History of Philosemitism." In *Philosemitism in History*, ed. Jonathan Karp and Adam Sutcliffe, 1–26. Cambridge, UK: Cambridge University Press, 2011.

Tal, Uriel. "On Modern Lutheranism and the Jews." in *Religion, Politics and Ideology in the Third Reich: Selected Essays*, 171–190. New York: Routledge, 2004.

Thiersch, Heinrich Wilhelm Josia. *Das Verbot der Ehe innerhalb der nahen Verwandtschaft, nach der heiligen Schrift und nach den Grundsätzen der christlichen Kirche*. Nördlingen. Beck, 1869.

Thornton, Helen. *State of Nature or Eden? Thomas Hobbes and His Contemporaries on the Natural Condition of Human Beings*. Rochester, NY: University of Rochester Press, 2005.

Thouard, Denis. "Hamann und der Streit um die Poesie der Hebräer." In *Die Gegenwärtigkeit Johann Georg Hamanns: Acta des achten Internationalen Hamann-Kolloquiums an der Martin-Luther-Universität Halle-Wittenberg 2002*, ed. Bernhard Gajek, 321–334. Frankfurt am Main: Peter Lang, 2005.

Tilgner, Wolfgang. *Volknomostheologie und Schopfungsglaube: Ein Beitrag zur Geschichte des Kirchenkampfes*. Göttingen: Vandenhoeck & Ruprecht, 1966.

Toomer, Gerald James. *Eastern Wisdom and Learning: The Study of Arabic in Seventeenth-Century England*. Oxford: Oxford University Press, 1996.

Tudor, Henri. *Political Myth*. London: Macmillan, 1972.

Tzoref-Ashkenazi, Chen. *Der romantische Mythos vom Ursprung der Deutschen: Friedrich Schlegels Suche nach der indogermanischen Verbindung*. Göttingen: Wallstein, 2009.

Vazsonyi, Nicholas. "Montesquieu, Friedrich Carl von Moser, and the 'National Spirit Debate' in Germany, 1765–1767." *German Studies Review* 22, no. 2 (May 1999): 225–246.

Vierhaus, Rudolf. "'Patriotismus': Begriff und Realität einer moralisch-politischen Haltung," In Deutschland im 18. Jahrhundert, Göttingen: Vandenhoeck & Ruprecht, 1987, 96–109.

Voigts, Manfred. "Das Ende der David-Tradition: Jakob Frank und die Französische Revolution." In *König David – biblische Schlüsselfigur und europäische Leitgestalt*, 249–279. Fribourg, Switzerland: Universitätsverlag Freiburg, 2003.

Volkov, Shulamit. "Talking of Jews, Thinking of Germans: The Ethnic Discourse in 19th Century Germany." In *Tel Aviver Jahbuch für deutsche Geschichte* 30 (2002): 37–49.

Wees, Hans van. "Genocide in the Ancient World." In *Oxford Handbook of Genocide Studies*, ed. Donald Bloxham and Dirk Moses, 239–258. Oxford: Oxford University Press, 2010.

Weidner, Daniel. *Bibel und Literatur um 1800*. Munich: Wilhelm Fink, 2011.

———. "'Menschliche, heilige Sprache': Das Hebräische bei Michaelis und Herder." *Monatshefte für deutschsprachige Literatur und Kultur* 95, no. 2 (2003): 171–206.

———. "Politik und Ästhetik: Lektüre der Bibel bei Michaelis, Herder und de Wette." In *Hebräsiche Poesie und jüdischer Volksgeist: Die Wirkungsgeschichte Johann Gottfried Herders im Judentum Mittel- und Osteuropas*, ed. Christoph Schulte, 35–66. Hildesheim: Olms, 2003.

———. "Scripture and Secularization: Johann Gottfried Herder's Reading of the Bible." *New German Critique* 94 (2005): 169–193.

———. "Ursprung und Wesen der Ebräischen Poesie." In *Urpoesie und Morgenland: Johann Gottfried Herders "Vom Geist der Ebräischen Poesie,"* ed. Daniel Weidner, 113–151. Berlin: Kadmos, 2008.

———, ed. *Urpoesie und Morgenland: Johann Gottfried Herders Vom Geist der Ebräischen Poesie.* Berlin: Kadmos, 2008.

Weissberg, Liliane. "Juden oder Hebräer? Religiöse und politische Bekehrung bei Herder." In *Johann Gottfried Herder: Geschichte und Kultur*, ed. Martin Bollacher, 191–211. Würzburg: Königshausen & Neumann, 1994.

Wheeler, Roxann. *The Complexion of Race: Categories of Difference in Eighteenth-Century British Culture*. Philadelphia: University of Pennsylvania, 2000.

Whitford, David M. *The Curse of Ham in the Early Modern Era: The Bible and the Justifications for Slavery*. Farnham, UK: Ashgate, 2009.

Wickenden, Nicholas. *G. J. Vossius and the Humanist Concept of History*. Assen: Van Gorcum, 1993.

Wiesehöfer, Josef, and Stephan Conermann, eds. *Carsten Niebuhr (1733–1815) und seine Zeit: Beiträge eines interdisziplinären Symposiums vom 7.-10. Oktober 1999 in Eutin*. Stuttgart: Franz Steiner, 2002.

Willi, Thomas. *Herders Beitrag zum Verstehen des Alten Testaments*. Tübingen: Mohr Siebeck, 1971.

Williamson, George S. *The Longing for Myth in Germany: Religion and Aesthetic Culture from Romanticism to Nietzsche*. Chicago: University of Chicago Press, 2004.

Wirtz, Michaela. *Patriotismus und Weltbürgertum: eine Begriffsgeschichtliche Studie zur deutsch-jüdischen Literatur 1750–1850*. Tübingen: Niemeyer, 2006.

Witte, John. *Law and Protestantism: The Legal Teachings of the Lutheran Reformation*. Cambridge, UK: Cambridge University Press, 2002.

Wittmann, Reinhard. "Der Gönner als Leser. Buchwidmungen als Quellen der Lesergeschichte." In *Parallelwelten des Buches: Beiträge zu Buchpolitik, Verlagsgeschichte, Bibliophilie und Buchkunst*, ed. Wulf D vonLucius, Monika Estermann, Ernst Fischer, and Reinhard Wittmann, 1–28. Wiesbaden: Harrassowitz, 2008.

Wokoeck, Ursula. *German Orientalism: The Study of the Middle East and Islam from 1800 to 1945*. London: Routledge, 2009.

Zakai, Avihu. *Exile and Kingdom: History and Apocalypse in the Puritan Migration to America*. Cambridge, UK: Cambridge University Press, 2002.

Zammito, John H. *The Genesis of Kant's Critique of Judgment*. Chicago: University of Chicago Press, 1992.

Zantop, Susanne. *Colonial Fantasies: Conquest, Family, and Nation in Precolonial Germany, 1770–1870*. Durham, NC: Duke University Press, 1997.

Zbinden, Jürg, "Heterogeneity, Irony, Ambivalence: The Idea of Progress in the Universal Histories and the Histories of Mankind in the German Enlightenment," *Storia della Storiografia* 29 (1996): 109–115.

Zedelmaier, Helmut. *Der Anfang der Geschichte: Studien zur Ursprungsdebatte im 18. Jahrhundert*. Hamburg: Felix Meiner, 2003.

———. "Die Sintflut als Anfang der Geschichte." In *Sintflut und Gedächtnis: Erinnern und Vergessen des Ursprungs*, ed. Jan Assmann and Martin Muslow, 253–261. Munich: Wilhelm Fink, 2006.

Zell, Michael. *Reframing Rembrandt: Jews and the Christian Image in Seventeenth-Century Amsterdam*. Berkeley: University of California Press, 2002.

Zschoch, Hellmut. "'Mit Gott für Freiheit, Recht und Vaterland!': Ernst Moritz Arndts deutsche Befreiungstheologie." In *Orientierung für das Leben: Kirchliche Bildung und Politik in Spätmittelalter, Reformation und Neuzeit*, ed. Patrik Mähling, 245–258. Berlin: Lit, 2010.

Index

Abraham, 2, 17–30, 33–37, 39n17, 40n29, 54, 68–70, 77–80, 88, 118, 132
Absolutism, 62, 118
Adam, 20–22, 24, 26, 54, 87–88
Adultery, 47–48, 51–52, 55
Africa, 29–30, 32–34, 79–80
Ahab, 129
Alexander VI (pope), 70
Allegory, 3–4, 38, 61, 97
America, 28–31, 33, 36, 70–71, 73–76, 82
Antisemitism, 1
Arabia, 25, 28, 31, 33
Arabic, 17, 24, 28, 88, 145
Arabs, 25, 31–32, 35, 52, 54–58
Aramaic, 24, 28, 118
Ascenas, 88
Assmann, Jan, 66
Assyria, 100
Augsburg, 47
Augusti, Joahnn Christian, 122
Augustine, 2, 37
Augustus, 132
Austria, 45, 95, 130

Babor, Johann, 113–114, 126
Babylon, 4, 26, 37, 100
Babylonian Exile, 37
Bahrdt, Karl Friedrich, 118, 124
Baroque, 88, 90, 95
Bauer, Gerorg Lorenz, 34, 114–115
Bayle, Pierre, 148
Bayreuth, 29
Bedouins, 2, 26, 34–35
Beer Sheba, 77
Ben Israel, Menasseh, 28
Berlin, 27, 96, 114, 129, 133
Bestiality, 31, 47, 74
Bethel, 104
Biblical criticism, 6–8, 101
blood revenge, 55–56

Bodmer, Johann Jakob, 89, 91–92
Bohemia, 121
Bolingbroke, Henry, 4, 70–71
Bonaparte, Napoleon, 129–130
Bourgeoisie, 89, 130
Brandenburg, 46, 48–49
Brandenburg, Maria Amalia von, 46

Cain, 18
Calmet, Augustin, 67
Calvin, Jean, 50
Calvinism, 48, 105
Campe, Joachim Heinrich, 118–119, 124, 128
Canaan, conquest of, 11, 18–19, 31, 36, 66–82, 131
cannibalism, 73
cantillation, 23–24
Carpzov, Benedikt, 47–48
Carus, Friedrich August, 115
Catholicism, 43, 47–48, 70–71, 105, 121
Celts, 88
Chaldea, 27, 31, 34
Chorites, 18, 36
Chosenness, 1, 4, 9–10, 20–22, 37–38, 39n17, 69, 71, 73, 79–81, 96, 102
Circumcision, 33–34, 44, 55, 59
civil society, 36, 55, 57
classical antiquity, 1–2, 7, 12, 30, 50, 67, 87, 89–94, 98, 116, 120, 130, 132, 136
climate, 58–59, 86
Colonialism, 36, 70–71, 80, 82
Conquistadors, 70
Conservatism, 23, 44, 67, 71, 73, 75, 81–82, 119, 123, 137, 146
Cosmopolitanism, 97, 124

Danton, Georges, 121
Dauernheim, 126
David, 2–3, 21, 37, 86, 94, 98, 109

David's Lament, 121
De la Mothe Cadillac, Antoine, 29
De Wette, Martin Leberecht, 27, 126, 130–133
Deism, deists, 4–5, 29–32, 37, 67–76, 81, 99, 101, 116–117, 129, 136, 145–146
Denmark, 28
Dessau, 135
Ditmar, Theodor Jakob, 27, 36, 114
Dobruška, Moses. *See* Thomas von Schönfeld
Döderlein, Johann Christoph, 122
Duel, 57–58, 60, 94

Echzell, 126, 128
Edelmann, Johann Christian, 21, 72, 75, 128
Education, 4, 23, 37, 81
Egypt, 6, 21, 23, 31, 46, 48, 54, 66–67, 78, 82, 102–104, 106, 111, 115
Eichhorn, Johann Gottfried, 59, 67, 113–114, 116, 122–125, 132
Elijah, 129
emancipation, Jewish, 136
Empfindsamkeit, 89
Enlightenment, 1, 8–12, 18–23, 26, 28, 35, 38, 57, 60–61, 66, 68, 71, 75–76, 79, 82, 90, 99, 102, 104, 106, 114, 124–125, 134, 138, 145–146
Epiphanius, 73
Erlangen, 134
Ethnicity, 6, 8–9, 11, 27, 44, 49, 70, 81–82, 133
Ethnography, 2, 6, 11, 17–19, 24, 27–36, 44–46, 50, 52, 55–60, 79, 88, 127, 132, 135, 145
Euphrates, 26

Faber, Johann Ernst, 17–19, 32, 67, 78–79, 126
Federation, 100, 129–130, 146
Ferguson, Adam, 105
Feudalism, 57
Flood, 18, 20, 22, 29, 35, 44, 56–57, 73, 77, 86, 125, 134
France, 1, 4, 12, 21, 53, 67–68, 71–72, 87, 89, 95, 123, 126–127, 130
Francisco de Vitoria, 74
Francke, Hermann, 49
Frank, Jacob, 121
Freemasory, 102, 121, 129
Freidenker, 67, 72, 82
French, 87, 89

Friedrich II, 45, 51, 118–119

Gabler, Johann Philip, 125, 132
Gatterer, Johann Christoph, 78
Ge'ez, 32
Geddes, Alexander, 115
genocide, 82
German language, 86, 87–89
Germanic tribes, 86, 94
Gleim, Johann Ludwig, 95
God, 33; Germanic, 94; National, 95–104, 147; of Abraham, 25–26, 34; of history, 76–77; of Israel, 4, 20–21, 35, 37–38, 69, 74, 79, 81, 134; Zebaoth, 97
Goeschen, Georg Joachim, 95
Goethe, Johann Wolfgang von, 86, 89, 97, 107, 115–116
Golden Calf, 104
Gomer, 88
Goths, 70
Göttingen, 5, 17, 19, 23–24, 49–50, 60, 120
Gottsched, Johann Christoph, 22, 89
Greek (language), 2, 28, 88, 119
Greeks *see* classical antiquity
Grotius, Hugo, 74

Habakkuk, 123
Halle, 23, 29, 34, 49
Ham, Hamites, 79–81
Hamann, Johann Georg, 89–90, 93, 107
Hanmann, Enoch, 88
Hardenberg, Karl August von, 118
Hartmann, Anton Theodor, 115, 129
Hasenkamp, Friedrich Arnold, 114
Haskalah see *Maskilim*
Hebrew language, 7, 12, 17, 24–25, 28, 32–33, 88–91, 118–119, 128, 135, 145–146
Hebrew poetry, 11–12, 86–87, 89–94, 97–101, 104, 113–114, 119–121, 127, 131–133, 135–137, 146
Hebron, 77
Hegel, Friedrich Wilhelm, 1, 86, 138
Helicon, 94
Herder, Johann Gottfried, 4–7, 10, 12, 17, 19, 36, 62, 86–87, 132; and Hebrew language, 89, 91 and Kant, 116; on the origin of

Israel, 26; on the extermination of the Canaanites, 67, 79–82; influence, 114–117, 120–123, 126, 129–138; on Hebrew poetry, 96–99, 127; on Klopstock, 93; on myth, 106–107, 125, 133; on nationalism, 96–98, 105–106; on the National God, 101–104; on the Orient, 90; on the Jews, 134–135; on theocracy, 99–101
Hermann (Arminius), 94
Herodotus, 18
Hessen, 125–126, 129–130
Hessen-Darmstadt, Ludwig von, 126, 129–130
Heyne, Christian Gottlob, 107
Hezel, Johann Wilhelm Friedrich, 126, 128
Hivites, 18, 67
Hobbes, Thomas, 55
Hochstetter, Johann Friedrich, 20
Hohenzollern, House of, 46
holy history, 20, 22, 25, 35, 38, 92, 93
holy war, 79, 81, 96
Homer, 128, 134
Horst, Georg Conrad, 123–125, 127–130
Hufnagel, Wilhelm Friedrich, 117, 124, 128, 134
human sacrifice, 31, 72, 74, 79, 118
Humanism, 20, 33
Hume, David, 107
Huns, 70–71
Hurons, 36, 91

Idolatry, 20–21, 54, 66, 69–72, 76, 80–82
Incest, 50, 52, 74
India, Indians, 22, 129, 133
interpretation, allegorical, 3–4, 38, 61, 97
interpretation, Christological, 61
interpretation, historical, 32, 61, 131
Iroquois, 29
Isaiah, 94
Italy, 87

Jacobins, 121, 129
Jahn, Johann, 114, 126
Japheth, 88
Jefferson, Thomas, 9
Jena, 17, 32, 46, 102, 120, 122, 131, 147
Jericho, 74

Jeroboam, 100
Jerusalem, 131
Jerusalem, Friedrich Wilhelm, 67, 76
Jesuits, 29, 73
Jesus, 1–3, 5, 21, 48
Jewish state, 38, 103
Jews, 1, 3, 6, 10, 21–24, 28–31, 37–38, 43–44, 48, 51, 61, 69, 71–72, 118, 134–136
Jonah, 30
Jordan (river), 18, 77–78, 93–94
Joseph II, 45, 61, 98, 121
Joshua, 3, 82n4
Josiah, 131
Judah Maccabeus, 130
Judah, Kingdom of, 68, 86, 94, 131–132
Justi, Carl Wilhelm, 120
Justi, Johann Heinrich, 58

Kabbalah, 121
Kant, Immanuel, 116–117, 124, 131, 133
Kennicott, Benjamin, 24, 40, 116
Kiel, 17
Klopstock, Friedrich Gottlieb, 11, 87, 89, 91–95, 98, 101, 104, 107, 115–116, 121–122, 127, 133–135, 137
Köhler, Johann Bernhard, 135
Kolbe, Peter, 29–30, 34
Königsberg, 135
Krosigk, Friedrich von, 29
Kuhnöl, Christian Gottlob, 114

Labat, Jean Baptiste, 33
Lafitau, Joseph-François, 29–30, 33
Latin, 34, 91, 115, 117, 132
Leipzig, 46
Leland, John, 67, 73–74
Lescarbot, Marc, 29
Lessing, Gotthold Ephraim, 4, 37, 72, 81, 94, 102, 104, 106, 116–117, 147
liberalism, 9, 24, 44, 137–138, 148
Locke, John, 56, 67, 73
Lowositz, 95
Lowth, Robert, 24, 31–32, 90–91, 136
Luther, Martin, 2–3, 11, 21, 37, 43–44, 50, 59, 61, 138, 147–148
Lutheranism, 37, 46, 48, 91, 105, 118

Magdeburg, 46
Maimonides, 54
Manna, 17
Marcion, 68
Marriage, 46–52, 55, 80
Maskilim, 134–136
Melanchthon, Philip, 20, 50
Melchizedek, 21
Mendelssohn, Moses, 32, 96, 117, 120–121
Meslier, Jean, 68
Mesopotamia, 18, 24, 34, 77
Messianism, 9, 121
Michaelis, Johann David, 5, 7–8, 10–11, 24–25, 27, 44–45, 94, 113, 131–134, 145, 148; and Faber, 17, 19; and Lowth, 32, 90; and Maimonides, 54; and marriage laws, 49–52; and Mendelssohn; and nationalism, 58–62; and the Jews, 59–60; ethnographic methods, 27–28, 33–36, 53, 55–58; Influence, 113–116, 119, 126, 128; on the origin of the Israelites, 23, 25–26; on the right to the Land of Canaan, 67, 75–79, 81–82
Mission, 33
Monotheism, 66, 68, 106
Montaigne, Michel de, 73
Montesquieu, 45, 53, 58, 62, 107
Morgan, Thomas, 4, 69
Moritz Wilhelm von Sachsen-Zeitz, 46
Moser, Friedrich Karl von, 58
Moses, 17, 21, 26, 32, 37–38, 43–44, 48, 50, 52–57, 59–62, 66, 69–70, 72, 75–76, 79–80, 82, 96, 98, 100, 102–105, 118, 121, 127, 130–131, 134–135
Muhammad, 147–148
Müller, Philipp, 46
myth, mythology, 1, 2, 10, 12, 38, 94–95, 101, 105–107, 114, 118, 125, 128–133, 137–138, 147–148

Napoleonic Wars, 96, 129–130
national character, 32, 53, 61, 95, 115
national culture, 1, 86, 138
national literature, 96, 104–105, 117, 121, 133
national poetry, 98–101, 117, 135, 148
national religion, 12, 99, 101–102, 106, 146
nationalism, 1, 6–10, 96–97, 104–106, 118, 125, 131, 133, 148
Native Americans, 28–33, 36, 52, 73, 91
Natural Law, 10, 43, 46, 49, 53–54, 62, 68
natural religion, 69, 95, 124
Naturvölker, 33
Netherlands, 7, 9, 21, 24, 46, 88, 105, 138
New Testament, 2, 7, 9, 44, 61, 87, 90, 94, 101, 104, 124, 126, 147
Nibelungenlied, 133
Nicolai, Friedrich, 120
Nidda (Hesse), 126
Niebuhr, Carsten, 28
Noah, 2, 18, 20–21, 26, 37, 56, 73, 80
Nomadism, 6, 11, 18, 26, 31, 36–37, 52, 54, 56, 72, 75, 77–79, 145–148
Novalis, 133, 147

Oder, 134
Oldendorp, Christian Georg, 32
Opitz, Martin, 88
orientalism, 6, 8, 17, 23, 25, 27, 31–34, 45, 52, 58, 60, 88, 113–116, 122, 125–128, 145
Ossian, 120

paganism, 103, 137
Palestine, 18–19, 22–26, 35, 67, 77
particularism, 12, 147
patriarchs, 2, 10–11, 19, 23, 29, 32–37, 54, 56, 77, 87, 116, 128
patriotism, 6, 87, 95–98, 104–106, 122–124, 127, 135, 137, 146
Paul, 2, 31, 33, 43, 59, 61–62, 147
peasantry, peasants, 2, 43
Penn, William, 29
Philippsohn, Moses, 135
Phoenicians, 4, 26, 77–79, 106
Pietism, 10, 12, 20, 23, 32, 34, 49, 72, 87, 92, 96
Pindar, 91, 93–94
Poland, 121
political Hebraism, 11, 105
polygamy, 52, 55
Procopius, 79
Progress, 18, 23, 26, 30–31, 35–36, 57, 106, 117
prophecy, Prophets, 2–3, 43, 91–93, 96, 104–105, 116, 122–124, 127, 129, 133

Protestantism, 5, 9, 11–12, 20, 24, 28, 37, 44, 47–48, 59–61, 77, 87, 94–96, 104–105, 119, 133, 137–138, 146–148
Providence, 38, 76, 104–106, 130, 147
Prussia, 45, 51, 95–96, 118, 130, 136
Psalms, 2–3, 92–99, 103, 117–118, 120–121, 138, 148
Psychology, 115
Pufendorf, Samuel von, 46
Puritans, 71, 105

Querelle des Anciens et des Modernes, 89

Reaction, 95, 136–137
Red Sea, 77–78, 96
Reformation, 3, 5, 7, 13, 15, 21, 43–47
Reich, German, 46–47, 50, 62, 130
Reimarus, Hermann Samuel, 21, 72, 75, 116, 124, 128
Reinhold, Karl Leonhard, 102
Renaissance, 2, 6, 22, 33, 40, 90
Revelation, 6, 19, 21, 23, 25, 30, 37, 61, 74, 81, 92, 123, 147–148
Revolution, French, 119, 121–122, 127, 129
Richter, Johann Andreas Lebrecht, 136
Rousseau, Jean-Jacques, 56, 107

Sabbateans, 53, 103
Sabians, 54
Sachsen-Anhalt, 88
Samuel, 129
Sarah, 27, 29
Saul, 37, 121
Saxony, 14, 47, 49
Schelling, Friedrich Wilhelm, 125, 131, 147
Scherer, Ludwig Wilhelm, 125–130, 137
Schiller, Friedrich, 38, 89, 98, 102, 104, 106, 116
Schlegel, Friedrich, 133, 147–148
Schmied, Johann Heinrich, 96
Schönfeld, Thomas von, 121–122
Schottel, Johann Justus, 88
Schultens, Albert, 21, 88
Scotland, 24, 33, 48, 115
secularization, 5, 7–8, 82, 92, 119, 146
Semler, Johann Salomo, 94, 102, 116, 119

Seven Years War, 12, 58, 95–96, 104, 106
sexuality, 52
Shem, 21, 73, 80
shepherds, 11, 18–19, 23, 25–27, 36, 69, 77–78, 86
Siona and Teutona, 95
social contract, 55
Sodomy, 47, 74
Song of Deborah, 120
Song of Moses, 135
Song of Songs, 52, 120
Song of the Sea, 95, 120–121
Spain, Spaniards, 70–71, 74–76, 87
Spalding, Johann Joachim, 134
Spencer, John, 54, 99
Spener, Philipp Jakob, 10
Spinoza, Baruch, 4, 14, 21, 72, 146, 148
spirit of the nation, 53
Starck, Johann August von, 129
State of Nature, 55–57
Sturm und Drang, 11–12, 87, 89–92, 95, 117, 127, 137
Sweden, 9, 95
Swisserland, 68
Syriac, 24, 28, 32

Tacitus, 88
Tahiti, 33–34
Talmud, 21
Ten Lost Tribes, 28, 33
Terah, 20
Teutonians, 86, 94
Theater, 90, 98
Theocracy, 10, 99–101, 117, 124, 132, 148
Thirty Years War, 46, 68
Thomasius, Christian, 26, 46–49, 61
Thorowgood, Thomas, 28–30, 33
Tindal, Mathieu, 69–71, 74
tolerance, 77–78
translation, 7, 28, 52, 71, 74, 75, 105–106, 119–123, 126, 128, 134–136
Troglodytes, 18–19
Tychsen, Thomas Christian, 114

universal history, 19–20, 38, 77
Universalism, 46, 61, 69, 147–148

Vandals, 70
Vienna, 114, 121
Virgil, 52, 132
Voltaire, 1, 4, 22–23, 31, 67–68, 72–73, 88

Wachler, Johann Ludwig, 129
Walther, Friedrich Andreas, 22
Warnekros, Friedrich Ehrenfried, 36
Weimar, 89, 131

Wessely, Naphtali Herz, 13, 134–136
Westphalia, Peace of, 46
Wieland, Christoph Martin, 120
Winckelmann, Johann Joachim, 89–90, 148
Wolfenbüttel, 71–72, 116, 118, 134

Yemen, 28

Zedlitz, Karl von, 118

OFRI ILANY is a postdoctoral fellow at the Polonsky Academy for Advanced Study in the Humanities and Social Sciences at the Van Leer Jerusalem Institute and a lecturer at Tel Aviv University. He has published numerous articles on the history of ideas, German-Jewish relations, and the history of sexuality. He is also an essayist and literary critic.